Making the Difference

Making the Difference

Essays in honour of Shirley Williams

Edited by Andrew Duff

First published in Great Britain in 2010 by
Biteback Publishing Ltd
Heal House
375 Kennington Lane
London
SE11 5QY

ISBN 978-1-84954-052-0

10 9 8 7 6 5 4 3 2 1

A CIP catalogue record for this book is available from the British Library.

Set in Bembo
Printed and bound in Great Britain by TJ International Ltd, Padstow, Cornwall

Contents

About the authors

Sir Menzies Campbell QC has been Liberal Democrat member of Parliament for North East Fife since 1987. He was the party's spokesman on security and defence issues for many years, opposing the UK's involvement in the invasion of Iraq in 2003. From 2006–7 Campbell was leader of the Liberal Democrats.

Andrew Duff has been the Liberal Democrat member of the European Parliament for the East of England since 1999, and is spokesman on constitutional affairs for the Alliance of Liberals and Democrats for Europe (ALDE). He has been president of the Union of European Federalists since 2008, and was director of the Federal Trust for Education and Research, 1993–9. *Saving the European Union: The Logic of the Lisbon Treaty* was published in 2009.

Sir Jeremy Greenstock has been the director of the Ditchley Foundation since 2004, having previously served as the UK's permanent representative to the UN in New York (1988–2003) and the UK's special envoy for Iraq (2003–4).

Germaine Greer is Professor Emeritus of English Literature and Comparative Studies at the University of Warwick. Born in Australia, she is a feminist writer and broadcaster. Her many publications include the best-selling *The Female Eunuch* (1970) and, most recently, *Shakespeare's Wife* (2007).

Richard Harries is Gresham Professor of Divinity. He was Bishop of Oxford from 1987–2006, and is now a life peer (Lord Harries of Pentregarth). He is the author of a number of books, most recently *Faith in Politics? Rediscovering the Christian Roots of Our Political Values* and *Issues of Life and Death: Christian Faith and Medical Intervention.*

Peter Hennessy has been Attlee Professor of Contemporary British History, Queen Mary, University of London since 2001. He is a noted journalist and broadcaster on constitutional issues. Among his publications are *Cabinets and the Bomb* (2007), *Having It So Good: Britain in the Fifties* (2006), and *The Prime Minister: The Office and Its Holders since 1945* (2000).

David Howarth is Reader in Private Law at the University of Cambridge, fellow of Clare College and associate fellow of the Centre for Science and Policy at the Judge Business School. His research concentrates on the relationship between law, politics and economics. From 2005–10 he was Liberal Democrat member of Parliament for Cambridge, serving as shadow Secretary of State for Justice and as shadow Energy Minister, and as a member of the Commons' Justice and Environmental Audit Committees.

Dame Jennifer Jenkins is the widow of Roy Jenkins (Lord Jenkins of Hillhead). She was chairman of the Consumers Association from 1965–76. A distinguished conservationist, she became chairman of the National Trust from 1986–90.

John Kampfner is chief executive of Index on Censorship. He has worked for the *Daily Telegraph*, *Financial Times* and the BBC's flagship *Today* programme. He was editor of the *New Statesman* 2005–8. His latest book is *Freedom for Sale* (2009); and his pamphlet *Lost Labours: Where Now for the Liberal Left?* was launched by Nick Clegg in March 2010.

Charles Kennedy is the Liberal Democrat member of Parliament for Ross, Skye and Lochaber, having first won its predecessor seat as a member of the SDP in 1983. He is president of the European Movement in the UK, rector of Glasgow University and between 1999 and 2006 was the leader of the Liberal Democrats.

Helena Kennedy (Baroness Kennedy of the Shaws) is a Queen's Counsel, practising in the field of human rights and civil liberties. She is president of the School of Oriental and African Studies, chair of Justice, the British arm of the International Commission of Jurists, and a trustee of the British Museum. She is a former chair of the British Council and of the Human Genetics Commission.

Anthony King has been Professor of Government at Essex University since 1969. A Canadian by birth and a former Rhodes Scholar, he has also taught at Oxford, Princeton and the University of Wisconsin-Madison. He is best known for his journalism and broadcasting on politics and elections. His most recent book is *The British Constitution* (2008).

Roger Liddle is chair of Policy Network, the international progressive think tank. He worked in 10 Downing St as European adviser to Tony Blair from 1997 to 2004 and then in Brussels for three years, working first in the cabinet of Trade Commissioner, Peter Mandelson and then as a policy adviser to the President of the Commission, José Manuel Barroso. Roger Liddle recently joined the Labour benches in the House of Lords.

John Lloyd is a contributing editor for the *Financial Times* and director of journalism at the Reuters Institute for the Study of Journalism at the University of Oxford, director of the Axess Programme on Journalism and Democracy and a columnist for *La Repubblica*. He was editor of the *New Statesman* in the 1980s and of *Time Out* in the 1970s. His books include *Loss without Limit: The British Miners' Strike*; *Rebirth of a Nation: An Anatomy of Russia*; and *What the Media are Doing to Our Politics*.

Clifford Longley is a Catholic journalist, broadcaster and author. He is editorial consultant, columnist and leader writer for *The Tablet*, and consultant to the Catholic Bishops' Conference of England and Wales for the production of *The Common Good and the Catholic Church's Social Teaching* (1996) and *Choosing the Common Good* (2010).

Robert Maclennan has been a Liberal Democrat member of the House of Lords since 2001 (Lord Maclennan of Rogart). He was successively Labour, SDP and Liberal Democrat member of Parliament for Caithness and Sutherland for thirty-five years. He was president of the Liberal Democrats 1992–6. From 1995–7 he co-chaired with Robin Cook talks between Labour and the Lib Dems on constitutional reform.

David Owen (Lord Owen of the City of Plymouth) was Labour and then SDP member of Parliament for Plymouth from 1966–92. Under Labour governments, he served as Navy Minister, Health Minister and Foreign Secretary. He was co-founder of the Social Democratic Party established in 1981 and its leader from 1983–7 and 1988–90. He sits as an independent social democrat in the House of Lords. From 1992–5 Lord Owen served as EU peace negotiator in the former Yugoslavia. In 1999 he established New Europe, which worked with Business for Sterling in the 'Yes to Europe, no to the euro' campaign. He is currently director of the Centre for International Humanitarian Cooperation, and has business interests in America and Russia.

Robert B. Reich is Professor of Public Policy at the University of California at Berkeley. He has served in three national administrations, most recently as US Secretary of Labor under President Bill Clinton. His many publications include *The Work of Nations* and *Supercapitalism*. He is the co-founder of the *American Prospect* magazine. His newest book, out in September, is *Aftershock: The Next Economy and America's Future*. He blogs at www.robertreich.org.

Bill Rodgers (Lord Rodgers of Quarry Bank) was Labour and then SDP member of Parliament for Stockton-on-Tees 1962–83. He was a member of James Callaghan's 1976–9 Labour Cabinet and one of the SDP's 'Gang of Four'. He succeeded Roy Jenkins as leader of the Liberal Democrats in the House of Lords, 1997–2001.

Robert Skidelsky (Lord Skidelsky of Tilton) was a professor at Warwick University, first of International Studies, then of Economics. He was made an SDP life peer in 1991 and now sits on the Cross Benches. He is mainly known for his three-volume biography of John Maynard Keynes and has recently published *Keynes: The Return of the Master*. He and Shirley are on the advisory board of the Moscow School of Political Studies. He has always been interested in education.

David Steel (Lord Steel of Aikwood) was a Member of Parliament from 1965 to 1997. He became leader of the Liberal Party in 1976, and in 1977–8 he championed the Lib–Lab pact. He led his party into alliance with the SDP, leading in 1988 to union as the Liberal Democrats. David Steel played a key role in the re-establishment of the Scottish Parliament, and was its first Presiding Officer until 2003. Among his publications are *A House Divided*, and his autobiography *Against Goliath*.

Sir Crispin Tickell is the Director of the Policy Foresight Programme at Oxford University. Between 1984 and 1987 he was the Permanent Secretary of the Overseas Development Administration (now DfID), and between 1987 and 1990 British Permanent Representative to the United Nations in New York. He then became Warden of Green College Oxford until 1997. He is an author and contributor to many publications on environmental and related issues. His interests include governance, business, climate change and the early history of the Earth.

Sir Stephen Wall was for thirty-five years a member of the British Diplomatic Service. He was Foreign Policy Adviser to Prime Minister John Major, and then UK Permanent Representative to the EU from 1995-2000. He was EU adviser to Prime Minister Tony Blair and Head of the European Secretariat in the Cabinet Office from 2000–2004. His book on Britain's EU policy, *A Stranger in Europe*, was published in 2008.

Preface

Eightieth birthdays are always worthy of a celebration. This book of essays celebrates that of Shirley Williams.

Shirley was born on 27 July 1930. Her parents were George Catlin and Vera Brittain. She was first elected to Parliament for Hitchin in 1964, and was a junior minister by 1966. In 1974 Shirley entered the Cabinet as Secretary of State for Prices and Consumer Protection, transferring to Education and Science from 1976. She lost her Hertford and Stevenage seat at the election in 1979 which swept Margaret Thatcher to victory. By 1980-81, disillusioned with Labour, Shirley joined with Roy Jenkins, David Owen and Bill Rodgers to form the Social Democratic Party. She became SDP MP for Crosby from 1981–3, and President of the party. From 2001–4, as Baroness Williams of Crosby, she was Leader of the Liberal Democrats in the House of Lords. From 2007–10 she advised Prime Minister Gordon Brown on issues of nuclear proliferation. Parallel to her parliamentary career, Shirley Williams lectured at the John F. Kennedy School of Government at Harvard.

Shirley was married first to the English philosopher Bernard Williams, in 1955, and second to the American political scientist Richard Neustadt, in 1987.

Three of Shirley's own books are referred to in this: her autobiography *Climbing the Bookshelves* (2009); *God and Caesar: Personal Reflections on Politics and Religion* (2004); and *Politics is for People* (1981).

I am most grateful to the essayists for their contributions, particularly for writing at a time of great turbulence and distraction both at home and abroad. And many thanks, too, to Iain Dale and his colleagues at Biteback for their energetic publishing enterprise.

Readers will not be surprised that the matter of coalition politics recurs through these pages. They should not expect to find a definitive diagnosis or a single prescription. There is yet disagreement, especially among the ranks of the centre left where Shirley Williams resides, about whether the Lib–Con coalition government is going to be good for the country in domestic and foreign affairs, and about the long-term effect of this coalition on the political system. Clearly, the referendum on electoral reform, postulated by the government for 5 May 2011, will be a determining event. The referendum campaign should boil down to a choice between coalition politics and single-party rule. If the voters say 'Yes' to the AV system, coalition governments are likely to become the norm rather than the exception. Suddenly the UK will look rather European.

Such a systemic change poses huge issues for all the political parties, but none more so than the Liberal Democrats. In 1926, when the Liberals were having to come to terms with being the third party in British politics, John Maynard Keynes mused about its future role. 'Possibly the Liberal Party cannot serve the State in any better way than by supplying Conservative Governments with Cabinets, and Labour Governments with ideas' (*Liberalism and Labour*).

In my capacity as commissioning editor of these essays, I draw no conclusion other than, first, that it takes British politicians a very long time to get things right and, second, that economists, diplomats, journalists, lawyers, poets, soldiers, priests and philosophers can sometimes help – but not always.

All those who contribute to this book have been associated with Shirley Williams in one way or another through her long career. We may not agree with each other (as the reader will quickly deduce) but we share admiration for Shirley's intellectual and political gifts and her proven ability to make a difference.

Making the Difference is not really a memoir, still less an academic Festschrift. I hope the essayists and their chosen subjects reflect at least something of the breadth of Shirley's interests and accomplishments. Shirley herself will be the best critic of this tribute.

Shirley Williams stands out from the crowd. A woman. A Roman Catholic. Pro-American. Pro-European. An inspired teacher. A consummate broadcaster. Her influence has been, and is, enormous: often controversial, usually forthright, sometimes passionate, always thoughtful.

Peter Mandelson is far from alone as a young man in having found Shirley 'dazzling', with 'the extraordinary talent of both talking and listening to young would-be politicians as if they were the fully finished article . . . She seemed to epitomise a liberal, thinking core in the [Labour] party that recognised a need to combine our traditional values with policies that were relevant to a changing world.' On hearing of her defeat in Stevenage, Peter dropped a bottle of wine in the Tube (*The Third Man*, 2010).

Prime ministers apart (and not all of them), Shirley is possibly the best-known politician in Britain: a walk with her down a public street can take ages as she is approached for a chat by friendly strangers who call her, simply, 'Shirley'. Still engaged at eighty, witty, humane and determined.

Andrew Duff
Cambridge
July 2010

Part one

Parliament and the constitution

The British constitution shimmers through: the 'hung' general election of May 2010

Peter Hennessy

Should a young social anthropologist turn his or her attention to the behaviour patterns of the guardians of the British constitution, they would find three characteristics powerfully shaped their collective make-up. First, a profound reluctance to write anything down if it could be avoided. Second, a belief, as a former Cabinet Secretary put it, privately naturally, of making it up as we go along and calling it being flexible. Third, that there is no problem so acute that it won't yield to a weekend of decorous and discreet discussion between eighteenth-century limestone walls at a mansion somewhere deep in the English countryside.

What has this to do with the British general election of May 2010? A good deal, as it happens. And a definite constitutional spoor can be traced between said country mansion and Buckingham Palace, via the Cabinet Office and the House of Commons, between early November 2009 and mid-May 2010 when, bit by bit, the hung parliament patch of what Sidney Low, in *The Governance of England* (1904), called the 'tacit understandings' of the unwritten constitution moved from the back of an envelope to the cold print of a code (or the draft of a new *Cabinet Manual*, to be precise).

Come with me first to Ditchley Park in north Oxfordshire, home of the Ditchley Foundation, impresario since its creation in 1958 by the Wills family (devotees of the Anglo-American membrane) for innumerable off-the-record conferences which have broadened considerably from the politico-military preoccupations of the Cold War into which it was born. With considerable prescience it hosted a gathering between 5 and 7 November 2009, chaired by the former Prime Minister, Sir John Major, on 'Managing the Machinery of Government in Periods of Change'.

The theme was transitions and Robert Hazell from the Constitution Unit at University College, London and Peter Riddell and Catherine Haddon of the Institute for Government brought with them impressive primers on the subject produced by their respective institutions.* American and Canadian participants came with plentiful comparative experience of their ways of doing it. Among the attendees were the Queen's Private Secretary, Christopher Geidt, and Alex Allan, Chairman of the Joint Intelligence Committee who, at the time, was deeply involved in helping the Secretary of the Cabinet, Sir Gus O'Donnell, with transition planning for the 2010 general election (as Principal Private Secretary in Number 10 in May 1997 he had seen John Major out and Tony Blair in).

Ditchley operates on deep 'Chatham House' rules. But its Director, Sir Jeremy Greenstock, writes a 'Note' after each conference to which is appended a list of participants. One reads it to the sound of some decorous fixing:

> As regards the UK scene, we had a healthy discussion about the procedures that might have to be followed if the election produced a hung parliament. There was no modern precedent for a situation of great uncertainty as to which political leader might be invited to form a government [the 'hung' result of the February 1974 general election being the last]. Moreover the provisions of the 'Caretakers Convention', which covered the arrangements for government in the meantime, were not widely known. Participants regarded it as extremely important to avoid a situation where a government might appear delegitimized, or the sovereign put in an impossible position, by a failure to draw up sensible arrangements in advance.
>
> There were precedents mentioned, particularly from New Zealand,

---

* Robert Hazell, *Elections, Transitions and Government Formation* (Constitution Unit, 2009); Peter Riddell and Catherine Haddon, *Transitions: Preparing for Changes of Government* (Institute for Government, 2009).

which might have relevance. It was firmly suggested that unwritten rules or gentlemen's understandings were no longer adequate in the modern world. The current expenses scandal in parliament was an indication of that. We also heard an interesting input from recent Canadian experience, where the dual role of the prime minister as political leader and constitutional adviser had been seen as awkward [in the autumn of 2008 Stephen Harper had asked the Governor-General of Canada to prorogue Parliament when he found himself in difficulties in the House of Commons in Ottawa. She concurred; but it led to controversy].

'Participants', Sir Jeremy Greenstock's Note reported, 'felt that there would be a willingness on all sides to take a very careful approach to this eventuality.' In his concluding list of 'priorities' for the UK, Sir Jeremy included the recommendation that: 'All predictable eventualities surrounding a hung parliament should be studied with some urgency, with clear guidelines written for the principal players, to the extent possible'.

What one might call the Ditchley Protocol resonated in Whitehall. The Cabinet Secretary, Sir Gus O'Donnell, convened a meeting over a sandwich lunch in the Cabinet Office in mid-February, and at the end of the month he presented its written product to the all-party Justice Select Committee of the House of Commons. In so doing, Sir Gus named the outsiders who had helped draw up the 'Hung Parliament' section of the new draft *Cabinet Manual* (which drew heavily on the existing New Zealand one). And there was a considerable overlap with the Ditchley attendees the previous November, as Sir Gus made plain in his evidence to the Justice Committee on 24 February 2010. Christopher Geidt, Alex Allan, Professors Vernon Bogdanor and Robert Hazell, plus Professor Rodney Brazier (who had not been at Ditchley), Peter Riddell (who could not make the Cabinet Office meeting but sent in material) and the author. Also there were senior officials from the Cabinet Office and the Ministry of Justice.

Those meetings at Ditchley and at 70 Whitehall marked a significant shift in UK constitutional history. I had been keen since the early to mid-1990s for the 'tacit understandings' about 'hung parliaments' to be written down and made public. In an inaugural lecture at Queen Mary on 1 February 1994, I urged what Philip Ziegler has called the 'golden triangle' (the Cabinet Secretary, the Queen's Private Secretary and the Prime Minister's Principal Private Secretary) to reconsider the desirability of this and overcome their reluctance to pick up their collective pen:

> For the Queen's advisers, on this patch of the constitutional terrain, are, in their ever courteous way, living proof of the vitality of [George] Dangerfield's observation on their equivalents at the time of the House of Lords crisis in 1910–11 who refused 'to conjure a great ghost [of a constitution] into the narrow and corruptible flesh of a code'.*

I argued that evening, with one of the then current 'golden triangle', Sir Robin Butler, the Cabinet Secretary, chairing the lecture beside me that

> the time has come for the 'great ghost' to be exorcised. With the mid- to late 1990s threatening to be a potentially volatile period in electoral terms (and any form of proportional representation, if the UK adopted it, would almost certainly produce a hung result every time), and with the monarchy discomfited by the personal problems of some members of the Royal Family, this is not the moment for the guardians of the constitution to risk any suggestion of politicisation or any trace of controversy in the areas covered by the remaining personal prerogatives [the monarch's powers to dissolve Parliament and appoint a prime minister].

I finished by urging the 'golden triangle' to 'consider the dangers very seriously and advise the monarch and the PM [at that time John Major] accordingly. All-party agreement is necessary. . . It is too important for the political parties, for Parliament, for the monarch and for the public for such matters to be left to "instantly invented precedents" – a kind of DIY constitution knitted together in private by a handful of unelected officials operating on the assumption that it will-be-all-right-on-the-night.'†

---

* George Dangerfield, *The Strange Death of Liberal England* (1935).

† 'Searching for the "Great Ghost": The Palace, the Premiership, the Cabinet and the Constitution in the Post-War Period', *Journal of Contemporary History*, Vol. 30, No. 2, April 1995.

The 1990s 'golden triangle' did consider such questions. But they sided with Jim Callaghan, the former prime minister, who had said in a 1991 BBC Radio 4 *Analysis* documentary I had made with Simon Coates about hung parliaments, the Queen and the constitution: 'Well, it works, doesn't it? So I think that's the answer, even if it is on the back of an envelope and doesn't have a written constitution with every comma and semicolon in place. Because sometimes they can make for difficulties that common sense can overcome.'* By the end of the decade, the 'golden triangle', past and present, had still to be persuaded. And in 2000, I reported their thinking like this:

First, that flexibility is all important; precise contingencies cannot be predicted, no two are alike. Published principles would bring rigidity to a part of the constitution which works well partly because of its capacity to adapt successfully to the unforeseen.

Second, why should the Queen be the one person to be tied down? Party leaders might, under the pressure and heat of events, be capable of causing difficulties, but the monarch could find herself trammelled by principles agreed with a set of departed party leaders while she remained in post being the one figure in public life who can never retire (privately she has always ruled out the possibility of abdication).

Finally, there is the doctrine of inappropriate time – that a period of trouble for the royal family is the wrong moment to suggest that the head of state may not be in a position to carry out this part of her job safely and satisfactorily, if required, without change to past practice.[†]

I also made a stab at writing down that which the 'triangle' then wished to remain unwritten by distilling the essence of the Queen's two remaining personal prerogatives:

*   Only the monarch can dissolve Parliament, thereby causing a general election to be held.

* Peter Hennessy and Simon Coates, *The Back of the Envelope: Hung Parliaments, the Queen and the Constitution*, Analysis Paper No. 5, University of Strathclyde, 1991.

† Peter Hennessy, *The Prime Minister: The Office and Its Holders since 1945* (2000).

- Only the monarch can appoint a prime minister.
- After an indecisive general election, the monarch is required to act only if the incumbent prime minister resigns before placing a Queen's Speech before Parliament or after failing to win a majority for that legislative programme in the House of Commons.
- The overarching principle at such delicate times is that the Queen's government must be carried on and that the monarch is not drawn into political controversy by politicians competing to receive her commission to form a government.
- Normally an outgoing prime minister is asked to advise the monarch on the succession, but the monarch has to ask for it, and, if given, it is informal advice which can be rejected, rather than formal advice which must be acted upon.
- After an inconclusive result, if the incumbent prime minister resigns the monarch will normally offer the first chance to form an administration to the party leader commanding the largest single number of seats in the House of Commons.
- A prime minister can 'request', but not 'demand', a dissolution of Parliament. The monarch can refuse. The circumstances in which this might happen would be, in Lord Armstrong's words, 'improbable' [Lord Armstrong of Ilminster, who had sat on two points of the 'triangle' as first Principal Private Secretary in Number 10 and later as Cabinet Secretary, had participated in *The Back of the Envelope* radio documentary]. But the power to withhold consent could be a check, in Lord Armstrong's words, once more, on the 'irresponsible exercise of a prime minister's right to make such a request'.
- The circumstances in which a royal refusal could be forthcoming are, according to Sir Alan ('Tommy') Lascelles, George VI's Private Secretary, if 'the existing Parliament was still vital, viable and capable of doing its job' or if the monarch 'could rely on finding another Prime Minister who could carry out [his or her] Government for a reasonable period, with a working majority in the House of Commons'.

Lascelles conveyed his views pseudonymously, writing as 'Senex', or wise man, to *The Times* on 2 May 1950 when Labour's majority of six seats after the February general election caused a flurry of speculation that Clem Attlee's second administration might not endure (in fact, it did so until October 1951). Lascelles's letter, which served as the British constitution on hung parliaments until Lord Armstrong gave his interview to the BBC Radio 4 *Analysis* programme forty-one years later, and which included a third ground for a monarch refusing a prime minister's request for a dissolution – that it 'would be detrimental to the national economy' – had been, I reported in 2000, quietly dropped in the intervening years. But in 2010, as we shall see shortly, the condition of the economy *did* contribute to the political and constitutional weather system created by the parliamentary arithmetic of the May general election.

When, at last, the precedents and the 'tacit understandings' of the hung parliament contingency – or contingencies, to be more precise, because there are degrees of hungness – struck the page in the draft *Cabinet Manual* Sir Gus O'Donnell sent to Sir Alan Beith, Chairman of the Justice Committee on 23 February 2010, what were its ingredients? (They were made public on 24 February, the day the Cabinet Secretary appeared before the Justice Committee.) Sir Gus had split them into two subdivisions of draft chapter 6, 'Elections and Government Formation', appearing in the Justice Committee's report *Constitutional Processes Following a General Election* (29 March 2010).

First, '*The principles of government formation*'.

> 14. Governments hold office by virtue of their ability to command the confidence of the House [of Commons] and hold office until they resign. A Government or a Prime Minister who cannot command the confidence of the House of Commons is required by constitutional convention to resign or, where it is appropriate to do so instead, may seek a dissolution of Parliament. When a Government or Prime Minister resigns it is for the Monarch to invite the person whom it appears is most likely to be able to command the confidence of the House of Commons to serve as Prime Minister and to form a government. However it is the responsibility

of those involved in the political process – and in particular the parties represented in Parliament – to seek to determine and communicate clearly who that person should be. These are the principles that underpin the appointment of a Prime Minister and formation of a government in all circumstances.

15. If an incumbent Government retains a majority in the new Parliament after an election, it will continue in office and resume normal business. If the election results in a clear majority for a different party, the incumbent Prime Minister and Government will immediately resign and the Monarch will invite the leader of the party that has won the election to form a government. . .

Next, the ' *"Hung" Parliaments*' section was captured in five paragraphs:

16. Where an election does not result in a clear majority for a single party, the incumbent Government remains in office unless and until the Prime Minister tenders his and the Government's resignation to the Monarch. An incumbent Government is entitled to await the meeting of the new Parliament to see if it can command the confidence of the House of Commons or to resign if it becomes clear that it is unlikely to command that confidence. If a Government is defeated on a motion of confidence in the House of Commons, a Prime Minister is expected to tender the Government's resignation immediately. A motion of confidence may be tabled by the Opposition, or may be a measure which the Government has previously said will be a test of the House's confidence in it. Votes on the Queen's Speech have been traditionally regarded as motions of confidence. 17. If the Prime Minister and Government resign at any stage, the principles in paragraph 14 apply – in particular that the person who appears to be most likely to command the confidence of the House of Commons will be asked by the Monarch to form a government. Where a range of different administrations could potentially be formed, the expectation is that discussions will take place between political parties on who shall form the next Government. The Monarch would not expect to become involved in such discussions, although the political parties and

the Cabinet Secretary would have a role in ensuring that the Palace is informed of progress.

18. A Prime Minister may request that the Monarch dissolves Parliament and hold a further election. The Monarch is not bound to accept such a request, especially when such a request is made soon after a previous dissolution. In those circumstances, the Monarch would normally wish the parties to ascertain that there was no potential government that could command the confidence of the House of Commons before granting a dissolution.

19. It is open to the Prime Minister to ask the Cabinet Secretary to support the Government's discussions with Opposition or minority parties on the formation of a government. If Opposition parties request similar support for their discussions with each other or with the Government, this can be provided by the Cabinet Office with the authorisation of the Prime Minister.

20. As long as there is significant doubt whether the Government has the confidence of the House of Commons, it would be prudent for it to observe discretion about taking significant decisions, as per the pre-election period. The normal and essential business of government at all levels, however, will need to be carried out.

This cluster of paragraphs represented a great advance in terms of access to and precision of a particularly sensitive element of a hitherto unwritten part of the British constitution. And yet, there was a problem with it which became apparent once the election campaign was fully under way.

The all-party House of Commons Justice Committee had made public on 29 March that: 'We welcome the evidence of significant thought and effort being put into preparations for the full range of parliamentary election outcomes by the Government, and the Cabinet Secretary in particular.' But Sir Gus had not consulted the Conservative or Liberal Democrat leaders directly and both sounded rather iffy about the newly written 'hung' parliament conventions when asked about them by journalists.

On 25 April, as reported in the *Sunday Times*, Nick Clegg said: 'I read that the civil service has published some book a few weeks ago . . . that in an environment like that [Labour third in share of votes but in possession of largest number of seats], he would have first call to form a government. Well, I think it's complete nonsense. I mean, how on earth? You can't have Gordon Brown squatting in Number 10 just because of the irrational idiosyncrasies of our electoral system.' Mr Clegg added: 'Whatever happens after the election has got to be guided by the stated preferences of voters, not some dusty constitutional document which states that convention dictates even losers can stay in Number 10.'

Quite apart from the means by which 'some book' published 'a few weeks ago' can mutate, in the space of a couple of sentences to 'some dusty constitutional document', the wider question remained of what the British constitution *is* rather than what a party leader in the heat of an electoral race might *wish it to be*. David Cameron on 3 May in *The Independent*, albeit more tersely, appeared to be making a similar point to Nick Clegg when he said: 'There is convention and there is practice and they are not always quite the same thing.'

At the very least, the Clegg/Cameron line on the draft *Cabinet Manual* added to the sense of the British constitution going on heat when the exit poll was released at 10 p.m. on 6 May. From almost that moment on, arguments were made (starting with Theresa May in the first discussion on BBC1's *Election 2010* programme) that, if the exit poll turned out to be accurate (which it did), that Gordon Brown had lost and should go. (To recall, the exit poll predicted Conservatives 305; Labour 255; Liberal Democrats 61; others 29. The actual result was Conservatives 306; Labour 258; Liberal Democrats 57; others 28.)

The Cabinet Office's piece of paper, however, turned out to be immensely useful to those who had, as it were, to incarnate the constitution *as it is* across a range of television and radio studios as the 'hung' parliament unfolded during the small hours of Friday 7 May. If we had had only the Lascelles letter of 1950 and the 1991 transcript of *The Back of the Envelope* to wave around, our task would have been far tougher.

The Cabinet Office had 'war gamed' a variety of 'hung' outcomes twice in the weeks before the election. The Permanent Secretaries devoted much of their annual spring conference at the National School of Government in Sunningdale to related matters. Teams of four civil servants were ready to help with advice and assistance for post-'hung' negotiations from the afternoon of the Friday. An office in the Cabinet Office was established for Christopher Geidt as a forward base from which he could report developments to the Queen. Gordon Brown had given the Cabinet Secretary permission for this ahead of the election. He confirmed it on the morning of 7 May when he returned to Downing Street.

The strong advice from the Cabinet Office, the Treasury and the Bank of England was that the clock was ticking and that the bonds and the currency markets might move if deal-making took too long and that a statement of intent on deficit reduction would be desirable on the Sunday evening before the markets opened on Monday morning. This happened when William Hague for the Conservatives and Danny Alexander for the Liberal Democrats did just that.

In fact, after a flurry of Liberal Democrat/Labour talks on the afternoon of Monday 10 May and the morning of Tuesday 11 May, the Liberal Democrat and Conservative negotiations moved towards a coalition agreement on the Tuesday evening as Gordon Brown prepared to call upon the Queen with his and his government's resignation. It had taken one day longer to reach the final outcome than in 1974 when Ted Heath drove to the Palace to resign on 4 March.

Sir Martin Charteris, the Queen's Private Secretary in 1974, later relived the weekend for me when Ted Heath hung on, having lost his majority in the 28 February election, and tried to do a deal with the Liberals. He said 'it was all very dicey'.* The five days that shook the British political system in May 2010 were not entirely dice-free. Neither David Cameron nor Nick Clegg ran against the conventions. And thanks in considerable part to the understandings for 'hung' parliaments having been written down just over three months earlier, the British constitution had shimmered through. It did its stuff. It got us there with the royal prerogatives in place, a government capable of commanding the House of Commons and a monarch unsullied by political taint or the slightest whiff of controversy. The 'great ghost' was no more.

---

* Interview with Lord Charteris of Amisfield for Wide Vision Productions/Channel 4 TV, *What Has Become of Us?*, 6 June 1994.

The Lords renewed

Robert Maclennan

The nature of political debate in the United Kingdom has changed in the last half century from a preoccupation with the implementation of political ideology to a more pragmatic concern to identify ways and means of delivering widely agreed societal goals. The Westminster model of parliamentary government has never been considered apt for export without modification. In the United Kingdom itself, despite progressive changes made possible by flexible constitutional procedures and conventions, reform has not kept pace with the needs of good governance. Britain's anachronistic structures are sometimes defended by pointing to examples of creditable outcomes. But widespread concerns remain that systemic flaws contribute to the failures to deliver what the public seeks from government.

At national, European and global levels the demands upon a government are manifold and complex and the price for poor decision-making can be not merely disappointing but dangerous. The role of Parliament is not only to provide the individual decision-makers for government but also to continue thereafter directly to influence the process of governmental decision. To accomplish this task with successful outcomes there is a clear need to adapt the parliamentary institutions to equip them for the new contemporary political challenges. Two elected chambers should be assisted by the appointment of a Council of State as an advisory body mandated both to reflect on the issues brought to Parliament and those which it decides merit Parliament's attention.

The main political parties in Parliament have now committed themselves to altering the basis of membership of the second chamber, the House of Lords, to provide for a predominantly or wholly elected body in its place. Since such a development was presaged in the Parliament Act of 1911, this progress may not be considered untimely. But as government and Parliament approach the time for decision, the particular choices for reform and their probable consequences need to be made more explicit. A banner headline is not enough.

The overriding purpose of reforming the House of Lords should be to enhance its capability, and that of Parliament as a whole, to serve the public needs. From time to time some politicians have called for the abolition of the upper House, perhaps considering that the institution was superfluous, or easier to remove than to reshape. But few who have observed the workings of the United Kingdom Parliament at close quarters would doubt the value of its second chamber in the legislative process, even if it is only to allow open reconsideration of policy proposals from the executive arm of national government. Bicameral parliaments are the norm in other democracies. In New Zealand, where the appointed upper chamber was abolished in 1950, an appointed commission, under the chairmanship of a former prime minister, was later set up to give pre-legislative scrutiny and advice to the unicameral Parliament. An interactive dialogue between two chambers of Parliament does allow issues considered in one to be raised in the other; mistakes and oversights can be recognised before legislation is enacted. The current debate in the United Kingdom appears now to favour reform, not abolition.

Parliamentary workload

There is also growing awareness that if the so-called 'prerogative powers of the Crown', currently exercised by ministers – including powers of public appointment, powers over armed conflict and treaty-making powers – are to be subjected to parliamentary oversight and control, there are great new burdens to be shouldered. The territorial devolution of power within the realm may have diminished the need for the same number of elected representatives from the devolved territories to oversee devolved matters. But reserved matters, and the cross-territorial impact of devolved government, make the domestic role of the MP little less heavy now than it was twenty years ago. Externally, since the Treaty of Lisbon formally provided for input from the national parliaments of the European Union in European law-making, the responsibilities of British parliamentarians have been further increased.

The work of Select Committees of the House of Commons in shadowing departments of state has grown since their introduction in the 1980s. Other longstanding bodies such as the Public Accounts Committee and more recent creations such as the Public Administration Select Committee also demand considerable commitment of time from dedicated MPs. It is not simply to suit the convenience of ministers that the work of the Standing Committees of the House of Commons in scrutinising legislation is now frequently subjected to a timetable which truncates their consideration of bills. New areas of policy, such as the protection of human rights following the incorporation of the European Convention of Human Rights into our domestic law, are now subject to systematic scrutiny. In that particular case, the work is shared between the two Houses of Parliament in a joint committee. It is also easily authenticated that the constituency case-workload of MPs has grown over recent decades. It follows that the reform of the chambers of Parliament must take account of the fact that MPs are considerably overstretched.

The present functions of the House of Lords are largely complementary to those of the House of Commons. The legislative deliberation in the Lords is not limited by timetable and, usually, bills are open to consideration at all their stages by the full House. Sometimes government bills originate in the Lords and the groundwork is covered extensively by peers with particular knowledge of the subject matter. Private Members' bills are also introduced there and do sometimes become law. In its investigative role the Lords has a less comprehensive structure of committees than does the Commons, save in respect of the European Union, the activities of which are scrutinised and reported on by a Select Committee with six subcommittees focusing on discrete areas of European policy and legislation. This is work not paralleled in the Commons. In the parliamentary session 2009/10 there were 137 peers serving on the main subject committees such as those on Science and Technology, the Constitution and Economic Affairs. In respect of subordinate legislation the Lords has a distinctive role, particularly in the work of its Delegated Powers and Regulatory Reform Committee, which considers whether new bills delegate powers appropriately and for which there is no Commons equivalent.

The reform of the composition of the second chamber will offer the best opportunity to reconsider the functions of both chambers with a view to ensuring not just an appropriate division of labour but also to raise the salience of the work done by each. If Parliament is to secure the trust of the public and, indeed, to benefit from its interactive input, then the nature and content of the work in progress needs to be better understood. The process of differentiation of the work of the two chambers was begun, again in the Parliament Act of 1911, by limiting the powers of the House of Lords over money bills. It would not, however, meet the challenge to produce better governance if the outcome of reform were either to marginalise the second chamber or to reduce it to a mere echo-chamber of the House of Commons. These are both serious risks.

Elections make a difference

One of the largely unquestioned nostrums of the debate on Lords reform has been that, whatever changes are made, the new chamber should not be in a position to challenge the primacy of the House of Commons. The deference of an unelected body to an elected chamber whose composition determines who shall govern the country is not merely understandable. It was an historic, democratic achievement. The directly representative nature of the House of Commons gives it in almost all circumstances the right to have the last word.

If, however, reform of the second chamber results in its composition being determined by election by the public then that new elected body will enjoy a new democratic legitimacy as well. Its powers and functions will have been determined by the Act of Parliament which set it up. But it will not be entirely clear to the elected members of the second chamber, nor indeed to the public who elected them, what advantage accrues to the country from their maintaining the subordinate role of their unelected predecessors. Unless power is shared, the problem of Commons' overload will not be effectively tackled. The tendency of political power to be centripetal will not be checked. The view that the second chamber is like a fifth wheel would be likely to gain currency. Moreover, the attractiveness to active, public-spirited people of standing for election to such a body is questionable. It would be even more questioned if the continuing presence of appointed members in the second chamber was seen as a device to retain political patronage, thereby reducing the democratic legitimacy of the second chamber and ensuring its ultimate subordination to the House of Commons.

The main weakness of Britain's constitutional structures is that they allow exclusive concentration of power in the hands of the executive arm of government and of the prime minister in particular. The institutional checks and balances are widely acknowledged to be more apparent than real. At any level of government the centre will always tend to be overburdened. But if the quality of governance is to be sustainably improved it cannot depend entirely on finding wise and fully aware individuals to make every ultimate decision. Even the brightest and best sometimes need to hear another point of view. The two chambers of Parliament when elected by the public will both have an undoubted right to be heard. The test of success in reforming the second chamber will be to ensure that it is worth listening to it and that its best advice is heeded.

It may well be argued that the House of Lords in its present form is worth listening to and, since in recent parliaments around 40 per cent of the amendments to government legislation which it has passed have been subsequently accepted without cavil by government, it is also being heeded. It is true that what is passed by the Lords and accepted by government is not always the preferred solution of either but rather the result of compromise, as in the case of the length of detention without charge of suspected terrorists. But such a modifying role is of value and that at least should be preserved when the chamber is reformed.

Both in its legislative and investigative roles a popularly elected chamber must be heard. Whether it will be a truly authoritative arm of our parliamentary democracy will depend considerably upon its standing and the quality of the contribution of its members to scrutiny and debate. The size and nature of the membership of the reformed chamber will both affect the regard in which it is held.

Size and composition

The public is unlikely to welcome the election of more than one thousand representatives to the two chambers of the Westminster Parliament. That would result from the addition of 350 elected members of the reformed second chamber, as adumbrated in earlier proposals, to the existing membership of the House of Commons. That would far exceed the size of bicameral legislatures in many larger countries. The proposed size of the reformed second chamber is more a reflection of the current number of active peers than a recommendation which would strengthen the standing of the elected second chamber. The Senate of the United States and the Bundesrat of the Federal German Republic are highly effective bodies both with substantially smaller full-time membership. It may be suggested that the requirements of Britain, once described as a unitary state, are different from those of nations with federal constitutions having constituent states with their own legislatures.

But Britain is now a constitutional hybrid. The approved trend is towards increasing decentralisation. There is a growing acceptance of the principle of subsidiarity, which implies that higher tiers of government should only have responsibility for what cannot be effectively decided at a lower tier. It would be perverse to reform the structure of our Westminster Parliament to accord with a passing unitary constitutional model. It would in particular be damaging to pile regional responsibilities on top of the national and international duties of the second chamber. To command attention the improved chamber needs to be eminent as well as legitimate. A smaller reformed chamber with real and discrete powers should more readily attract the calibre of candidate required to improve the quality of governance.

In Germany the upper chamber has approximately 11 per cent of the membership of the lower chamber. In the United States the upper chamber has approximately 23 per cent of the number of the lower chamber. For the United Kingdom with its smaller size perhaps the proportions might fall nearer the lower end of the range to, say, 15 per cent, or 111 members.

Such a change would, of course, directly impact upon the capability of the reformed chamber to replicate the full scope of work of the House of Lords. The reformed chamber with its full-time membership would doubtless be capable of revising government legislation and undertaking some serious scrutiny of the business of government in committees set up for the purpose. The differences between the pre- and post-reformed chambers, however, would be great and would flow from two factors.

First, as in the present House of Commons, new members would mostly be generally informed rather than particularly experienced. They might choose to be strategic in their input since there would be limited time for specialisation in preparation for particular investigative undertakings or for legislation. They would, doubtless, bring to their work the ability to amplify the representations made to them, whether by their electors or specialist interest groups. They might also reflect in their contributions the opinions of the parties to which they belong and which had supported their election. In any event there would inevitably be many issues for consideration beyond the direct knowledge of any of the members. Second, elected members are representative of their electors and must, if their democratic mandate is to be sustained, take account of their views, interests and concerns. It is difficult to see how such quotidian responsibilities could be avoided without damaging the reputation of the parliamentarians themselves. It is also difficult to see how these responsibilities could be discharged without further encroachment upon the time of the members to carry out their main duties in the reformed chamber. The delegation of constituency work to appointed staff would be unavoidable, expensive and probably not wholly satisfactory to the public.

Council of State

It has been suggested that to counter this difficulty the elected member should serve for only one term of, say, fifteen years. This could help to free the member from constituency work and, further, help to ensure their independence from party political constraints after their election. But if such a proposal were to be enacted it would remove the accountability of the member to the public. The purpose of election would in part be avoided. The preferable course of reform would be to follow the practice in elections to the US Senate of electing a third of their membership for a term of six years every two years and to leave to the electorate the choice of whether to re-elect their representatives at the end of the six-year term.

The change in the nature of the membership following elections to the reformed chamber needs to be addressed. The loss to Parliament of the knowledge and specialised experience which is directly brought to bear on the current deliberations of the House of Lords would be considerable. On the other hand, the authority of the reformed chamber to stop nonsense would be increased by its elected status and its powers to do so ought to be secured in the enabling legislation. But the dilemma is how to retain for Parliament as a whole the advice of the senior, meritorious, knowledgeable and widely experienced people who have justified the recent work of the House of Lords in Britain's democratic decision-making. Their direct participation in the process has contributed greatly to better governance. It would be no substitute to hear from them sporadically in a letter to *The Times*.

It has been suggested that the inclusion of such people in a top-up of the reformed chamber would meet the need. It would not. Apart from diluting the legitimacy of an elected chamber it could not possibly provide the range of experience represented in the House of Lords, particularly if the elected proportion of the chamber were to be predominant. A better solution would be to acknowledge the ongoing value of such people to all law-makers, in both chambers of Parliament, and to provide for a new parliamentary institution, the Council of State, to which suitably qualified people would be independently appointed.

The appointment of the Counsellors of State should be made by an independent statutory body, at arm's length from the government, and the members themselves should be broadly experienced. Nominations could be invited from the public or from the would-be counsellors themselves. To keep the council refreshed there should be a rolling membership, which should be properly staffed and remunerated. The term of appointment, however, should be long enough to ensure stability and continuity of operation.

If, as suggested, the reformed chamber consisted of 110 members and the Council of State had, say, 150 members, their combined numbers would be less than one-third of the present membership of the House of Lords. The role of the Council of State would be, in particular, to provide for pre-legislative scrutiny, possibly including hearings, on government legislation. It might also engage in post-legislative scrutiny to offer advice on outcomes. Their input into legislation would be provided for in the timetabling for the consideration of bills, but the role would be advisory, including proposing, or offering advice on, amendments, but with no power of decision or to obstruct the will of either elected chamber. The council would have a wider advisory role at its own hand or as requested by either of the two chambers.

It is worth considering when undertaking the reform of the House of Lords the case for some further separation of powers within the constitution. The existing practice is to appoint a few peers to serve in ministerial position and, additionally, to parachute a few more ministers into the House of Lords since their services are sought by the prime minister and, conventionally, ministers must belong to one or other House of Parliament. The convention no longer seems appropriate. Certainly the prime minister's choice of particular individuals to serve in government should not be circumscribed by the talent having to be found in Parliament. But from the point of view of elected legislative chambers it would be preferable that their interaction with the executive arm of government should be with the particular responsible minister.

At present, the House of Commons does not invite ministerial members of the House of Lords into its chamber, although it does hear them sometimes in select committees. The Lords most frequently hear from a junior spokesman for a department who is not necessarily a minister in that department. Fully elected chambers considering government bills should as a matter of course hear from the minister in charge of the legislation. Similarly, in both chambers members should be entitled to put their parliamentary questions to the responsible minister. Parliament should decide that a proportion of the ministers of the government need not sit in either chamber but that all ministers should be answerable to both. Membership of the House of Lords has not been the normal route to political preferment. It would help to avoid the risk of the mere replication of the role of MPs by elected members of the reformed chamber if the distinction were made clear by the second, reformed, chamber having no members directly participating in the executive arm of government.

The ethos of the second chamber and the focus of its legislative and investigative work would undoubtedly be transformed by such innovations. Together, however, they could help to generate greater public awareness of what is happening in Parliament. If, as has been proposed, the second chamber is elected by proportional representation then there may well be a more territorial flavour to its debates which could arouse greater local interest. But the principal role of the reformed chamber must be to enlarge the effectiveness of the parliamentary oversight of government and to achieve that will require a readiness to depart from time-honoured parliamentary conventions and radically to reshape the parliamentary institutions.

Women in Parliament

Germaine Greer

As long ago as 1974 two women were given the important job of drafting the Labour Party manifesto. They were 64-year-old Barbara Castle, and 44-year-old Shirley Williams. In 2010 Baroness Williams, speaking of women in Parliament, finds herself saying, 'We're slipping backwards – it's terribly depressing – and not just in numbers but influence. . . Now you have to hunt for a woman'. Unless you are looking for the bedfellow of a male leader, that is. Samantha Cameron, Sarah Brown and Miriam González Durántez (the only party leader's wife who still uses her own name) were the three women who mattered in the May 2010 election. Some looked at the list of women candidates and groaned that we didn't even have a Hillary Clinton. What the example of Hillary Clinton teaches us is that the best way to get ahead in US politics is to marry a man who gets himself elected president. Condoleezza Rice might be a more hopeful example, if she hadn't simply been plucked from Stanford University to serve in the Bush administration, and returned there as soon as Bush left office. Though she was for four years the most powerful woman in the world, Rice is not a career politician and so far has not chosen to subject herself to the rough and tumble of the hustings.

Barbara Castle was committed to electoral politics from her earliest youth. She was born into the staunchly socialist Betts family in 1910, and first stood as a Labour candidate in mock elections at her school. As an undergraduate at Oxford she joined the University Labour Club, and rose to become treasurer of the club, the highest office a woman could hold at the time. She found life at Oxford difficult, because of both her sex and her class, and could manage only a third in PPE. In 1937 she stood for election to St Pancras Borough Council and was elected; in 1943 she addressed the Labour Party conference. In the 1945 election which Labour won by a landslide, Betts, now Mrs Ted Castle, won the seat of Blackburn, which she was to hold through various changes of boundary until 1979.

Shirley Williams's career follows Castle's twenty years later, with the difference that she was a brilliant graduate and a Fulbright Scholar. Like Castle she joined the Oxford University Labour Club. Women were by then eligible to chair the club, which Williams did in 1950. In 1959 she stood as Labour candidate for Southampton, and duly lost; in 1964 she stood for Hitchin and won. Ten years later she was working with Castle on the Labour Party manifesto. Neither career was meteoric; both women had to be much smarter and more effective, and rather more patient, than the men competing with them for posts of influence. The Labour Party was the ultimate beneficiary.

While both Castle and Williams would have wanted to see more women among their colleagues, it would never have occurred to either of them to demand all-women short-lists for pre-selection. Women who have fought their way up through the ranks, competing with equally driven men and worsting them by sheer ability, are unlikely to advocate the kind of affirmative action that would install an arbitrary number of women in positions that they had not been able to attain through their own efforts. If we examine the records of distinguished female politicians we will find that they expressed conflicting views on the question of all-women short-lists. Ann Widdecombe was characteristically forthright, dubbing them 'an insult to women'. Though Lynne Featherstone, now one of only seven females among fifty-seven Lib Dem MPs, finds the current situation 'atrocious', she rejects all-women short-lists as a solution. 'We believe local people should decide on their choice of candidates and intervention from the centre isn't welcome. You can't just drop people in.' At the Liberal Democrat party conference of September 2001, when only five of fifty-two Liberal Democrat MPs were female, Baroness Williams supported Jackie Ballard's motion for all-women short-lists, saying: 'At the moment the

Conservative Party is dissolving into irrelevance. Do you really want the Liberal Democrats to be seen as profoundly backward and old-fashioned in attitudes to gender?' But Lyn-Sue Floodgate of Liberal Democrat Youth and Students opposed it: 'The proposers are telling me I cannot fulfil my dream of becoming an MP without this motion. They underestimate me,' she said.

Harriet Harman, Clare Short, Mo Mowlam and Tessa Jowell all supported the introduction of all-women short-lists. Harman and Jowell are now asking that the shadow cabinet be 50 per cent female. Quotas are in the wind; stock exchanges as diverse as those of Norway and Australia are demanding that listed companies show 40 per cent female representation at all levels in the organisation, including the boardroom, or be de-listed. Some hard-headed women are bucking the trend; as provost of Stanford, Condoleezza Rice has cancelled the university's policy of affirmative action in the granting of tenure posts.

How Labour's long-standing women MPs regarded the arrival in the house of sixty-four starry-eyed neophytes in 1997 we may never know. They have all been too loyal to say. They probably did not realise that younger and far less experienced women would be given the kinds of jobs in government that they might have expected for themselves. We cannot know but can imagine how they felt about being included in the derogatory class of 'Blair's Babes'. Kate Hoey and Clare Short did not turn up for the famous photograph of Blair standing on the steps of Church House surrounded by smiling women, but Gwyneth Dunwoody and Margaret Beckett were both there, smiling as rapturously as all the others.

Women like Castle and Williams were aware – none more so – of exactly how much better a woman had to perform than a man if she was to be given a top job. They had both seen men of far less ability promoted to positions above them, but they also knew that if women were to survive in adversarial politics they had to have considerable skill, real hunger and extraordinary powers of endurance. Simply to give an arbitrary number of women what men and other women had had to fight for, could not produce a governing class that knew what it was doing, or how and why.

All-women short-lists

The introduction by the Labour Party of all-women short-lists in 1995 was part of the process of 'modernisation' of the party. With female membership of the House of Commons at less than 10 per cent Britain could hardly figure in the world as a forward-looking democracy. Sporadic attempts were made by all parties to encourage women to stand for pre-selection and to provide special training for motivated women, but no improvement ensued. For the general election of 1992 the Labour Party insisted that at least one female candidate should appear on all pre-selection short-lists, but, as hardly any of the female candidates were selected to contest winnable seats, the dearth of women members continued unchanged. At the Labour party conference of 1993, in a paper written by Clare Short, it was announced that half of all the seats judged winnable would be required to put up all-women short-lists for pre-selection for the election of 1997. Psephologists had argued, apparently persuasively, that women vote more conservatively than men. The considered response of New Labour was to court more women. If, as seemed to many, 'modernisation' of the Labour Party was simply another name for the abandonment of socialist principles, the apparently radical policy of all-women short-lists was an effective way of guaranteeing timidity and conservatism on the part of the parliamentary party, and a particularly underhand way of disenfranchising the left. Cultivating a generation of neophytes would not only bring a 'better class of totty' into the House, it would also sideline the party's female left wing, and the party's most experienced women politicians.

It was only a matter of time before two male members of the party challenged the legality of all-women short-lists, and, supported by the Equal Opportunities Commission, brought a court action against the party; in December 1996 an industrial tribunal found that the all-women short-lists were illegal under the Sex Discrimination Act of 1975. The result was a compromise: while the unfinished selections from all-women short-lists were suspended, thirty-eight women already selected from all-women short-lists were allowed to stand in the 1997 election. Writing on the eve of the 2010 general election, *Daily Telegraph* journalist Liz Hunt referred to the outcome as 'the debacle of the Blair babes who simpered into Westminster thirteen years ago only to leave no discernible legacy other than the belief that most of them weren't up to the job'.

The selection of 'winnable seats' that would be required to mount women-only short-lists for pre-selection was anything but random. The seats had not only to be winnable by Labour but also winnable by women. And the constituency had to co-operate. Much depended on the composition of party membership at constituency level. A constituency party that was dominated by men, or that cultivated a macho atmosphere that was intimidating to women, would be unlikely to feature many women in the overall membership or among office-holders. Investigation of sexual politics at the branch level in any party would seem to be a necessary preliminary to demanding more women at the top. The other parties talked of training more women in the techniques of electoral government, in organisation, canvassing, formulating policy, networking and so forth, so that they acquired the necessary skills to work their way up from constituency party level. The women meanwhile went on stuffing envelopes and making tea.

New Labour needed to look new. If women who were willing to stand could not be found in the local branches, they would import them. Four constituency parties rebelled and refused to select any candidate at all. When the landslide victory was announced, twenty-seven Conservative-held seats had fallen to women selected from Blair's all-women short-lists, and seven seats had been held for Labour. Besides the thirty-four women who had arrived via the all-women short-lists, and thirty-seven veterans, there were thirty other women MPs who were taking seats in the House for the first time. These women were to prove more conspicuous than women recruited via the all-women short-lists, most of whom were happy to remain backbenchers, on message, and work hard as constituency MPs. Karen Buck, who survived the 2010 election to hold her seat for a fourth term, in 2001 turned down a place in the Whips' Office and chose to remain on the back benches. A few of the newcomers had been groomed by the party, but most, whether they had come via the all-women short-lists or not, found the Commons a bizarre and intimidating environment. Their ignorance was compounded by the fact that as a rule they were significantly younger than the male MPs, who found it easy to treat them as juniors, and even dared to harass them with ribald observations and comments. One woman described the atmosphere in the house as 'Neanderthal'. Even so the thirty-four women from the all-women short-lists have performed as well in the Commons as many of their colleagues, and they have tended to show rather more stickability. Only nine had left office before the 2010 election, and nine survived it to serve a fourth term.

No beneficiary of the all-women short-lists rose higher than Jacqui Smith. She held a succession of cabinet posts before being appointed Home Secretary by Gordon Brown in June 2007, becoming only the third woman to rise to such a level in the administration. Her two-year reign was an unimpressive series of gaffes, culminating in the expenses debacle, in which her behaviour in claiming for her actual home in Redditch as her secondary home was described as 'near fraudulent'. Humiliatingly, she was found to have claimed for two pornographic films. She was asked to apologise to the House but did not. She was later reported as saying: 'When I became Home Secretary, I'd never run a major organisation. I hope I did a good job. But if I did, it was more by luck than by any kind of development of skills. I think we should have been better trained. I think there should have been more induction'. One can only imagine what Barbara Castle would have had to say about that.

The plastering of the Commons with inexperienced and ill-prepared women was the worst kind of gesture politics, and the principal sufferers in the event were the women themselves. The most vocal critic of parliamentary mores was Tess Kingham, who had won Gloucester in open contest. As she struggled to balance her responsibilities to her three children with her parliamentary timetable, she was appalled to find that debate was deliberately prolonged by time-wasting tactics and that almost no issue was debated on its merits. The female newcomers waited hours to be called to speak only to be silenced on technicalities. When to the rigours of attending the House, the demands of the constituency and caring for a family were added, the women found themselves existing in a permanent state of exhaustion. Hopes that the parliamentary timetable would be reformed, and become more family-friendly proved vain, despite (or perhaps because of) the efforts of the modernising committee led by veterans Ann Taylor and Margaret Beckett, for whom no such concessions had ever been made.

Possibly the most ambitious of the female newcomers of 1997 who had been groomed for high office was Patricia Hewitt, who had been rewarded for her efforts as one of the chief architects of Labour's modernisation by being selected for the safe seat of Leicester West. She was appointed to her first government post in 1999 and to the cabinet in 2001. Her patchy performance as Secretary of State for Health was not improved by a series of reckless indiscretions, which ended in a vote of no confidence in the House. When Brown took over as Prime Minister, Hewitt was dropped from the cabinet and within weeks had taken up a lucrative post on the board of Alliance Boots. She was eventually suspended from the Parliamentary Labour Party as a consequence of having been secretly filmed apparently agreeing to help a client obtain a seat on a government advisory group in return for a fee of £3,000 a day. Clearly Hewitt is a different kind of political animal from Castle and Williams.

Combining the rigours of the parliamentary routine with those of pregnancy cannot really add to a member's effectiveness, but it did not interfere with the prospects of the female insiders in New Labour's first administration. Though 29-year-old Ruth Kelly was heavily pregnant when Blair came to power, and would eventually bear four children while she was in office, she was regularly promoted. Yvette Cooper was not persuaded to delay her child-bearing either, and in 2001 became the first serving cabinet minister to take maternity leave. Claire Curtis-Thomas had been told so often by her constituency that she could not possibly win the seat of Crosby, that she had decided to try for a third child. When she discovered that she had taken the seat with a huge swing, and that she was going to have to move house and travel up and down to Westminster throughout her pregnancy, she wept. Though she had one child with learning difficulties, her plea for a crèche in the Commons was greeted with ridicule. Julia Drown invoked the male members' worst nightmares when she campaigned for the right to breastfeed in the House.

Pressure to include women and members of ethnic minorities in the House of Commons is usually justified by the perception of a need to make Parliament 'more representative' of Britain's cultural diversity. The underlying assumption is that parliamentarians have all sprung up from the grassroots. They are more likely to have been drawn into parliamentary politics by what used to be called the 'old boys' network'. This was associated with the right wing, but Labour politics has its own systems of patronage and promotion which work in a very similar fashion. We should not be surprised to find then that a fairly high proportion of the new female intake in the election of 1997 was connected to the old intake in one way or another. Of the women from the all-women short-lists, Maria Eagle, selected for Liverpool Garston, is the twin sister of Angela Eagle, MP for Wallasey since 1992, Ann Keen, who was selected for Brentford and Isleworth, is married to MP Alan Keen, Ann Cryer, selected for Keighley, is the widow of one MP and the mother of another; Julie Morgan, who was selected for Cardiff North, is the wife of the MP for Cardiff West; and Dari Taylor, who was selected for Stockton South, is the daughter of a former MP for Burnley. And so on. Nothing about this is surprising.

The women who were already familiar with the parliamentary regime had an advantage; the rest were given no induction into an arcane system and had little choice but to do as they were told, that is, when anybody bothered to tell them. Dari Taylor was twice in trouble for misusing Commons stationery. She seems not to have realised that what she had done was a serious breach of the rules and did not apologise. When the House of Commons Committee on Standards and Privileges fined her £500 and demanded a written apology, she said that the rules were too confusing and she had tried her best to stick to them. Kali Mountford was suspended from the House for five days, after she made the classic blunder of leaking a committee report to the government. The plea of inadvertence cannot be made in the cases of the many women MPs who fiddled their expenses as adroitly as the most seasoned men.

Counter-productive

The effect of the all-women lists was not to encourage more women to enter the political fray, but apparently to discourage them from seeking selection without them. The election of 2001 returned six fewer women Labour MPs than in 1997. The Labour government then introduced the Sex

Discrimination (Election Candidates) Act (2002), which legalised positive discrimination in selecting candidates. All-women short-lists were used again in the 2005 election, which brought the number of women Labour MPs to 98 out of a total of 128 for all parties, an improvement of only two. The all-women lists were used again in 2010 but this time Labour lost the election. Even so eighty-one women MPs were returned for Labour, more than for all the other parties combined. Women make up 31 per cent of the Parliamentary Labour Party but only slightly more than 20 per cent of the membership of the House. Harriet Harman has interpreted this as meaning that the Labour Party represents the 'voice of women'. This is to stretch a point to breaking.

If all-women short-lists were meant to boost the numbers of women in Parliament, they were far less effective than was hoped. If the immediate effect of introducing an inexperienced group of women to an intensely competitive masculine environment was to cause them grief and embarrassment, and to have many of them stand down within a term or two, then it can be seen actually to have retarded the emergence of women and women's issues into mainstream politics. If the original intention was to produce a biddable House of Commons for a presidential prime minister who tended to sideline his cabinet, the strategy seems to have worked, greatly to the detriment of party democracy. Back benches crowded with naive women who are on message can be more easily manipulated by the centre than old campaigners like Gwyneth Dunwoody or Clare Short. Most of the new women MPs of the 1997 intake were good constituency members, who worked hard for their constituents and would have had little trouble being selected for second and third terms, if so many of them had not chosen to stand down.

Great historical changes cannot be made in a hurry; papering a female face onto a misogynist House of Commons will be ultimately self-defeating. The process must start where it started for Barbara Castle, at school, where young women should be encouraged to form political parties, to develop agendas, to defend policies and to canvass their mock electorate. Only by starting at the beginning can we raise a generation of women who will have the skills, the motivation, the toughness and the stamina to reform an absurdly laddish House of Commons – and to enjoy doing it.

Part two

The centre left

The beginnings: a personal memoir

Bill Rodgers

In 1951, I made a note in my personal diary about some of the Oxford stars who were about to go down from their university years. Among the rising young politicians there was Jeremy Thorpe, later to become the Liberal leader; another was William Rees-Mogg, who became editor of *The Times*. There was Robin Day, Dick Taverne and, briefly, Norman St John Stevas.

There were two layers of political involvement open to the undergraduates: through the highly prestigious (and self-regarding) Oxford Union debating society; and through the main political clubs – Conservative, Labour and Liberal – each of which recruited well over a thousand members each term. But although it is now hard to believe, women were excluded from the Oxford Union, except to sit in the galleries and admire the male speakers below or silently rail against their exclusion. However, there were no restraints for women to play a full and leadership role in the political clubs and in the Michaelmas Term (autumn) of 1950, Shirley Vivian Brittain Catlin was elected Chairman of the Oxford University Labour Club. Her political career had begun.

I saw a lot of Shirley as I was her deputy in the Labour Club and out of this grew a long working relationship in politics and a close personal friendship. She was, I wrote in my diary, 'a rare character, a unique combination of mental ability, physical energy, friendliness and ambition', plus an element of straying from the whole truth, especially in order to avoid abrasive encounters. I found her 'soft' on issues that required unpopular decisions

(I was left to make them) but, in turn, she thought me unreasonably hard.

Shirley sat, as Chairman (this was long before 'Chair' or 'Chairperson'), at packed meetings addressed by leading ministers in the closing days of the Attlee government, among others Hugh Dalton, the former Chancellor of the Exchequer, and the young Parliamentary Secretary of the Admiralty, James Callaghan. Shirley persuaded Victor Gollancz, the Left Book Club publisher, to speak and she was host to a 'Left Luncheon' for the leading actor Paul Schofield.

She also sat on the Executive Committee and with college organisers, future MPs (and ministers) including Dick Marsh and Gerald Kaufman (and, in addition, a future ambassador, a future civil service permanent secretary as well as several future heads of Oxbridge colleges). She wrote to me from her address, 2 Cheyne Walk, Chelsea: 'The Labour Club is hungrily eating up the days of my vacation. Goodbye to all the intense academic work I honestly believed I'd do.'

Even in those student times, Shirley had a marvellously rich speaking voice, seductive in conversation and urgently persuasive on a public platform. Typically, her opening Chairman's message to the club was date-lined New York because during the summer vacation she had been in a touring production of *King Lear*. She was already familiar with the United States and also with India. She was not one of the invited members of the undergraduate Oxford University Strasbourg Club but she was fully aware of the significant political European changes in the post-war world. In only a few years she was to write two substantial Fabian pamphlets pointing towards Britain's future in the emerging European Economic Community.

Sixty years ago, Shirley had an emotional response to politics, committed to redistributing wealth and opportunity in what our friends called 'a just society'. She was slightly uneasy in being comfortably off and she occasionally tried to diminish her status and become – as I put it in my diary – 'one of the people'. But she was a genuine egalitarian, treating socialism 'as much of the heart as of the head'.

In the language of the time, the word 'socialism' was routine but the ideas and values were social democratic, not heavily dogmatic or ideological. Through her family, she was linked to Herbert Morrison, the former Home

Secretary and deputy leader of the Labour Party; but in the years ahead she never formed a strong individual relationship with any major leader. She respected Hugh Gaitskell on his merits when he was the Labour leader but she was not a 'Gaitskellite'; she held Roy Jenkins in high regard but she was not of his intimate circle.

Soon after leaving Oxford, in a short pause before her new career, she was the constituency election agent to the Labour candidate in Chelsea and three years later she fought her own first parliamentary seat at a by-election in Harwich. It was another stage of her political ascent.

In my 1951 diary, I speculated about Shirley's future. She had, I thought, few crises in her life but one day a crisis would confront her. How would she manage it? At Oxford she had lived a charmed life in a goldfish bowl, handling people with subtlety, communicating with them skilfully and getting away with a few liberties. Would she survive in the rough, cruel world of real politics?

The answer as we now know is a resounding 'Yes'. Despite her long ministerial career, Shirley lost her seat in Hertford and Stevenage and again in Crosby, where she had triumphed in her SDP 1981 by-election. She left the Labour Party to become one of the 'Gang of Four', a very painful and high-risk break. She never really enjoyed the collegiate atmosphere of the House of Commons and is not a natural House of Lords person. But despite that, in the broad scope of public life she has done brilliantly, in a straight line for sixty years from the Oxford Labour Club to yet another outstanding performance in *Question Time* and to another distinguished international conference. It is a remarkable story.

The reform agenda: the SDP and its legacy

David Owen

Inside the Labour Party, even before she was elected to Parliament in 1964, Shirley Williams had been its most popular politician. The first time we got to know each other was in 1972 on a working party established by the British Association. We were set the fascinating task of studying the scientific, social, ethical and legal implications of all the recent advances in genetics and biology. Under the scientist Walter Bodmer, we grappled with in vitro fertilisation and the moral dilemmas; Shirley, the converted and devout Roman Catholic and I, in spirit, from my grandfather, still a member of the Welsh disestablished Church. We were cabinet ministers together from 1977–9 and Shirley was very generous over my rapid promotion. I remember, during that time, how we tried, but failed, to persuade the Cabinet to make the European Convention on Human Rights and Fundamental Freedoms, which the UK endorsed in 1951, justiciable in the UK courts. Yet that reform, along with devolution to Scotland, Wales and Northern Ireland, Freedom of Information, a Ministry of Justice and proportional voting became key reforms espoused by the SDP.

All these reforms, except proportional representation for electing MPs, were introduced, to their credit, by New Labour. I judge that the combined effect of these reforms, along with the EU treaties, has been to give the UK a written constitution. I see the challenge for the twenty-first century, for constitutional reformers like Shirley and me, as being to introduce proportional representation voting for the House of Commons elections, to elect the second chamber, and, since both of us have an admiration for the US constitution, to gradually establish a greater separation between Cabinet as the executive and Parliament as the legislature. We have not really discussed the newly created Supreme Court but I want to see it overtly given the task of safeguarding and defending this new constitution, and our country and our people, from conflicting legislation whether from national parliaments, the European Court of Human Rights, the European Union and its European Court of Justice. I see this as somewhat analogous to the German Constitutional Court. On this overall ambitious agenda, I hope, at least for the major part, that Shirley and I will be in harmony.

The Gang of Three

In May 1979 Shirley fell victim to the swing against Labour and lost Stevenage and in 1980, as she was no longer in the House of Commons, we had fewer opportunities for talking. Somewhat surprisingly, neither of us had ever been to each other's homes in London or in the country. In fact I had to ask Bill Rodgers for her phone number in order to fix a meeting for the three of us to meet at her flat to talk about the state of the Labour Party. Bill had known Shirley well since Oxford and because our families saw each other he was surprised that Shirley and I did not know each other better. The day before we were due to meet, John Silkin signed a statement saying he was going to attempt, at the autumn Labour Conference, to commit the party to withdrawing from the European Community with no renegotiation and without even a referendum. As a former Chief Whip of the Labour government, Silkin's was a major political challenge.

Next morning Bill and I met in Shirley's flat. The papers were full of the impending row within the Labour Party over the European Community. We decided to issue a joint statement to catch the Sunday newspapers. Shirley's was the main draft; all three of us contributed words and sentences. We declared that for the Labour Party to make a manifesto commitment to leave the European Community in 1983 or 1984 would be 'irresponsible, opportunistic and short sighted' and added that we could have no part in it. We asked 'Is this decision to be endlessly reopened? Are the old divisions to be stirred up again and again weakening our national self-confidence and our ability to contribute constructively to economic, energy and social problems?' We ended by saying 'there are some of us who will not accept a choice between socialism and Europe. We will choose them both.' That was the first indication we had ever given that we could contemplate leaving the Labour Party for a new social democratic party. We decided to meet over the next few weeks to draft a much more comprehensive statement covering economic and social questions for we knew that Europe was too narrow a platform to have much appeal within the Labour Party. Yet in press terms the Gang of Three was born. Shirley was, from the start, the key figure in winning over Labour MPs and voters. Her great gift of empathy had given her unique appeal, particularly to women Labour Party members and those in the Cooperative Movement.

Our defiance was headline news in the *Sunday Times*. It was an important milestone in the birth of the SDP for it brought together a critical mass needed to attract other Labour MPs. It was also a positive partnership with good humour and give-and-take. Our decision to fight together did not imply we were ready to accept Roy Jenkins's earlier dream of a Centre Party. On Monday 9 June he had spoken to the Parliamentary Press Gallery saying that there was no question of his flickering back to British politics, like a moth to a candle, before he finished his Presidency of the European Commission on 6 January 1981. However, he talked of an experimental plane, his way of describing the Centre Party, with which the press associated him.

Not surprisingly, the anti-marketeers hit back at our Gang of Three statement, and Peter Shore and John Silkin got involved in the growing controversy. Jim Callaghan, now Leader of the Opposition, stepped in, calling all those in the Shadow Cabinet, who were arguing in public, to a meeting in his room in the House of Commons. Shirley, therefore, was not involved. Jim asked us to try to defuse the controversy but Bill and I replied that we could not stay silent; the danger to the European Community was now a very real one, because after Silkin's intervention the anti-marketeer Safeguards Campaign had circulated to constituency parties a resolution demanding withdrawal from the Community. If we did nothing it would become official Labour Party policy within months. All we could promise, in deference to Jim, was that we would try our best to keep personalities out of the conflict.

The Labour Party Commission of Enquiry was having a meeting to finalise its report on reforming the party's constitution on the weekend of 14–15 June 1980 at the ASTMS training college at Bishop's Stortford. On the Sunday, the conference turned to the question of leadership. Suddenly Jim Callaghan was told for the first time by the unions about their concept of an electoral college, with power to elect the party leader and to control the party manifesto, made up of 50 per cent MPs and 25 per cent trade union representation; 20 per cent representing constituency parties and 5 per cent others covering the Cooperative Party and Fabian Society. By the early evening Jim had endorsed it. It was incomprehensible and quite out of character that he put his name to such an indefensible proposition without consulting with MPs and the wider party. Peter Jenkins, writing in *The Guardian* on 18 June 1980, and using his old links as an industrial correspondent to winkle out what had really happened in Bishop's Stortford, wrote:

> The relevant question in British politics at this moment is not what prospect there is for a new Party but rather what is the chance of the old Party splitting. Dr David Owen, Mr William Rodgers and Mrs Shirley Williams will have serious decisions to make . . . Mr Jenkins might find himself joining their Party instead of trying to recruit them to his.

For the three of us the main preoccupation now was to draft a more comprehensive policy statement. Prior to the publication, we had a number of meetings on what became an open letter in *The Guardian* published on 1 August. Our long piece went through different drafts with each of us adding and subtracting phrases or words. By the end it was genuinely the product of all three of us. Throughout, the major issue with which we had to grapple was how far we went in implying that we were ready to leave the Labour Party and help create a new party. On 3 July, with a redraft of Bill's initial draft, I wrote to Shirley:

The hardest question I find to resolve is whether we should explicitly raise
again the question of another socialist party. Again on balance I conclude
we should, but fairly indirectly, and I think we need to guard against being
thought to be 'opting out' rather than 'fighting on'.

On 1 August our piece appeared, prominently positioned in *The Guardian*.
The opening sentence read: 'The Labour Party is facing the gravest crisis in
its history – graver even than the crisis of 1931.' This was followed by three
sections – on the commitment to the mixed economy, the commitment to
international socialism and the commitment to representative democracy.
However, the sting was in the tail and it was over these words that we had
wrestled.

If the NEC remains committed to pursuing its present course and if,
consequently, fears multiply among the people, then support for a Centre
party will strengthen as disaffected voters move away from Labour. We
have already said that we will not support a Centre party for it would
lack roots and a coherent philosophy. But if the Labour Party abandons
its democratic and internationalist principles, the argument may grow for
a new democratic socialist party to establish itself as a party of conscience
and reform committed to those principles. We are not prepared to abandon
Britain to divisive and often cruel Tory policies because electors do not
have an opportunity to vote for an acceptable socialist alternative to a
Conservative Government.

There are those who say that the Labour Party cannot survive its present
battles but must now tear itself to pieces. Others believe that soft words and
a little skilful evasion of the issues can paper over the cracks again. We do
not share either of these views. If there is one lesson it is that there can be
no compromise with those who share neither the values nor the philosophy
of democratic socialism. A Labour Party committed to these values and
this philosophy can defeat Tory reaction. We shall fight for such a Labour
Party. We ask all those who share that conviction to fight for it too. It is
Britain's best hope.

In *The Guardian*, it was 'The Three Musketeers Take Up Arms'; in the *Sunday Times*, 'Why the Gang of Three Are Right'. The hard fight ahead was the Blackpool Labour Party Conference. This was to prove far more disastrous than any of us expected and on Monday 29 September, the Campaign for a Labour Victory had a meeting in the Baronial Hall of the Winter Gardens. Shirley, alarmed like we all were over the mounting pressure over reselection of Labour MPs, in a very harsh sentence warned that there was such a thing as a fascism of the left. That evening in Shirley's room in the Imperial Hotel we heard that Clive Jenkins was confident of swinging the trade union votes to win on an electoral college and on withdrawal from the Community. Fellow MPs started to talk for the first time about leaving the Labour Party without qualifying what they were saying. Ironically, many of those who spoke most fervently eventually stayed with the party. But that night we all felt doom laden.

The withdrawal from the European Community motion was carried on a card vote by 5,042,000 to 2,097,000. The requisite two-thirds majority was not there to ensure it was in the manifesto but nobody listening to that debate could have had any doubt that Labour would fight the next election on an outright commitment to withdraw and, what is more, that if it won it would take Britain out despite the 1975 referendum decision to stay in. By the Thursday morning the conference seemed determined to convince the country that it was totally in the grip of the far left by proceeding to vote for unilateral nuclear disarmament.

These blows, coming one upon the other, were shattering. Shirley, on Thursday, was already in full cry at another Campaign for Labour Victory fringe meeting by the time Bill, who had spoken to the press after his speech on defence, joined us. It was clear that the electoral college question was going to be referred to a special conference and Shirley said that we would take our battle there. It showed how these deeply important issues had to be dealt with rapidly, almost instinctively. Events were moving so fast that we could hardly anticipate them.

Jim Callaghan announced he was stepping down as leader and Shirley and I wanted all the candidates for the party leadership election to say whether they were prepared to commit themselves to one member, one vote in every constituency to select an MP, to sack an MP and to elect the leader of the party. Things were more complex with Bill, for though he could see the tactical advantages of one member, one vote he genuinely believed that it was better for MPs to choose the leader and preferred to stick to this option, while agreeing not to do anything to damage the cause for one member, one vote.

The Shadow Cabinet decided to go ahead with MPs electing our new leader and the Parliamentary Labour Party supported this. On 4 November the first ballot results from the leadership election were announced. Denis Healey had 112 votes, Michael Foot 83, John Silkin 38 and Peter Shore 32. It was obvious that Michael could win on the next ballot. On Monday 10 November, he duly did so, beating Denis Healey by 139 to 129 votes.

A few days later, the Parliamentary Labour Party voted against one member, one vote to elect their leader but supported a modified version of an electoral college proposed by Roy Hattersley. What was revealing was the apathy of Labour MPs; barely half attended and the motion was only carried by sixty-eight votes to fifty-nine. It then had to be discussed between the Shadow Cabinet and the National Executive to see if they could compromise their respective texts. Soon afterwards, Bill and I went over to Shirley's flat to discuss the general situation. I came with a letter which I intended to send to my constituency party the next day explaining why I had decided not to seek election to the Shadow Cabinet. Shirley and Bill seemed stunned that I was determined to leave the Shadow Cabinet and they both tried to persuade me to stay. Shirley then said that if I were to stand down she would not be able to go ahead with her nomination as a prospective parliamentary candidate in Stevenage, due to be agreed shortly at a constituency meeting. I argued, though I was not fully convinced, that it was perfectly possible for her to go ahead if she wished and also for Bill to be a member of the Shadow Cabinet. We did not have to act in an identical fashion. It was a good-natured argument, and eventually it was agreed that Bill and I would go our separate ways but without any rancour.

Shirley said that she would not now agree to be nominated for Stevenage. This was a very big decision for her. She had been the MP from 1964–79 and yet she sensed that if she went ahead and was selected it would be much harder for her to pull out a few months later. In retrospect, hers was a crucial decision, making it possible to bring our membership of the Labour Party to a head after the disastrous special conference in January 1981. Shirley warned me, quite rightly as it turned out, that the press would interpret my decision as being a major step towards leaving the Labour Party. Bill misread Shirley, saying to me as we left her flat that he had known her a lot longer than I had and she would be persuaded to go ahead and become the prospective Labour candidate for Stevenage. Shirley, however, stuck by her decision to withdraw her candidature and I knew, because I was taking the same step, that it required a lot of courage to tell old friends in her constituency of her decision. In personal terms these were agonising days and many old friends were affronted and relationships permanently damaged.

Shirley was a member of the Labour Party National Executive Committee and in early December, the NEC had to decide on an electoral college. She and Tom Bradley had decided, after discussing it with friends, not to resign from the NEC but to argue their case against at the meeting. Then at the Parliamentary Labour Party meeting on 11 December Bill and I supported an amendment urging the PLP to decline to accept the electoral college as legitimate and democratic since the NEC and Shadow Cabinet had, as we expected, failed to reach an agreed solution on one member, one vote within the trade union section of the electoral college.

Towards the end of 1980 the three of us then tried to decide about Roy who, on 6 January 1981, was due to cease being the President of the Commission. The media would, we knew, demand a single figurehead, particularly if we widened the Gang of Three to Four. I argued, in a memorandum, which was stolen from my room and became public, that there were two options: we three, while the fight was continuing within the Labour Party, should launch all initiatives with Roy supporting them, while clearly taking, for a time, a secondary role; or, if there was collective leadership of four of us, Shirley should become the openly acknowledged leader of the group until any initiative was underpinned by democratic elections. While all this was going on Bill was re-elected to the Shadow

Cabinet but this proved a poisoned chalice; Michael Foot did not keep him as defence spokesman and he resigned.

The Limehouse Declaration

The Limehouse Declaration was published on 25 January 1981, the day after the special Labour conference endorsed a flawed electoral college. The Gang of Three was no more and the Gang of Four was born with the new Social Democratic Party being launched in a fanfare of publicity on 26 March. Shirley was under pressure, from all of us, to become an MP urgently. In hindsight, she needed more time for her family and herself. The by-election in Warrington was an ideal Labour seat for her to stand in; the polls showed only she, of likely SDP candidates, could hope to win but her friend, Tony King, was against her standing, fearing after Stevenage she might be seen as a two-time loser. Despite my pleading for her to delay a decision at a Gang of Four lunch, she declined and Roy wisely seized the opportunity to fight. He managed to skilfully portray a good second as a moral victory. Shirley, having not fought, never recovered her position as the most likely leader. She was in a weak position later to demand of David Steel that he support her to fight the next by-election opportunity in Croydon, which was well suited to her, and the SDP. She then had to fight the naturally Conservative seat of Crosby in a by-election, which she brilliantly won. But the SDP needed her in a seat she could win at a general election and where she could hammer home our message to Labour voters that under Michael Foot's leadership Labour was bound to be an electoral disaster. Any politician is shaped in part by their constituency. It is both the strength and the weakness of the single-member constituency. Shirley, despite a valiant fight and some boundary changes, lost Crosby in 1983.

The old adage that in politics 'everything depends on where you sit' had its inevitable impact on where SDP MPs ended up after the split in 1987. It affected my own stance; for despite being surrounded by Liberal and later Liberal Democrat MPs in Devon and Cornwall, Plymouth remains to this day impervious to their appeal as the seats shift between Labour and Conservative MPs. Since the end of the Second World War the city has never had any significant number of Liberal or later Liberal Democrat councillors. Perhaps this continued association with Labour is a reflection of Plymouth being a Cromwellian city. Perhaps it is a legacy of Leslie Hore-Belisha, a Liberal MP before World War Two. In the dockyard Labour people would say to my SDP supporters 'David will do a Hore-Belisha', who ended up as a Conservative and losing at the 1945 general election. I never doubted that I could only keep my Devonport seat as a Social Democrat and this undoubtedly influenced my opposition to the persistent demands from early 1981 onwards that the SDP should slowly merge with the Liberal Party.

Initially Shirley, Bill and I were modernists within the SDP Parliamentary Party and we did not seek refuge in abstaining on the Conservative 1982 legislation over the closed shop. We had twenty-seven MPs who took the SDP Whip; five voted against, one abstained, and all the rest voted in favour. The SDP championed the need to bring the trade unions back to their members through a one member, one vote democracy. It was not until John Smith became the leader of the Labour Party after their 1992 defeat that Labour accepted in principle one member, one vote for trade unionists in the Labour leadership electoral college. Yet even in 2010, the actual practice of this principle leaves something to be desired.

Shirley and I were surprised when one member, one vote for the SDP leadership was rejected by the still appointed National Committee, with Roy supporting Bill for the MPs choosing the leader followed by the party voting to endorse. However, a party referendum reinstated one member, one vote. A joint SDP/Liberal Commission was established on voting reform for Westminster that decided to support the Single Transferable Vote. This choice was not inevitable for those members who came from the Labour or Conservative parties. Shirley, Bill and I had defended 'First Past the Post' in the past and Roy had moved his position only a few years earlier. Yet we were all convinced that STV would provide a better government, making it easier for voters to assent to decisions even if they did not agree with the decisions.

At all stages I wanted Shirley to be the leader of the SDP. I felt she would have been the guarantee as leader that the party would be a social democratic one in action as well as in words; but it was not to be. Eventually it was decided to have four distinct roles in a collective leadership with two of us, Bill and me, in Parliament, and Roy and Shirley outside. This held until the summer of 1982 when with all four back in the House of Commons an election was held for leader and a president of the party. I was determined that there should be a leadership contest but held off announcing my nomination until Shirley returned from holiday. I then offered to support her and not stand, or stand with her but encourage my supporters to make their second preference for her. Sadly, Shirley preferred to stand for President of the SDP against Bill rather than stand against Roy for the leadership. I stood against Roy and lost by 26,300 votes to 20,900.

In the 1983 general election, the SDP/Liberal Alliance got 25.4 per cent of the vote, but the SDP was left with only six MPs and Shirley and Bill both lost their seats. It was inevitable that the Gang of Four did not remain a power structure within the party. It was also inevitable that the SDP, to survive, would have to take the leadership in the ideological battleground of British politics from 1983 onwards: otherwise we were in grave danger of ceasing to exist or slipping into irrelevance. Sadly, we had first to have an ideological battle within the SDP and my relations became very strained with Shirley, Bill and Roy, who did not like many of the new SDP policies endorsed by the party conference in 1985, particularly on the social market and nuclear deterrence.

In the 1987 general election the SDP/Liberal Alliance still managed to poll 22.6 per cent of the vote, well above all subsequent Liberal Democrat general election results, until the 2010 election in which they polled 23 per cent, but even then they polled half a million fewer votes than the Alliance in 1987. Roy and Ian Wrigglesworth lost their seats and the SDP Parliamentary Party went down from eight MPs to five. Of our two by-election victories, Rosie Barnes held her Greenwich seat but Mike Hancock lost in Portsmouth by a mere 205 votes.

SDP policy ideas have had a major influence on British politics for nearly thirty years – first and foremost, in the creation of New Labour from 1994–7. The social market, a term disliked by Liberals, became enshrined, in 2007, in the Lisbon Treaty so that old argument no longer has any relevance. A minimum UK nuclear deterrent became not just accepted unequivocally by New Labour but also a little later by the Liberal Democrats under Paddy Ashdown. The continuing SDP, up until its demise in 1990 from insufficient members, contributed much to policy development, not just on these but many other issues as diverse as an internal market in the NHS, a national lottery, greater independence for the Bank of England and a graduate tax.

Could the Alliance have held together until 1992?

In the summer of 1987, a substantial group within the SDP shared Shirley, Roy and Bill's view that we should merge with the Liberals. However, there was also a sizeable group within the SDP who would never choose to merge and all five of the SDP MPs, celebrating their election victory in their constituencies, were initially against merging. In the few days before the SDP's National Committee was due to meet on the Thursday, tired after a gruelling campaign, I agonised over what to do personally and what to recommend to the party. I talked to many key SDP members whose position on merging was not clear, and to a few Liberal MPs who wanted me to lead a merged party. On policies, there were still important areas where the parties' positions were incompatible. There was no legitimate way I could envisage of forcing people into working for and representing a party with which they did not feel in harmony. Nor in taking away from those elected SDP MPs and councillors the right to continue to call themselves Social Democrats.

I upset Shirley after the election by refusing to meet until I had made up my mind as to what to recommend. The truth was that I did not dare expose to her my indecision since she would be bound to tell others, and it would have been interpreted that I was wavering over merging. By the Wednesday afternoon I had decided and drawn up a resolution for a consultative ballot to create an 'amicable divorce' within the party to find out who wished to negotiate collectively to merge and who wished to stay in the SDP as a separate party, to be followed by an agreed split. In all the haste, I presented the typed resolution that afternoon to the Parliamentary

Party without prior one-to-one discussions. The other four MPs, John Cartwright, Bob Maclennan, Charles Kennedy and Rosie Barnes, were surprised and rejected my view that divorce was inevitable. They wanted to fight any merger and they were strongly supported by the leader and deputy leader of the SDP peers, Lord Jack Diamond and Baroness Phyllis Stedman. I was alone in my judgement and frankly rather shattered to be disowned, yet it did not seem right to resign then as leader. Instead, I told my colleagues that they would have to take the lead in the National Committee and Bob Maclennan was charged with drawing up a resolution to negotiate a new relationship with the Liberal Party. Perhaps I should have widened the initial Parliamentary Party meeting to include Shirley, the President of the party, and perhaps Bill and Roy as well, who were fervently advocating merging, but it would not have been easy to obtain the agreement of the MPs to this who were, by then, very critical of the other members of the Gang of Four.

At the National Committee next day, I felt I could not put forward my own detailed resolution for a ballot among party members so it was never properly discussed. Perhaps in that larger meeting I might have been able to persuade them, in the words of my resolution, of 'the dangers of a deeply divisive debate being undertaken in which members of the party explain why they do or do not believe that a merger of the parties is desirable against the background of 'winner takes all'. Events were to prove that my amicable divorce provided the only mechanism to go our separate ways with goodwill. Instead, the Parliamentary Party meeting settled on Bob Maclennan drafting words for a separate but deeper relationship with the Liberals as the alternative to full merger. On 6 August, a ballot of members showed 57.4 per cent to 42.6 per cent in favour of negotiating a full merger with the Liberal Party and I immediately resigned as leader, since I could not participate in good faith in such negotiations. Shirley invited Debbie and me to her wedding celebration (to Dick Neustadt) in the midst of all this bitterness, which was a beautiful thought, and we went with great pleasure.

A political divorce leaves its mark as it normally does with divorced couples, but it says much for Shirley's personality that she has always been referred to affectionately in our family, and still is today, as 'Shirl the Pearl'. Twenty years later, she came to stay in our holiday home in Greece and we had very frank talks about all that had happened over those intervening years, during which a new friendship grew. She told me how deeply upsetting it had been to be shut out from any dialogue prior to the critical Parliamentary Party meeting after the 1987 election. We walked, talked, sailed and swam together with Debbie and it was great fun.

To this day, thinking back, I am not sure whether those horribly divisive National Committee meetings, with Charles Kennedy changing his position, as he was fully entitled to do, could have been avoided. It was no accident that the eventual split among the five MPs followed the nature of their seats: the three of us staying SDP were in normally held Labour inner-city seats; the two who became Liberal Democrats had rural seats with a large Liberal vote. If – and that is admittedly a big 'if' – we had split amicably then I was ready to accept that as a much smaller party the SDP would have been the junior partner in an Alliance with a newly formed Liberal Democrat party. The Liberal Democrats would also have provided the leader of any Alliance at the next election.

Call it cussedness if one wants to, but I still believe that had we in the SDP been more patient and given the electorate more time to get used to two parties working together, a Liberal/SDP Alliance would have been able to hold the balance of power after the 1992 general election in a hung parliament. There can, of course, be no certainty; but with Margaret Thatcher no longer the Tory leader, it would have been possible for us all credibly to state before the 1992 election (as it had not been in 1987) that in the event of a hung parliament the Alliance would negotiate with either John Major or Neil Kinnock. By 1992 Neil Kinnock's position on Europe, defence and much else besides, was very different. He was also by then, and I believe remains today, a true supporter of proportional representation. In all probability the Alliance, with the Liberal Democrats the larger element, would have formed a coalition with Labour and that coalition would have probably introduced the Alternative Member System (AMS) voting system practised by the Federal Republic of Germany for the Bundestag.

To some extent, Paddy Ashdown tried to portray during the 1992 general election a Liberal Democrat even-handedness and readiness to work with either the Conservatives or Labour if there were to be a hung parliament. But this attempt never carried much conviction with the electorate, who saw the Liberal Democrats as being far closer to Labour. Paddy Ashdown charged David Stephen, my political adviser when I was Foreign Secretary, who became a Liberal Democrat, with opening up a private dialogue with the Conservative government prior to the election. But John Major surprised everyone by winning outright. The opportunity of the Liberal Democrats holding the balance of power never appeared realistic to the voters in the subsequent general elections of 1997, 2001 or 2005. Interestingly, very late in the 2005 campaign, worried about the Liberal Democrats creeping up on them, a Labour cabinet minister approached me to endorse Labour. I decided not to do so because, by then deeply disillusioned with Tony Blair, I wanted the Liberal Democrats to do well.

The build-up of the Liberal Democrats

During the twenty-two years of the party's existence Shirley Williams has played an outstanding role in building up the Liberal Democrats and representing an authentic strand of social democracy. She followed Roy as the leader of the Liberal Democrats in the House of Lords and was herself succeeded by Bill and later Tom McNally. Throughout these years, she made a prodigious effort in helping to build up the profile of the Liberal Democrats in the constituencies. Many of the former SDP MPs have also had key roles, not least Charles Kennedy who as a young leader courageously gave a parliamentary voice to all those in the country who in principle opposed the war in Iraq in 2003. Even though I did not share his view, I saw the value, in a diverse democracy, of the Liberal Democrat position. Other former members of the SDP, like Vince Cable and Chris Huhne, have contributed to the more market-orientated new thinking on the economy – in an old Liberal tradition espoused by Jo Grimond and brought up to date in *The Orange Book*. Other ex-SDP members such as Anthony Lester and William Goodhart in the Lords were at the core of an informal coalition to protect civil liberties that worked with crossbenchers and many Conservative peers to block some of the more outrageous attempts of the Labour government to ride roughshod over basic freedoms in an overreaction to terrorist and other threats.

During those twenty-two years, unlike Shirley, my time has been spent outside mainstream politics and for the most part earning my living in international business and only part-time as an independent social democrat crossbencher in the House of Lords.

I have focused instead on three main political areas:

- The social market economy: believing that the balance between the social element of any economy and the market element is often a left–right ideological issue that only voters can resolve. The Social Market Foundation (SMF), which I helped found, still makes an important contribution; and I have championed a social democrat's interpretation of the social market in articles and speeches, some drawing at times on my experience of being chairman and non-executive director of various companies in the UK, America and Russia.

- Foreign affairs: my determination has been to restore cabinet government and political bipartisanship over foreign policy, hitherto commonplace. This can only be done when the deceit and manipulation of Parliament that underlay Eden's conduct over Suez and Blair's over Iraq is fully recognised and checks are put in place so it never returns. Also the non-federalist Europeanism of Churchill, Attlee, Macmillan, Wilson, Home, Callaghan, Thatcher and Major needs to be restored and the federalist vision of Heath and Blair needs to be decisively rejected, as appears may be happening. All three parties having promised a referendum on the Constitutional Treaty in the 2005 election, it was an abuse of power for the Labour Party and the Liberal Democrats to vote against a referendum on the Lisbon Treaty. Had there been such a referendum, despite the appalling negotiating result, with the utmost reluctance I would have campaigned for a 'Yes' vote.

- The euro is a currency I am strongly against for the UK, primarily, but not exclusively, on economic grounds. I refused Tony Blair's personal invitation in 1996 to rejoin Labour mainly because of his enthusiasm

for UK membership of the euro zone. In 1999, I helped create New
Europe with people from all parties who had to be in favour of EU
membership while being opposed to euro membership. With Business
for Sterling, we successfully campaigned until 2005 through speeches,
pamphlets, meetings, adverts and film to maintain a level of public
opposition so that Tony Blair was never in a position to call, let alone
win, a euro referendum. The euro argument having been won, New
Europe disbanded. But pressure to join the euro zone will return and
then the political arguments against are likely to become more dominant.

The continuing reform agenda

What of the still outstanding reforms which the UK needs if it is to prosper?
In our long discussions in Greece in 2008, Shirley and I both agreed on
one major matter that was very different to the SDP position throughout
the 1980s. Proportional representation for Westminster elections could
now come about only through a referendum, and not by a negotiated fix
between the parties. This was, in part, a reflection of the referenda held
prior to Scottish and Welsh devolution but also the now wide acceptance
of referenda prior to constitutional change.

We also both agreed that Gordon Brown's attempt to widen the base
of government as is commonly done in the United States was worth
encouraging. In 2007 Shirley had been asked, and accepted, to advise the
government on nuclear non-proliferation, an issue on which we both
have had a longstanding concern, commitment and always considerable
agreement. Soon after becoming Prime Minister, Gordon Brown had also
wanted me to advise him on the NHS but I was reluctant for a number
of reasons. First and foremost, in my heart of hearts I did not believe the
New Labour project was capable of being rescued even if Gordon Brown
was to fulfil my hopes of being a better Prime Minister than Tony Blair. In
addition, it had been thirty-four years since I had been Minister of Health
and I felt I was too out of date. I wished him well and believed then he
would call an election within weeks. It did not surprise me that Shirley
and I both felt that Gordon Brown might reassert social democratic values

within a Labour Party where too many had long since been abandoned. We were both to be sadly disappointed.

Gradually, over these last twenty-two years, the Liberal Democrats have developed into a stronger political force in Westminster and in council chambers up and down the country. In Liverpool, as Chancellor of the University, I appreciated and worked well with the governing Liberal Democrats. The mantle of national leadership changed three times and in due course settled on Nick Clegg. I respected his Europeanism. Multilingual, having been an MEP and worked in Brussels, inter-party negotiations and coalitions are part of his political DNA. All this I reflected on when Politico's decided to republish my autobiography *Time to Declare*, adding *Second Innings* to the title to reflect that their editor had both substantially cut the original and added new material from my speeches and other books. When the book was published in 2009, it surprised some Liberal Democrats for its different tone and my advocacy of their party being in a government of national unity at the next election.

Nick Clegg's greatest skill was to find a formula in late 2009 for the forthcoming election that did carry conviction with the electorate, if not all of his Liberal Democrat activists. He stated he would negotiate, in the event of no party having an outright majority, with whichever party, Conservative or Labour, had the 'strongest mandate'. During the election period he then clarified that by saying he would negotiate first with whichever party had both a majority of MPs and a majority of votes. He was clearly emerging as a Liberal in the continental tradition, at ease with the market economy, perfectly happy with being seen by the electorate as able to negotiate with either Conservative or Labour. He also wisely saw that such flexibility was the essential prerequisite for ensuring that his minority party would be able to influence and carry clout in any negotiations after an election where no single party had an outright majority. Liberal Democrat councillors were taking responsibility in council chambers up and down the country and some were working with Conservatives. More and more Liberal Democrat MPs were growing fed up with mere protest and wished to be part of a government. Meanwhile the electorate, disillusioned by the parliamentary expenses scandal, seemed unwilling to trust either Conservative or Labour with absolute power. The time appeared riper than for many decades for a government made up of more than one party.

I wrote in *The Times* in October 2009, when the Conservatives were still way ahead in the opinion polls, that they were unlikely to win outright. On this, Mike Thomas, a Labour and subsequently SDP MP, agreed wholeheartedly. Together we created over the next few months, with support from friends in all main parties, a website, Charter 2010. The aim was to inform and convince the electorate that in the event of a hung parliament the situation could be turned from deadlock to a stable government provided there was a commitment to a fixed-term parliament. Personally, all I wanted was a successful coalition government. It did not much matter to me whether the largest party in that coalition was Labour or Conservative. I had become very alarmed by the precariousness of the UK's fiscal position. I felt that the size of our structural fiscal deficit meant we had to take more account of the need to maintain the UK's credit rating and capacity to sell government gilts. In all the discussion about global economic policies and the academic debate surrounding Keynes v. Hayek dating back to the 1930s, the necessity of maintaining the confidence of the international financial community was being given too little importance.

On the Friday after polling day in May 2010 the Conservatives were very clearly in the position of having the largest number of MPs, but not an outright majority, and as well the largest number of votes. To his immense credit, Nick Clegg kept his word to the electorate that he would negotiate first with the Conservatives, since that party had the strongest mandate. He was wisely letting the voters determine the most likely coalition partner since the Liberal Democrat party had not been ready to choose openly before the election Labour or the Conservatives as their preferred partner. It was legitimate to keep open the possibility of a coalition with Labour; and when the Liberal Democrats formally started negotiations with Labour as well, it may have helped concentrate David Cameron's mind on the need to offer Nick Clegg something on the Alternative Vote (AV), in order to carry his party with him into a coalition. In truth, however, Cameron had made a surprisingly 'big, open and comprehensive offer' on the Friday afternoon before Clegg spoke.

Technically, the arithmetic of the House of Commons might have allowed the Liberal Democrats to form a voting arrangement or a coalition with Labour and to deliver their support for a Queen's Speech put forward by Labour with the additional voting support of the Scottish and Welsh Nationalists, an independent and a Green MP. But such a working arrangement would never have been able to last for a five-year parliament. To most people it would have looked like a coalition of losers, and would never have had the same international credibility that the coalition quickly established over dealing with the UK's structural fiscal deficit. It would also probably have led to an election in the winter of 2010–11.

Labour will, as is right for an opposition, attack much of the coalition government's economic position but to be effective they must first recognise that a substantial part of the coalition's public expenditure cuts were part of Labour's legacy for the coalition, to which if they had won they were committed. The arguments within the coalition and between Labour and the coalition will rest mainly on which is the correct path for achieving sustained economic growth and how best to balance reduced expenditure and increased taxation levels with an interventionist monetary policy.

On the continuing overall reform agenda, it looks as if an elected House of Lords, probably with STV as the method of voting, will at long last be put on the statute book by all-party agreement. The more crucial question, for me, and I suspect for Shirley too, is can the Liberal Democrats in coalition with the Conservatives so conduct themselves that by their actions, the wider electorate becomes convinced that it has nothing to fear from coalition governments.

The 'miserable little compromise'

It perplexed and surprised me that the Liberal Democrats in 2009, prior to the 2010 election, supported Labour's opportunistic advocacy of a referendum not on proportional representation but on a choice between the Alternative Vote and First Past the Post. Nick Clegg referred to it then as a 'miserable little compromise' and said that he would only settle for 'AV+', that is, the Alternative Vote in most constituencies but a top-up element of MPs to ensure proportionality. Instead the Liberal Democrats settled, after some negotiations over AV without a referendum, on AV by a referendum. Legislation for that referendum, to be held in May 2011, has been announced but it will have to pass through both Houses of Parliament, along with a reduction to 600 new constituencies to be established by Boundary Commissions.

Firstly, the timing of the referendum: to choose a date for a referendum in May 2011, ten months in advance, is foolhardy. No one in the present circumstances can be sure what the state of public opinion will be with regard to the coalition's performance so far ahead. However, one thing that can be said with near certainty is that if the public felt the coalition was not working well and in their interests, the status quo argument for retaining FPTP will win that referendum. Presumably, the fear of later unpopularity and the need to get the new system in place in good time before the next general election influenced the Liberal Democrats to choose the earliest possible referendum date. But already in early July 2010, a YouGov poll has shown that a 'Yes to AV' vote in 2011 will only be won if Labour campaigns strongly for AV, itself a rather unlikely prospect. YouGov also used a deliberative polling technique that it used previously to predict successfully the 'No' vote in the referendum in the North East on regional government. There is a massive difference between how people respond to a question of AV when asked cold and how they respond after they have had time to weigh up the issue. Initially, over 60 per cent of voters see merits on both sides of the argument but when they are warmed up by becoming engaged with twelve arguments about AV, only 33 per cent support AV and 36 per cent are against.

It happens that YouGov's chairman, Peter Kellner, is a longstanding supporter of AV and gave evidence to the Jenkins Commission on electoral reform in support of it, which they rejected. So there is unlikely to be any question of bias against AV within the YouGov organisation. Most worrying for the Liberal Democrats, besides their own fall in popularity between May and July, is the finding that Labour voters flipped around on AV more than any other section of the electorate. Some 59 per cent in favour of AV when asked cold became 47 per cent against AV when warmed up. Common prudence should make Liberal Democrats put into the legislation that the timing of the referendum in the Bill will be determined by an Order giving around 6–8 weeks' notice. In this way while still heading towards May 2011 they keep their options open to delay until 2014 by which time they should be able to claim that the coalition had been a success and see their poll rating restored.

Secondly, parliamentary scrutiny will also focus on whether or not the referendum should be held, as announced, to coincide with the Scottish and Welsh parliamentary elections and the English local elections. The Liberal Democrat choice on this is blatant, because under devolution these voters will not vote using FPTP. It might also have been judged that London, which will have no local elections in May 2011, will have a low poll and this pattern will favour Liberal Democrat activists voting for AV. But even this calculation may work in favour of FPTP because Conservative 'No' activists may strongly outpoll Labour 'Yes' activists. A recent report of the House of Lords Select Committee on the Constitution (Twelfth Report of Session 2009/10, *Referendums in the United Kingdom*) points to a vigorous debate on this question and the views of the Electoral Commission will be important. Recommendation 145 says 'referendums should not be held on the same day as General Elections. For other elections, we recommend there should be a presumption against holding referendums on the same day as elections but that this should be judged on a case-by-case basis by the Electoral Commission.' Already a total of forty-five Conservative MPs have signed an Early Day Motion saying it is wrong to hold the referendum and the elections on the same day. This is an indication of how difficult the passage of the Bill may become on this and other aspects. The views of the Electoral Commission will be important, with a final ruling expected in September (although it seems an amber light has already been given).

Thirdly, parliamentary debate will focus on the fact that AV has already been considered in depth on at least three important occasions: by a commission established by the SDP and Liberal Party in 1982; by the Plant Commission on Democracy, Representation and Elections, established by the Labour Party in 1990; and by the Independent Commission on the Voting System, chaired by Roy Jenkins, established in 1997. All three of these reports rejected AV and they did so for solid reasons. While all voting systems are a compromise, the arguments over AV go back even to 1931 when Winston Churchill objected to the AV system in the Representation of the People (No. 2) Bill. In his speech to the Commons on 2 June 1931, Churchill claimed that AV meant that 'the decision is to be determined by the most worthless votes, given for the most worthless candidates'. Churchill, incidentally, argued in that debate in favour of STV instead of AV if any electoral reform had to take place. The reason why AV has such strong critics was made clear in the late Lord Alexander's note of reservation to the Jenkins Report. Alexander, a distinguished Conservative lawyer who was in favour of proportional representation, wrote about AV: 'It ignores the second preferences of the voters who supported the two candidates with the highest first preference vote, but allows the voters for the third or even weaker candidates to have their second votes counted so as to determine the result.' He asked: 'Why should the second preferences of those voters who favoured the two stronger candidates on the first vote be totally ignored and only those who support the lower place and less popular candidate get a second bite at the cherry. Why, too, should the second preferences of these voters be given equal weight with the first preferences of the supporters of the stronger candidates?' It is also a politically embarrassing fact that AV can produce under some circumstances a more disproportionate result than FPTP. Moreover, it is also a fact that the Jenkins Commission, in choosing AV as part of its recommended mechanism (the so-called AV+), albeit with a top-up list, was choosing a more disproportionate system than the Alternative Member System (AMS).

I put these facts forward not to argue a particular case – though I have never been convinced by the case for AV, a preferential rather than a proportional voting system – but to point out that it is the duty of Parliament to debate the choice being given to the electors in a referendum and not to feel pre-empted by the inter-party fix agreed as part of the coalition agreement. Yet fixes have their place in politics and it may be the coalition has the strength and the cohesion to put through this legislation without serious amendment and that the Liberal Democrats will go on to win a 'Yes' vote on AV, albeit with many of their supporters holding their noses.

Fighting referenda

Shirley Williams, however, knows better than any other person that referenda are quite unlike general elections. She played a very prominent role in the 1975 'Yes' referendum campaign for staying in the then European Community. The polls certainly swung from a definite 'No' vote to a 'Yes' in the six-month period prior to the vote but this was not because of the perceived merits of the European Community. As a single issue, staying in the EC remained unpopular with British voters throughout. In order to win, the campaign for a 'Yes' vote had to change the focus of the debate from the EC to another issue. They chose as the main issue to pose 'which politicians on Europe do you trust?' In Labour terms, Shirley or Tony Benn? In Conservative terms, Willie Whitelaw or the Northern Ireland Unionist Enoch Powell? A crucial part of changing the opinion of reluctant Labour voters was the part played by Harold Wilson and Jim Callaghan who in a low-key way came down on balance in favour of the so-called new negotiated terms and maintaining the status quo. Staying in was depicted as the steady, sensible course; changing course by coming out meant rocking the boat. In contrast to these two solid figures saying 'Yes', the Labour personalities Barbara Castle and Michael Foot saying vote 'No' were depicted as 'lefties'. That Labour-guided reformulation of the referendum question worked very well. So could a Conservative-guided reformulation question in 2011.

Some assume the fact that David Cameron, from the start, has announced that he intends to play a low-key role in supporting the existing First Past the Post system means that he is doing this to help win acceptance for AV. If so, then Cameron is still intent, as he foolishly promised at the start of his leadership, on being the 'heir to Blair', treating his party with contempt, pretending to go one way while steering it towards another, seeing merit in AV and believing that the coalition partners could encourage third or fourth preference votes to go towards the other. Such a cynical view would see a Con–Lib deal as the new norm under AV. Another reading of Cameron's relaxed low-key stance, of accepting the result either way, is that he is being very Wilsonesque by actually helping the maintenance of the status quo, which is sticking with FPTP. As Prime Minister, David

Cameron will be able to argue quietly, with some justice, that he has shown that the existing FPTP system is flexible in that it obliged him not to carry his own preference for a government with a single party mandate, but to listen to the electorate and forge a coalition government. In this way Cameron can say in a non-provocative way that he still believes it a good thing to have from time to time the clarity of a single party with a governing majority if the electorate so decide and he, therefore, favours, on balance, FPTP. That is not an unreasonable position, particularly when AV is neither proportional nor always fairer than FPTP. Also the 'No' campaign under Lord Leach, who led the successful Business for Sterling 'No' campaign against the euro, will be media savvy, using popular, not extreme or old-fashioned-looking, political figures.

No Liberal Democrat should count on Labour's support for a 'Yes' vote despite their continuing backing of a referendum on the AV system. Labour want only one result – that which damages the Liberal Democrats and weakens the cohesion of the coalition. At the last shadow cabinet meeting in July, a decision was taken to oppose the referendum legislation because it is coupled with the boundary changes. This, together with the Tory backbench disquiet, could seriously derail the passage of the Bill. There remain also many Labour electoral reformers, like the respected former MP Tony Wright, who have for years opposed AV. The argument that AV is a staging post to proportionality is at best dubious; at worst, a lost AV referendum could postpone proportional representation for many decades. It is a big ask to ditch the principled arguments for proportional representation, either AV+, AMS or STV, which have the great merit of all guaranteeing fairness. A new leader of the Labour Party would be well advised to come round during the legislative process on the referendum to championing proportional voting for electing both the House of Lords and the House of Commons: if they were to do so, the coalition's position might well be lost. We can expect to see a lot of odd voting alliances emerging as the legislation is debated: the Scottish and Welsh Nationalists, as well as Northern Ireland MPs, may well bargain their votes.

Another problem for the referendum campaign is that a vote on AV in 2011 will be before the new constituency boundaries are known and before

the coalition has a proven record of success. Were a referendum on AV
to be held at the end of the fourth or early in the fifth year of a coalition
government in 2014, many more people might have been convinced that
governments composed of more than one party can provide courageous
and coherent leadership and therefore be ready to vote for AV. It will still
mean some supporters of proportional representation swallowing hard. But
a lost referendum in 2011, following a divisive debate in the coalition, may
not wreck its ability to stay the course but it risks weakening the coalition's
capacity to sustain unpopular measures.

It would be far better for the coalition's legislation to allow for the
postponement of the referendum and to concentrate instead on the terms
of the Boundary Commissions' review of constituency boundaries. It will
take more than two years for the four Boundary Commissions in the UK to
report. Some people will want to judge the effect of AV on their particular
constituency. In 2011, finding it impossible to calculate the effect of AV
on their own local constituency at the next election, some potential voters
may lose interest, abstain or vote against. It is perfectly reasonable that
the legislation for the Boundary Commissions should not just instruct the
creation of constituencies with a more equal number of voters, but also
instruct that constituencies should have a more even spread of voters across
the political parties, so that they reduce the number of very safe seats and
increase the number of marginal seats. The Boundary Commissions could
also be instructed to suggest groupings for the new constituencies essential
for STV in the event that a later referendum included as one of the options
voting for the Single Transferable Vote. If almost all Labour MPs voted for
this with Welsh and Scottish MPs, there could be a Liberal Democrat revolt
sufficient to carry such an amendment.

I hope that more thought will be given within the coalition to these
issues so that a referendum on AV can be postponed, otherwise in May
2011 it could well be lost. David Cameron's initial offer, made in private
after the election, should be revived, to set up a joint commission to review
the terms of any referendum. In that review, Liberal Democrats could argue
the case for proportionality as a principle and with the coalition working
well the Conservatives just might be more likely to listen.

A new factor that the Conservatives, as well as the Liberal Democrats, might face would be if, as I predict, the Labour Party converts to STV or AV+. It is possible by then that the new constituencies would be better balanced between the main parties as part of the Boundary Commission changed instructions to create less safe seats and more marginal seats by 2014. In that case, it might mean that the list element in AV+, the part the Conservatives dislike the most, would be reduced in number and AV+ thereby made more attractive. At that stage, it would be tempting for the Conservatives to move their position to a referendum on FPTP v. AV+ rather than AV, or have a three-way option. Either way it would mean having a proper referendum on proportional representation. In this way, whether the referendum was won or lost for FPTP, it would maintain coalition unity. It would also pre-empt the Labour Party being able to appeal to Liberal Democrats over proportional representation during and after a 2015 general election which, by then, might well be in the Conservative Party's best interests.

★

For my part I believed that a Liberal Democrat coalition with Labour in 2010 necessitated Gordon Brown stepping down once the negotiations were completed, not waiting until September. I told Peter Mandelson this when he rang me up on the Friday afternoon after the election. I am not a paid-up supporter of the Conservative/Liberal Democrat coalition in the sense that I am a member of neither party, but I wish it well for on its success depends not just the critical task of closing the structural fiscal deficit but also of carrying a real cross-party reform agenda.

As an independent social democrat crossbencher in the House of Lords, I still hope that a continental social democratic Labour Party emerges over the next five years, one that imaginatively redefines the social part of a market economy and supports proportional representation for Westminster elections. After all, the Labour government was fully committed to STV being used in the UK for local government elections in Northern Ireland and Scotland, for European parliamentary elections in Northern Ireland, and in choosing the Northern Ireland Assembly. An all-through commitment to STV, as I would prefer, or a mixture with AV+ or AMS, would be a natural yet radical step for Labour to advocate. In 2012 Labour is likely to vote, on House of Lords reform, for STV to choose a second chamber; certainly no list system is appropriate unless you intend to snuff out any independent members being chosen.

Another important challenge for the younger generation of Labour MPs is to rediscover a commitment to civil liberties. Tony Blair identifying with Michael Howard's approach to much of the crime and punishment agenda was to go down a blind alley deserting the libertarian tradition of social democracy. Another New Labour folly was to embrace the Eurofederalism of the 2004 Constitutional Treaty. The French and Dutch rejection, in their referenda, came at a time when many continental social democratic parties, particularly in Sweden, the Netherlands and even Germany, were reassessing the federalist dream in large part under the pressure of public opinion. Tony Blair's Eurofederalism combined with undue subordination to the US ran not just against UK public opinion but counter to British diplomacy from the Treaty of Versailles negotiations in 1919 onwards.

By the time of Labour's spectacular victory in 1997, many SDP members were spread across all three parties and none. Most, I suspect, including some who had supported the Conservative government of John Major, believed in the value of the alternation of power and after seventeen years were content to see the return of Labour to government. By 2010, I suspect many of those, after thirteen years of Labour, were ready for them to lose power and see the Liberal Democrats negotiate a sensible agreement with the Conservatives as the party with the strongest mandate. If I am right about this, and there is still an SDP voting constituency with some ties with the past, particularly on the one big issue of electoral reform, we need to question carefully the case for settling in a 2011 referendum for a miserable compromise. If that constituency had wanted to support AV for the Westminster Parliament at any time, it could have done so from 1982 onwards. Why at the very moment that at long last we have a coalition government whose record, if successful, will of itself promote the case for proportional representation, should we compromise our beliefs?

I am very glad that over the years Shirley and Bill's wish to merge to form the Liberal Democrats and my wish to remain outside has lost much of its sting. But all three of us, in my judgement, still uphold in our different ways many social democratic principles. We came together in public again as the Gang of Three in 2008 when the University of Liverpool conferred honorary degrees on both Bill and Shirley with their Liverpool connections evident in their titles as Liberal Democrat peers: Bill's through the Quarry Bank school he attended in Liverpool and Shirley's through her neighbouring Crosby by-election triumph. We will all three be together to share the joy of Shirley's eightieth birthday party. She remains in her eighty-first year one of the great empathetic politicians of our age and will use her undoubted persuasiveness within the Liberal Democrats to fulfil what she wrote in 1981 at the beginning of the battle to decide what the new politics will be like. 'It is possible, just possible, that it will be a politics for people.'

The Liberal view

David Steel

It is an odd coincidence that as I sit at my desk at home writing this brief essay I am conscious of preparing for two events involving Shirley Williams – the first is a visit by her to stay with us at Aikwood Tower when she comes north next month for the Borders Book Festival (where the session on her autobiography *Climbing the Bookshelves* is already sold out). We are organising a lively dinner party which will include Chris Mullin (who is also here to promote his entertaining book on being a junior minister) and Ellie and Jim Naughtie, who are old friends. The second is an eightieth birthday dinner for friends organised by her old university and parliamentary colleague Bill Rodgers in London.

Shirley is a rare being in the world of politics: she is regarded as a national treasure, rather like the late Queen Mum. This came home to me some years ago when having been in Scotland with relatives she called in for a celebratory New Year drink on having been made a life peer. She was standing by the fire when our local blacksmith wandered in to deal with some repair or other. Without batting an eyelid at her unexpected presence he said 'congratulations Shirley' and went about his business.

Yet in my early years in politics our paths never crossed – she was a stalwart pillar of the Labour Party, and as a good Roman Catholic never supported my Abortion Bill. We might have got to know each other much earlier because she and I together with a senior Tory MP were due in the autumn of 1965 to go on my first official delegation as a new MP to Hong Kong, but at the last minute she dropped out. So it was that in the autumn of 1977 I wrote an open letter to her in *The Guardian*, just after she had been defeated for the deputy leadership of the Labour Party by Michael Foot, urging her to join in a realignment of the moderate left. She was Education Secretary at the time: we had never spoken, and of course it was tongue-in-cheek and she made no response publicly or privately.

After the 1979 general election, when she lost her seat, the Thatcher era began, and I had a long conversation in Brussels with Roy Jenkins (then President of the European Commission) about the need for realignment. This was followed by his historic Dimbleby lecture, to which Shirley responded, 'I am not interested in a third party. I do not believe it has a future.' My own autobiography describes further detailed meetings with Roy, while quite separately the Gang of Three – Shirley, Bill Rodgers and David Owen – were increasingly exasperated at threats that Labour would have us leave the European Community and embrace unilateral disarmament. In the summer of 1980 the three published an open letter in *The Guardian* to their party colleagues reiterating that they would not support a Centre Party but that support for such a concept was likely to grow. I responded with an open letter to them in the same paper and signed it 'Yours fraternally' – but they probably regarded me as meddling in a purely internal Labour debate. Again there was no response.

At the beginning of 1981 Roy returned from Brussels and the three began to meet with him as the Gang of Four. The 'Council for Social Democracy' was formed and I continued to smother them with public kindness and assume a putative alliance. A telephone poll gave such an alliance 51 per cent support, and the SDP was launched as a separate party in March.

In April I found myself with Richard Holme at the annual Königswinter conference on the banks of the Rhine. Bill (whom I had got to know during the 1975 European referendum) and Shirley were there together with John Roper. The five of us lunched in the open air at the Rheinhotel. On a paper napkin Richard drew up possible heads of agreement for the two parties to work together – on policy and organisation. After lunch we walked up the hill to the Drachenfels Castle in buoyant mood. Shirley sweetly asked, 'Does this mean I'll have to support proportional representation?'

In June we published a declaration of principles written by Richard Holme and David Marquand entitled *A Fresh Start for Britain*. In a famous photograph, Shirley and I held it in our hands sitting on the grass in the quadrangle behind Westminster Abbey, described merrily by one journalist as 'looking like superannuated student lovers'. The next happening was the by-election at Warrington – where as Shirley herself admits she chickened out of standing – leaving the field clear for Roy to do so, which he did spectacularly. It was the first joint battle for the SDP and the Liberals.

Then I had to face the annual Liberal Assembly in September in Llandudno with the proposal to enter a formal alliance. I decided to organise an eve-of-conference huge fringe meeting and persuaded Jo Grimond to join me with Roy and Shirley. The press described the reception we got as 'rapturous' and it overtook the actual debate completely.

Then came a by-election in Croydon where I tried unsuccessfully to persuade the lacklustre Liberal Bill Pitt to stand down in favour of Shirley as candidate. (Michael Meadowcroft – that self-appointed and wholly destructive keeper of the Liberal conscience – described my effort as maladroit.) Pitt would not budge, though pretended to consider it, and went on to win thanks to Richard Holme's success in keeping him away from the press: later, after losing it, he joined the Labour Party. Shirley had to wait.

In November 1981 her chance came with Liberal Tony Hill graciously standing down for a by-election in Crosby. Shirley fought a magnificent campaign. *The Economist* front cover pictured me, Roy and Shirley as 'Her Majesty's New Opposition'. In mid-1982 Roy was elected leader of the SDP against David Owen: Shirley, having once again ducked the contest herself, supported David. Who knows whether if she had stood and won the Alliance might have had greater public appeal? I am not certain myself. Roy and I being of such obviously disparate ages and experience made a comfortable partnership, and in any case the Falklands war put an end to our string of by-election successes and revived Mrs Thatcher's standing in the 1983 general election.

In the run-up to the 1987 election and in its immediate aftermath Shirley as President of the SDP played a crucial part in the growing together of the two parties and in the merger negotiations. The fault line in the Alliance lay not – as was so often misrepresented – between David Owen and me, but between David Owen and the trio of Roy, Shirley and Bill. David has written candidly about the cause of his two main disagreements in his own book: premature closeness with the Liberals and excessive Europhilia.

Shirley went on to lead the Liberal Democrats in the House of Lords with great distinction and high public profile. She played a crucial role both internally in the new Liberal Democrats and externally in convincing the public in gathering over three further elections the support which has led us at last back to government. She has the capacity which she shares with the late Nancy Seear, the last Liberal leader in the Lords, the capacity to speak without notes and without much notice on almost any subject convincingly and with fervour.

On her eightieth birthday Shirley's infectious enthusiasm is undimmed. She continues to delight us all.

A new politics, 1981 and 2010

Charles Kennedy

> I began to feel that Britain's problems were largely institutional, and that her institutions have bred attitudes, especially class attitudes, that militate against a common effort to resolve her problems. The institutions, most of them intended to improve the quality of human life, have become bastions for particular interests against those of society as a whole. Political parties have been used as the instruments of one group of institutions or another, for example business or trades unions or professional groups. (*Politics is for People*)

Shirley Williams penned those words in 1981, the year that the Council for Social Democracy broke away from the Labour Party to form the SDP, and the year she was returned to Parliament against the odds at the Crosby by-election. The sentiments echo down the years; there are still institutional problems in British politics, none more so than at Westminster. She spoke then of the 'gulf' that separated political parties and their 'preoccupations' from the 'world's circumstances'. Then she meant the navel-gazing of internal disputes and sectional interests, the twin spectacles of a Conservative government mired in economic crisis as a result of policy driven by ideology, and a Labour Party seemingly hell-bent on self-immolation due to internal strife. Politics, she blithely insisted, was for people.

Notwithstanding the ephemeral nature of some of the book's conclusions, this was a value that rested at the heart of her political mission from the day she was first elected as a Labour MP to her status today as one of the

Liberal Democrats' most influential figures. She has always been a towering presence in Liberal Democrat politics. You ignore her at your peril; not because of some misplaced fear of impending retribution (Shirley's characteristic even-handedness is well-documented), but because, in many respects, she *is* the party. Her story is the party's story: a reaction against extremes on both sides of the political divide; a desire to foster a new, co-operative politics with progress at its heart; the drive for an activist, radical centre. It is the story of the original Liberal Democrat attempt to build a new politics. I know it well – because her story is also my story.

When she and the other members of the 'Gang of Four' – Bill Rodgers, David Owen, and my own hero, the late Roy Jenkins – came forward to present the Limehouse Declaration which led to the foundation of the SDP, they were completing a process Jenkins had begun in his Dimbleby Lecture over a year earlier. Roy had been away in Brussels as President of the European Commission, and that critical distance had fostered a distinctive view of the state of British politics. There was, for Roy, an artificiality about political debate that in the long run did Britain a disservice and appealed more to theatre than to reality. 'There is too often', Roy noted, 'a shrill and unconvincing attempt to portray almost everyone on the other side as a fool or a knave':

> Each successive Tory government is the most reactionary since that of Lord Liverpool, or some other hobgoblin figure shrouded in the past. Each successive Labour government has been the most rapacious, doctrinaire and unpatriotic conspiracy to be seen this side of the Iron Curtain. Either might, I suppose, be true in the future, but it cannot all have been true in the past, and I do not believe that it either convinces or pleases the electorate. ('Home Thoughts from Abroad', BBC Dimbleby Lecture 1979)

This was the navel-gazing which Shirley was later to condemn. It was significant that a fortnight after Roy delivered his lecture, Shirley and Bill Rodgers came to see him. It had outlined in concrete terms the shared vision they held that a party of the radical centre was the only answer to the fake tribalism which scarred the political landscape. It was a clarion call which found an echo among a new generation of political campaigners, including myself. It was not, as the Limehouse Declaration later argued (January 1981), to be a politics of 'an inert centre, merely representing the lowest common denominator between two extremes'. What was needed instead was a 'realignment of British politics', the 'strengthening of the radical centre' Roy had called for in the Dimbleby Lecture.

Realignment

That search for realignment has had two aspects in the decades which have followed: the creation of that new, radical centre party – ultimately the Liberal Democrats – and, subsequently, the reorientation of the prevailing political landscape in favour of the values it espouses. Shirley was to the forefront of both. She understands, better than most politicians do, that it is pointless to have a vision if you are not prepared to carry that vision through yourself. She lived it. Campaigning in Crosby she was authentic in a way no spin doctor can match. People responded to her. This was no less true at the earlier Warrington by-election, where Shirley might have thrown her hat into the ring, only to hesitate and see Roy take the chance instead. Committed to the cause, she threw herself into the campaign; my old friend Dick Newby remembers an occasion during that campaign when, megaphone in hand, the car she was travelling in passed by a motorist tending to his broken-down vehicle:

> Its grease-stained owner raised his head from beneath the bonnet and found himself within a few feet of Williams. 'Hello, Shirley,' he said, grinning broadly as if greeting a long-lost friend. No other contemporary politician could have evoked such a warm, familiar response from a complete stranger. For me, it captured, in an instant, the Williams magic. (Liberal Democrat History Group)

Jenkins missed out in Warrington, though not by much. Williams's own challenge came in Crosby, a Tory safe seat suddenly vacant due to the death of the incumbent, Sir Graham Page. Crosby was then an unlikely venue for the new politics; north of Liverpool, it was solidly Conservative and comprised some of the most affluent areas in the north-west; according to *Newsweek*, 'a genteel suburb laced with Victorian mansions'. The Conservatives had held the seat and its predecessors since 1918. Little wonder then that when Shirley captured it for the SDP it sent shockwaves around the world. *Newsweek* spoke of 'Britain's new politics':

> The rules of British politics suddenly changed last week. In a remarkable changing of the guard, the Tories lost their Crosby bastion to Shirley Williams . . . and to her eight-month-old party, the Social Democrats. The stark message to Britain's Conservative and Labour parties couldn't be missed: if the Social Democrats could win in Crosby, they could win almost anywhere. 'This is the beginning for us of a great movement in history, an idea that has found its time,' said Williams on election night. 'It was the poet Dryden who said: "'Tis well an old age is out and time to begin anew."' (*Newsweek*, 7 December 1981)

Shirley believed in personal risk. She was a prominent Labour politician and had held two Cabinet posts, first as Secretary of State for Consumer Protection, and later, and most famously, as Secretary of State for Education. She had a lot to lose by helping to lead the fight for a new politics beyond the Labour Party. But she did it anyway – because she saw it as the only option. It was at no small personal cost. For years the Labour Party – and many of Shirley's former colleagues – regarded the Gang of Four and those who had followed them as egomaniacal traitors. The level of personal animosity they experienced was often extreme. The British left has always, after all, been fond of that invidious term 'splitter'. That is part of the reason, perhaps, that Shirley did come to love the Liberal Democrats and regard the party as her natural home. It did not escape Roy Hattersley's eye that when she took the ermine and became Baroness Williams it was Crosby that was included in her formal title, where she had spent a mere fraction of her parliamentary career. Representing Crosby was about more than just winning against the odds or proving others wrong for the sake of it (enjoyable though that can be at times); it was about showing the new politics could work.

I have written in *The Future of Politics* (2000) about Roy's influence on my political development, but Shirley's formative influence must also be noted. Like many young people in the early 1980s I was trying to understand what direction our politics might take. I knew I was a progressive, I knew I was a social democrat. Jenkins's lecture spoke to my concerns, as did the Limehouse Declaration. Now, through Shirley's victory, we saw that this was about more than words; it was about practical politics, about translating words and values into action. The new politics was not a mirage – it was a new era of possibility.

It was understandable in the circumstances that some got carried away. Some American periodicals in particular (including the *New York Times*) began to believe that Britain's two-party system might be swept away overnight, and they almost welcomed it. As one columnist put it, American liberals had reason to cheer for a centrist, progressive party that had no qualms about NATO.

It would be too much to claim that the aftermath of the Falklands War derailed the SDP. There was more to it than that. As Liberal Democrats we are keenly aware of the importance of community politics, and in 1983 the Alliance needed more of it. Where it had it, we were successful. And the share of the vote commanded by the Alliance proved there was a desire for the new politics, and it is a desire which has not waned since, even though without fair votes it might not always have translated into the right number of seats. During the troubled period leading up to the merger, Shirley was a tower of strength when others wavered. And in the aftermath, as the infant Liberal Democrats struggled to be recognised as a new force in British politics, she was in some respects the guarantor of our credibility. She never lost faith in the opportunities that our party's political journey offered for the country. For politicians such as me making my way in Parliament during those times it was invaluable to have such a stateswoman to guide us.

It helped that Shirley and I have much in common – former members of the Labour Party, SDP MPs, supporters of the merger with the Liberals, and, finally, leaders of the Liberal Democrats (she in the Lords, I in the Commons). On a more personal level, we are both Catholics, and we have both campaigned in parts of the world where religion is still a live issue in politics. In her book *God and Caesar* Shirley considered with characteristic honesty the challenges personal faith places on the politician who lives every day in the secular world of compromise.

Sometimes Shirley found compromise impossible, and that is surely right. Leaving the Labour Party was one of those moments. But later there were still more meaningful occasions, when she supported Paddy Ashdown's stance over Bosnia and travelled with Paddy to Kosovo in the build-up to war and ethnic cleansing. This was politics at its most real and important. When some began to doubt the wisdom of NATO intervention, after four weeks of airstrikes, she stood firm. She remembered why:

> With our own eyes we saw settlements burned down, houses whose foundations were knocked to bits so badly by grenades it would be impossible to rebuild them, and groups of people, mostly farmers, huddled into what small rooms remained, not daring to go out even to milk their cows, because of snipers. (*Herald*, 19 April 1999)

Serving as our frontbench spokesperson on foreign affairs in the Lords, she drove the point home. Before it became popular for politicians to refer to values as if they were a magic formula to deliver votes, Shirley lived them.

She was a great support and inspiration to me, before, after and during my time as party leader. Her personal backing during the 1999 leadership election was invaluable and her counsel indispensable. That's not to say we always saw eye-to-eye; but that is what speaks of Shirley's integrity – for someone who has in the past claimed that her greatest weakness is her desire not to offend, she always has a way of letting you know where she stands. This was particularly so for one National Front activist in the 1970s who decided to translate his prejudices into a physical attack on Shirley, who responded succinctly by punching him in the stomach. Sometimes actions really do speak louder than words.

Shirley Williams is the original Liberal Democrat. It took many of her former colleagues in the Labour Party a long time to realise the implications of what that meant. Reviewing *Climbing the Bookshelves*, Roy Hattersley wrote of Shirley that she 'is temperamentally a Liberal Democrat. She is part of its radical wing. But, more important than policy, it is where she feels at home.' The same could be said of myself.

Coalition

That is not to say that it is always easy to be a Liberal Democrat; far from it. Both Shirley and I were united in recent times by our scepticism in respect of the coalition deal which finally put the party back into power. We do seek a new politics – but for me, at least, it was difficult to see how that might be achieved in partnership with a Conservative Party which was still wedded to the legacy of Thatcherism. As she told *The Guardian* (9 May 2010), for Shirley, it was 'not in the Conservatives' DNA' to come to terms with liberal values. Yet even so, Nick Clegg owes a debt to Shirley; she described him as 'first generation Liberal Democrat – neither a Liberal nor a Social Democrat, but something new' (*New Statesman*, 12 May). That generation of Liberal Democrats – of people who did not identify themselves with the naked tribalism of the other two main parties – simply would not have been possible without Shirley's example. Long before David Cameron spoke of ending 'Punch and Judy politics', Shirley helped found a new, inclusive political party in an attempt to do just that.

And when coalition finally came Shirley was, as ever, measured in her response. There is no denying that the coalition negotiations brought forth a document that in many areas was in line with liberal values. As those steeped in the liberal tradition are only too aware, part of the challenge of government is what not to do, and it was significant that among the coalition programme, the end of ID cards, the demise of the national identity database, and greater regulation of CCTV were clear Liberal Democrat priorities achieved almost at a stroke. Nick Clegg has spoken passionately about the need for the greatest reforms in British politics for decades – in his eyes, since the 1832 Reform Act – and this is a view Shirley and I share. Westminster's reputation has seldom been lower. Shirley, with her decades of experience, is sanguine about this. In her view, Parliament was probably less industrious than it is today when she first tried to gain office in the 1950s. But today the media is less sympathetic, sometimes justifiably so, and the sense that politicians are out of touch is a real one. In that light, it is unsurprising that someone who has made her life's work a mission to connect politics with people should find cause for optimism in a coalition she initially found difficult to accept. There will be a national debate on electoral reform. There will be a renewed Liberal Democrat input into whole swathes of policy. And, from Shirley's point of view, the electorate demanded that we try to work together. Shirley and I agree on that. We simply differed with others on the form. As she puts it herself:

> Can we be certain that this new kind of politics will work? The realistic answer must be no. But the alternative was a message to the electorate that, whatever their instincts for co-operation, the politicians preferred the safe, long-established confrontation. We have an obligation to try to make it work.

You would expect no less from a politician who three decades earlier set out to break the mould of British politics, end the inadequacies of tribalism and – above all – ensure that politics works for people. We still have a long way to go on that score. But we still have that obligation to try.

Where next for the centre left?

John Kampfner

When Shirley Williams made her move, with the Gang of Four, away from Labour in the early 1980s she did so because the party that she had known and loved had become zealous and extreme. When I made a similar, and much less portentous, journey only this March, I did so out of a similar sense of despair, and also hope for a fresh start.

Yet the Labour Party 2010 could hardly be described as extreme. Perhaps listless might have been a better adjective? Or lifeless? It was this very lack of vim, of purpose that brought the New Labour hegemony to a close. As former ministers and advisers ponder the future, disorientated by the astonishing turn of events that has seen Nick Clegg join David Cameron in the Conservative–Liberal Democrat coalition, they have suddenly found time on their hands to think more deeply about the successes and failures of an era that began amid such jubilation in 1997.

So where now for the centre left? It is important to reprise the past in order better to understand the prospects for the future.

The conventional wisdom of the first decade is that Iraq destroyed Tony Blair. Without that Anglo-American crusading misadventure, the then Prime Minister would have secured a more positive chapter in the history books. The conventional wisdom of the past three years is that Gordon Brown foundered because of his lack of interpersonal skills and his failure to communicate. Both these conclusions point in the right direction, but they tell only part of the story.

The real tragedy was the Labour government's lack of self-belief. The bullying, media manipulation and hubris were mechanisms devised to compensate for a caution they could never shake off. The New Labour project was born of the traumas of the 1980s. It was based on the notion that centre-left governments can change society only at the margins. Unable or unwilling to battle against the causes of inequality, Blair and Brown confined themselves to tackling its effects. Having raised the white flag to the super-rich, ministers exerted their power elsewhere, seeking ever more ingenious ways of telling people how to lead their lives.

In a simple audit, Labour's first administration from 1997–2001 can be seen as by far the most successful. During that time it introduced the minimum wage, freedom of information, the Human Rights Act, devolution for Scotland and Wales and a plethora of other specific measures. The government, with colourful and radical figures such as the late Robin Cook and Mo Mowlam among its senior ranks, epitomised a more optimistic, pre-9/11 era. Yet even then, even with a majority to dream of, Blair ensured that Labour was defined not by what it was, but what it was not. It became a mirror image of its past. Old Labour equals anti-business: New Labour intensely relaxed about the filthy rich. Old Labour given short shrift by the White House: New Labour Prime Minister salivates alongside US President.

Iraq was the perfect example of Blair's ability to turn exigency (keeping on the right side of George Bush) into opportunity. In all areas of policy, tactics became convictions. Blair and Brown saw their mission as to turn the Labour Party into an election-winning machine. Any principle or policy that did not fall into that template was discarded.

Almost all the significant reforms of the early Blair era had been inherited from John Smith and Neil Kinnock. Many, such as the establishment of the International Criminal Court and measures to ban the use of landmines, were pursued reluctantly by Blair. The Prime Minister's office snorted at the idea of an ethical dimension to foreign policy, countermanding Cook's plan to limit arms sales to dictatorships.

Perhaps the greatest curiosity was Labour's approach to inequality. The tax and benefits system were used to considerable effect to direct money to impoverished children and pensioners. However, almost always these measures were done by stealth. But nothing was done to try to win over the public to the need for redistribution. Labour had accepted the economic settlement wrought by Margaret Thatcher. Blair, and even more so Brown, restricted their aims to offering limited palliative care for the most disadvantaged: redistributive bolt-ons.

Brown claimed to have found a magic formula for sustained and more equitable wealth creation. By 2008 boom had turned spectacularly to bust. The two drivers of growth had been exposed as brittle – a consumer binge based on excessive borrowing, and a financial services sector drunk on hubris. Brown and Blair did whatever it took to please the wealthy in general and the banking community in particular. They were operating in a global environment where free flows of capital were hard to control. Yet they consistently exaggerated the powerlessness of national governments to stem these tides.

Echoing the Thatcher-era mantras, they regarded as dangerous any form of subvention or intervention to help ailing industries. In so doing, they allowed a number of otherwise healthy companies to go to the wall, in contrast to governments in, say, France or Germany. As Nick Clegg pointed out in his pamphlet, *The Liberal Moment*, published by Demos in 2009: 'In their relentless courtship of the City, New Labour forgot the need for a balanced economy.' In consequence, Britain was 'immensely and uniquely' vulnerable to the global recession.

By the time of Blair's departure in 2007, the terms of the debate had begun to shift, albeit tentatively. Three of the five candidates for the deputy leadership – Jon Cruddas, Harriet Harman and Peter Hain – highlighted the societal problems of the wealth divide. Hain said Labour 'has not yet begun to reverse' the inequalities of the Thatcher years. 'It is time Labour is clear that the war we wish to wage is not just a war on poverty, but also a war on inequality.' Only very late in the day, once the financial crash had exposed the avarice and risk-taking of the financial services sector, did Brown himself see the need to talk about stronger regulation, defending ailing industries or taxing bank profits.

For many in Labour, Iraq was the final straw. The anger over not just the military decision, but the deceits and the short cuts along the way, accelerated a latent public discontent with politics. Three familiar processes were in play during the fraught road to war: the second-guessing of the media and the Conservative positions; the submission to the agency with power (in this case the US government); and the subordination of less trusted political actors and institutions (the Cabinet and Parliament) to the inner core of the party leadership. In each of these Blair and his allies began from a characteristically pessimistic position.

Bizarrely for a man often accused of hubris, Blair was driven by a minimalist view – that Britain was nothing if not America's best friend. Blair projected his Iraq intervention in crusading terms. Yet in so many areas Britain either acted or colluded in a fashion that was not just immoral but in contravention of international law. The government connived in the transport of terrorist suspects by the US government to secret prisons around the world, giving landing rights at British airports for these so-called 'rendition' flights, while proclaiming it had no knowledge of them. The most hideous episode was the complicity in torture.

During his second term, Blair was knocked off course by Iraq, and never recovered from it. Brown was distracted by his enmity towards Blair. Having spent so long agitating for the top job, he forgot somewhere down the line to prepare. Once he finally prised the keys to Number 10 from his rival, Brown seemed to have no idea what to do next.

New Labour Leninism

It might seem a strange observation to make, but throughout these thirteen years New Labour's tactics bore many of the hallmarks of a Leninist revolutionary cell. A clique within a party quickly took over that party and engineered its structures so that it would enjoy long-term hegemony within the party and beyond. Its most important task was to neutralise the potency of Fleet Street. For Blair and Brown two images remained vivid – the lampooning of Neil Kinnock as he fell backwards on Brighton beach in 1983 and the media assault of that same Labour leader in the 1992 campaign, with *The Sun*'s famous election headline 'Will the last person to leave Britain please turn out the lights'. As the philosopher Ralf Dahrendorf said: 'When you define yourself in others' terms, you allow them to determine your agenda.'

Which came first: the fear, the aggression or the ideological caution? They were indistinguishable. One might reasonably argue that the reason so many in New Labour acted in a thuggish manner is because their passion was based not in the desire to engineer change, but in one all-consuming purpose: re-election. Since 1997, their every working day was based around the task of prolonging their term of office. That preoccupation filled in the ideological hollow.

Blair and Brown believed that Britain was both a Conservative and conservative country. They were pessimistic, fatalistic perhaps, about their ability to change society. Back in 1997, a cabinet minister likened the mood to feeling like a squatter who had just broken into someone's home and did not know when he might be evicted. No matter how low was the stock of the Conservatives, Labour always felt haunted, and saw a perpetual need to triangulate the two positions.

In criminal justice, Blair assumed he would achieve little if he did not acquiesce to the tastes of the majority view as represented to him by pollsters and certain press magnates. Authoritarianism united arch-Blairites and many on the left. Both regarded those in the party who valued individual rights as deluded or dangerous. Labour became ostentatiously illiberal, hopelessly out of touch with the public mood.

All too often ministers appealed to the lowest common denominator. Jack Straw quickly set the tone. After his plans to limit trial by jury were attacked by the judiciary, he launched an attack on his opponents, labelling them 'woolly-minded Hampstead liberals'. His successor as Home Secretary, David Blunkett, was the most extreme of all, promising to stop 'bogus' asylum seekers from 'flooding' into Britain. He locked up suspected terrorists indefinitely, without trial, and fought off cabinet opposition to ID cards, batting away the concerns of civil liberties campaigners as 'airy fairy' whingeing.

In one of his typically perspicacious newspaper columns, Cook once wrote: 'It is revealing that Britain now has a prime minister who uses "liberal" as a term of abuse, in the way that a North American politician would use it – as a smear.' Cook drew a broader conclusion: 'As a short-run electoral tactic, the Blair style has been a success. You cannot argue with two landslide victories and a tenure in office without precedent in Labour's history. But as a means of shifting the political values of society, it is hopeless.' (*The Independent*, 23 July 2004)

The attacks of 11 September 2001 allowed Blair to elide his instincts with increased public fears over security. The attacks in London on 7 July 2005 continued that process, with his call that 'the rules of the game have changed'.

By the time Blair left office in 2007, he had bequeathed a surveillance state unrivalled anywhere in the democratic world. The thirteen years of New Labour saw an erosion of civil liberties without precedent in modern British history. The list includes: plans for an identity card that would store fifty pieces of personal information on each individual; a surveillance system allowing local councils to snoop on people for fly-tipping; a quarter of the world's closed-circuit television cameras; and plans to extend of pre-trial custody to lengths that would be unacceptable in all other civilised countries. Parliament passed forty-five criminal justice laws – more than the total for the whole of the previous century – creating more than 3,000 new criminal offences. Worst of all was the rise in the prison population, which reached a record level of almost 85,000.

As Clegg pointed out, the loss of faith over the government's authoritarianism extended beyond the Labour movement. 'Liberal Democrats share the sense of betrayal that all progressives have about the worst excesses of the Labour government over the last twelve years, from the illegal invasion of Iraq and subordination of Britain's foreign policy to the Bush administration through to the tough talk on crime that has put a generation of young men behind bars and jettisoned our long treasured and hard won civil liberties,' he wrote. 'These were not minor peccadilloes that can be swept under the carpet and ignored. They were fundamental betrayals of the progressive cause that has eaten away at the very meaning and soul of the Labour Party and its purpose in British politics.'

In several policy areas, the Brown era did mark an improvement. With his longtime aide Ed Miliband at the helm, he did try to pursue a bolder approach to international climate change negotiations; he did, eventually, raise the top rate of tax (although only under fiscal duress); he took a less dogmatic approach to private provision in the public services; he was less cavalier with his Cabinet and Parliament, but that was largely because of a shift in the balance of forces. That is about it. Brown could have used his brief time in office to have defined himself more clearly. Instead, he adopted the old methods of hiding behind an inner coterie, ever fearful of a centre-right-dominated media, and ever triangulating, seeking to second-guess and outmanoeuvre the Conservatives rather than simply getting on with the job of engineering change.

The verdict

So what is the audit of these thirteen years? One of the tests of a government is the extent to which its successor seeks to dismantle its legacy. One of David Cameron's first and most controversial decisions as Conservative leader was to pledge that the National Health Service would remain true to its founding principles of being free at the point of delivery. The minimum wage became inviolable. Sure Start children's centres, which made a major contribution to working families, were also belatedly accepted by the Conservatives. The country might now be paying a heavy financial price, but the heavy investment in the NHS and education did lead to major progress in waiting lists and major improvements in school and hospital buildings. Then there was the law introducing civil partnerships, a rare instance of the government moving ahead of public opinion, confident in the knowledge that ultimately a majority of voters would approve the change. The Britain of 2010 is considerably more socially tolerant than the Britain of 1997.

During the election campaign, Labour portrayed Brown as the man good in a crisis. He was. On those fevered days when banks were going bust, he did play a pivotal part in shoring up the global economy. But it was a crisis he also helped to create, encouraging financiers to believe that the world belonged to them. From his first months as Chancellor of the Exchequer, Brown signed a Faustian pact with the City. As the revenues flowed in, so he became increasingly dependent on these people making vast amounts of wealth. Those around Brown say that he felt distaste for the whole process, but believed he was trapped. The Labour peer, Lord Puttnam, puts it: 'Gordon had too much baggage'. Puttnam likens Brown's 1999 Mansion House speech, in which he extolled the virtues of the financial services industry, to 'Henry V at a bankers' Agincourt'.

How different that all feels from the Labour of Michael Foot's day that Shirley – along with Roy Jenkins, David Owen and Bill Rodgers – left back in the early 1980s.

And yet this same Labour government, which was so frightened of taking on vested interests, which was so in awe of the super rich, at the same time and again almost by stealth, saddled the country with a debt burden that will take years to redress. At each step of the way, as the new coalition government has pointed out, retrenchment will be extraordinarily painful and potentially divisive. The parties might have differed during the election campaign about the speed and depth of the initial cuts, but these arguments were disingenuous. There was going to be no other way.

So how did this happen on the watch of such a cautious Labour government? Again I put it down to displacement theory. Labour spent and spent its way, as it sought ever more ambitious means to administer palliative care. This is now its overriding legacy.

It is therefore, on one level, a dispiriting moment for anyone who counts him- or herself as of the centre left. If, however, Clegg does deliver on his promises to restore many of the UK's lost civil liberties and if he succeeds in his agenda for political and constitutional reform, then he will have achieved more in this respect than Labour did in thirteen years.

My reference point was the politics of the late Robin Cook. His ideological bearings were sensible redistribution, an ethical foreign policy, a more transparent politics, radical constitutional change, investment in public services and environmental protection.

The liberalism to which I have long been drawn is not the libertarianism of the centre right, with its message of keeping the state off people's backs. Left-liberals believe that liberty is something to be worked for, a set of positive rights. For the right liberty is an innate condition, an absence of impediments.

The model is the liberalism of L. T. Hobhouse and T. H. Green, who saw egalitarianism as a virtue and a mission, not just of itself, but also, crucially, as a means of delivering greater individual freedom. In the immediate post-war years the paradigms of social democracy and liberal democracy were often seen as intertwined. It was, after all, two Liberals, Keynes and Beveridge, who had been the intellectual architects of much that was best and most enduring – and, indeed, most cherished within the Labour Party – in the post-war transformation wrought by the Attlee government.

Tony Crosland's 1956 classic *The Future of Socialism* is imbued with the language of individual freedom. Although there is much collectivism in the book, Crosland's main aim was to increase the life chances of individuals. He even went so far as to say that social justice was not the end point of his vision of a better Britain. Rather, it was a precursor, albeit a fundamental one, to promoting freedom.

Liberty and equality are not alternatives, as Amartya Sen pointed out nearly two decades ago. They do not have to work in competition. In enlightened systems they complement each other. 'Liberty is among the possible fields of application of equality, and equality is among the possible patterns of distribution of liberty.'

The best purpose of the state is surely to intervene on a macro-economic level, through fiscal and other measures, to build the foundations for delivering greater social justice, rather than meddling in people's lives on a more day-to-day level as an alternative outlet for politicians' lack of courage.

It is remarkable how little 'liberal' thinking took place within the Labour Party during the first ten years of Blair–Brown rule. In the final few years of the era some thinkers in and around the Labour movement, from the pressure group Compass to the think tank Demos, asked themselves whether, after all the assaults on civil liberties, amid the centralisation and the brutalism, the Labour Party can yet be 'liberalised'. One of these was Phil Collins, a former adviser to Blair: 'For New Labour to survive, it must become more liberal,' he wrote. 'The key dividing line in politics is no longer between left and right but increasingly between liberal and authoritarian. The Labour government too often finds itself on the wrong side of this divide. One of the lessons Labour ought to have learned from eleven years in charge of the state is to be humble about the limits of that power.'

This is the biggest task facing the new Labour leadership. Its first task should be humility and candour. It should have no illusions about how deeply confidence has been corroded.

Skilful electoral tactics have temporarily overcome a longtime Labour decline. Even in his moment of triumph in 1997, Tony Blair gained fewer votes than did John Major in 1992. Since Labour's first 'landslide', it has been one-way traffic downwards. By 2005, Labour had lost four million supporters, and even Michael Howard gained more votes in England than Blair did. It is only thanks to the electoral system and the Tories' inability to break beyond their hardcore vote that Labour has survived in power for as long as it has.

When Brown took over from Blair in 2007, ending more than a decade of angry frustration, many who had abandoned Labour in 2005 toyed with the idea of a rapprochement. But the extent of the malaise was only highlighted by his brief and unhappy tenure. Yet the demise of a tribe also presents opportunities to create something better. I look forward to a new era of more pluralist politics, one that embraces constitutional and political reform and defines itself by values rather than self-perpetuation in power.

Labour had no opportunity to renew itself while in government. It was exhausted. It had lost its bearings. It now faces an entirely new challenge. Just as for the first time in half a century, the Liberal Democrats find themselves in government, so the country has only one single party of the centre left in opposition. That should provide Labour with an opening.

But in many ways, that is an old way of addressing the age-old question. To what extent is Britain a Conservative and conservative country? Clegg has taken the understandable – and perhaps only available – decision, to join with the Tories and to seek to influence change for the good from within.

He has taken a leap of faith, and asked his party to join him in it. He argued that a marriage of convenience would achieve little. His alliance with Cameron appears heartfelt. How then will he differentiate the Liberal Democrat appeal from that of the Conservatives? How will he convince left-liberals who came across from Labour that their decision was not in vain? These are conundrums of which is he well aware.

Politics is more fluid than ever before. Tribal allegiances are ever weaker. For a brief period, the Con–Lib coalition will be prised apart as, presumably, Clegg and his team join forces with most senior Labour figures and some from other parties to mount a referendum campaign for the Alternative Vote.

If all the key figures in the centre left, no matter which party they belong to, realise that the old ways of operating are over, then there is a chance for the twin causes of social justice and liberalism eventually to work together. It is a tall order, just as a centre right party gets into its stride. But after all the mistakes of the past decade and more, never has there been a more urgent need for this new kind of pluralist politics to take root.

Is the progressive alliance dead? A personal reflection

Roger Liddle

Shirley Williams has been a distinguished figure in British politics for over forty-five years. She has huge achievements to her credit, not just in her time as a member of the Wilson and Callaghan cabinets in the 1970s but in her work since on education, constitutional reform, civil rights and nuclear disarmament. More than any other living person, she represents the liberal conscience of the nation.

Yet she remains one of the great 'might have beens' of British political life. One great 'might have been' is if she had held her Hertford and Stevenage seat in 1979, Labour history could have been quite different. I remember that Friday after the election, driving down the A1 from Stockton where I had been working for Bill Rodgers, my then boss. In the era before mobiles, Bill got out at a call box to ring Shirley at her count. I still remain his ashen-faced look as he came back to the car. Had Shirley survived, she would have been the leading figure in the shadow cabinet opposing the Bennite turn to the left and the shabby compromises too many decent people saw no alternative to making. She would have put much-needed steel into Denis Healey's campaign for the leadership in the autumn of 1980. In the leadership election after Labour's 1983 defeat, with her base in the trade unions that regularly elected her to the Women's Section of Labour's National Executive, she would have been a strong and appealing candidate. But by then of course we were all members of the SDP.

Again fate had been cruel to Shirley. The Warrington by-election in July 1981 was the new party's first opportunity to demonstrate its electoral appeal. Shirley was the SDP's most popular figure, with impeccable Labour authenticity, and as a constituency, the old borough of Warrington seemed a natural for her – a traditional working-class seat with strong Roman Catholic ties. Roy Jenkins was hesitant about whether to go for it. Only when Shirley, for a complex of difficult (but understandable) personal reasons decided not to go ahead, did he bravely throw his hat in the ring. The consequence was that Roy, not Shirley, became the assumed favourite to become SDP leader. Four months after Warrington, having been damned by the press as a trimmer and equivocator, Shirley rashly plunged into a by-election in what was then the safe Tory seat of Crosby in Merseyside. She won spectacularly of course, but lost the seat in the 1983 general election after a vicious Tory campaign that pilloried her actions as a Labour minister in abolishing direct grant schools and joining the Grunwick picket line. This left the SDP leadership open for David Owen, who though brilliant as a tactical Opposition politician and farsighted in recognising that social democracy had to come to terms with Thatcherism, proved deeply flawed.

Shirley came to feel real revulsion at some of the high-profile stances Owen took. I remember one evening at the height of the 1984–5 miners' strike, in the room at her conference hotel, sharing our common feelings of despair at what we felt was the harsh and uncompromising stance David Owen was taking. There are many things over which I disagree with Shirley, but on the really big issues I always felt confident that she would come out the right way. She has an instinctive feel for where social democrats ought to be. That is why, if I were having a similar late-night drink today, I can only think that her private views of George Osborne and David Cameron would be incomparably more fierce and dismissive than the anger she felt for David Owen a quarter of a century ago.

For the past thirty years I have shared a common aim with Shirley Williams, albeit in a much less distinguished capacity. That aim has been starting together in the Labour Party, and then from different parties and perspectives, to create an enduring progressive alliance on the centre-left of British politics. Does the surprise creation of the Conservative–Liberal

Democrat coalition in the wake of the 2010 general election draw a final, definitive and (for me) painful line under this long quest? Were we wrong to think that the central question for the centre left was to provide an electable and effective governing alternative to the Conservatives so that British politics in the twenty-first century would not experience the same Conservative domination as the country had lived through in the twentieth? To put it brutally, after thirty years of trying, has the concept of a progressive alliance failed and should we forget the whole thing?

This is a risky essay to write, as given the time of writing, it is far too early to tell how the new centre-right coalition will fare. Some Liberal Democrats will argue that the circumstances of 2010 were unique. Labour, they will say, was at the end of the road after thirteen years in office and could not be propped up in office, however much they might have preferred otherwise. The House of Commons numbers did not really make a Lib–Lab coalition a viable proposition – though that is arguable. For all that, I find the enthusiasm with which leading Liberal Democrats have embraced the idea of a Conservative coalition more than a little shocking.

Was I wrong to think that there is no fundamental conflict of values and principles that forces apart the vast majority of Labour and Liberal Democrat committed supporters and activists? Are we not a compatible mix of social democrats and social liberals, who recognise the key role of the state in advancing individual opportunity: not economic liberals who believe in principle in cutting back the size of the state? Are we not both instinctively on the side of the underdog; both about extending opportunity for the many, not the few; both believing in an environmentally sustainable, social market economy, but not a market society?

I always thought Labour and the Liberal Democrats shared a politics of the public interest, not the protection of privilege or vested interest. We see decent public services as something to be valued, not wasteful bureaucracy that has to be cut. We want to extend democracy and people's control over their lives. We are passionately opposed to all forms of inequality. In global affairs, we are internationalists and multilateralists. Our strong commitment to Britain's membership of the European Union is central to our political values and worldview.

True there are some significant policy differences that need to be worked through, such as the degree of government intervention necessary to correct market failure; attitudes to nuclear energy; the balance between civil liberties and protection of the public against terrorism; the balance between local and central; and between equity and equal access to services on the one hand and freedom, choice and diversity in the provision of public services, on the other. But these second-order differences of view can be found within the broad coalitions that make up any political party.

Put it another way: can anyone point me to a significant philosophical statement of the underlying values that bind together Liberals and Conservatives? Clegg and Cameron look as though they are searching for a guiding policy based on a suspicion of state power and a view that the state ought to be smaller both in relation to economic and social policy, and civil liberties. This may appeal to a minority of anti-authority, anti-state Liberal activists. But it seems a long way to me from the enlightened liberalism of Hobhouse and Green, and goodness knows what figures like Keynes and Beveridge would make of Liberals sharing cabinet positions with the likes of George Osborne.

This in itself is not an argument that makes a coalition government impossible. The history of the British Liberal Party from 1885–1955 is littered with examples of Liberals who chose to prop up Conservative governments and enter into electoral alliances with the Conservative Party. But this history does cast doubt on whether this present Con–Lib alliance of opportunism can really claim to be a partnership of principle, still less a 'union of hearts' as in Gladstone's magnificent exposition of the case for Irish Home Rule and as I always hoped would prove possible in a progressive Lib–Lab alliance.

Because it is too early to forecast the future, this essay focuses on learning the right lessons from the past. The last thirty years have seen three successive attempts to 'break the mould'. The first was to save Labour from itself that began in the late 1970s, led to the SDP breakaway in 1981 and the construction of the Alliance with the old Liberal Party, and which, despite flying high for a time, ended in dismal failure with the SDP split in 1987. The second was to build some kind of progressive alliance between the resurgent Labour Party of the late 1980s and the newly merged Liberal Democrats, culminating in the 'Project' that Tony Blair and Paddy Ashdown tried hard but unsuccessfully to bring to fruition around the 1997 general election. The third was Gordon Brown's endeavour after 2007 to build a new 'progressive consensus' that crumbled to dust in the five days after the 2010 election when it became evident that the attempt to bring about a Lib–Lab coalition had collapsed.

Labour's decades

For the early part of Shirley Williams's political life, the question of a progressive alliance was not remotely relevant. For three decades after 1945 Labour was the hegemonic party of the centre left, regularly drawing over 40 per cent of the vote in general elections. The reason was not just the class structure of Britain at the time (after all, an overwhelmingly working-class electorate had supported Conservative and National governments in the inter-war years). Rather the strength of the 'historical myth' (as Kenneth Morgan described it to me) that the post-war Attlee Government created sustained Labour over decades. For all its travails, the post-war Attlee government was credited indelibly in people's minds with achieving full employment and creating the NHS and welfare state. As a result, Labour commanded the fierce and undisputed, almost tribal loyalty of a large section of the working class for an entire generation. Although diminishing, Labour can still tap into a reserve of that same loyalty. It remained sufficient to see off the SDP in 1983 and hold on to second place against Cleggmania in 2010, despite the fear at the centre of Labour's campaign that Labour support might be in meltdown.

Labour was not of course without its problems in the post-war era. Mark Abrams's pamphlet after Labour's 1959 defeat – *Must Labour Lose?* – analysed the factors that were weakening Labour's underlying support by highlighting structural changes in society that were leading to the emergence of a new aspirant class that found traditional 'labourism' deeply unattractive. This analysis has echoed down the decades, significantly in Giles Radice's seminal Fabian pamphlets after the 1992 general election on

Southern Discomfort as well as in the current analyses of Labour's heavy defeat in 2010 in southern and eastern England (outside London) that Liam Byrne and John Denham have made.

However these analyses do not in themselves prove that Labour was or is finished as a broad majoritarian party of the centre left. It would be a grave mistake for Labour now to come to think that because in the 2010 election Labour has retreated to its heartlands, the only future lies in alliances with other parties, the aim of which is to draw in support in parts of the country where Labour is now much weaker. Rather the history of the last half-century has shown that when Labour presents itself in an electorally appealing way, as most obviously in 1964 and 1966, or in the New Labour victories of 1997, 2001, and 2005, workable parliamentary majorities can be secured.

It is my contention that for Labour to reach out to others successfully, Labour itself has first got to restore its position and appeal as a One Nation party. Part, but only part, of this process involves reconnecting with 'our own people'. However to concentrate exclusively on that task is to surrender the centre ground of politics to the Con–Libs. Labour has to be a party of what Roy Jenkins liked to call the 'radical centre' – and it is my contention that it is only from Labour occupying this point of the political spectrum that a new progressive alliance can be constructed.

The big lesson of the SDP failure was the resilience of the Labour Party – despite the catastrophic disasters that pushed Labour to the brink in the early 1980s. In the 1970s Labour's most serious problems were internal and ideological. It failed in the 1950s and 1960s to make itself into a modern continental European social democratic party. It failed in government in the 1960s and 1970s to make work a corporatist solution to Britain's economic problems. And by the late 1970s it was riven internally and on the brink of a Cultural Revolution.

The position of the Gaitskellite intellectuals in the party had always depended on a fairly narrow base. Themselves liberal and cosmopolitan in outlook, they depended in the Parliamentary Labour Party on the votes of leadership-loyal right wingers, many of whom were former trade union activists. Inside their constituency parties, they could normally count on an old guard of longstanding councillors and Coop Women's Sections. At

Conference they relied almost wholly on the leadership of the right-wing trade unions to protect the party from the latest left-wing enthusiasms and to elect a sound National Executive to manage the party structures.

In the 1970s a big generational change took place at Labour's grassroots. The working-class old guard was gradually being replaced by first-generation graduates imbued with the rebellious spirit of 1968. Among them were feminists, black activists, gay liberationists and environmentalists who in their determination to make the world a better place began to take over constituency Labour parties. Some of this new generation were attracted to groups on the far left as British socialism appeared to be going through its last great revival. Some detected an upsurge of revolutionary spirit in the wave of strikes that hit Britain. Tony Benn was the prophet and potential future leader setting out a bold 'alternative economic strategy' to the compromises with British capitalism and the IMF which the 1974 Labour government had been forced to make. The truth is that once this surge of socialist idealism had burnt itself out, many of those left inside the Labour Party remained natural recruits to progressive alliance politics. In this process the revisionism of *Marxism Today* probably played as big a role as the impact of the SDP and Labour's 1983 defeat, as did the emergence of new thinking on the left in the form of communitarianism and Euro-communism.

The response of the 'old right' to this 'new left' upsurge was weak and divided. The 'legitimate left' – the standard bearers of the old Bevanite flame – gained ground in the PLP as a result of the right's divisions over Europe and their own personal rivalries, brilliantly chronicled in Giles Radice's *Friends and Rivals*, which played a key part in explaining why Jim Callaghan and not Roy Jenkins succeeded Harold Wilson as leader. The trade unions' normal willingness to throw their weight behind the leadership was blunted by the breach within the Labour government over the 1978–9 'Winter of Discontent'.

The Social Democratic Party

The SDP's Gang of Four painfully concluded that Labour was a lost cause. The SDP's founders had great clarity about their original aims. As

Bill Rodgers told Roy Jenkins in December 1979, 'I would want a Fourth Party eventually to take over 90 per cent of the existing Labour vote. It would be a party of the left, winning towards the centre as it discarded the outside left. I have no confidence in – and no great warmth towards – a party of the centre. It would not work.' And Shirley Williams publicly declared in a radio interview that she was not interested in a centre party. Such a party would have 'no roots, no principles, no philosophy and no values'.

But fulfilment of this ambition depended on an implosion of Labour internally. It never quite happened, though implosion may have been pretty close. It is widely assumed that if Tony Benn had beaten Denis Healey for the Labour deputy leadership in September 2001, many more Labour MPs might have departed for the SDP and key trade unions might have disaffiliated, including the Electricians and Engineers. But the reason Healey held on to the deputy leadership was because a critical group of some forty 'legitimate Left' Labour MPs, led by Neil Kinnock, had abstained rather than support Tony Benn. This vote was the critical first sign that the soft left could be separated from the hard left and so provide a new foundation of loyal leadership support on which Neil Kinnock after 1983 was then able to build. At the same time the right-wing unions finally got their act together to change the composition of the NEC: they started to expel Militant and protect the party against the entryism of the far left.

These changes proved enough for Labour to hold on to its base of support in the 1983 general election despite the massive unpopularity of Michael Foot. Conservative support had also consolidated as a result of the victorious Falklands campaign in spring 1982. The 1983 general election saw the First Past the Post voting system wreak its revenge on the SDP. With a record 26 per cent of the vote, but its support fairly evenly spread across the UK, the SDP/Liberal Alliance managed to win only twenty-three seats. Labour with a mere 28 per cent of the vote won 210 seats.

This shocking result for Labour contributed to a process of painful intellectual reassessment on the Labour left. It was helped by the increasing isolation of Tony Benn, who lost his Bristol seat, Margaret Thatcher's defeat of the miners' strike two years after 1983, and the marginalisation of left-wing councils such as Lambeth and Liverpool which had pushed their opposition to government spending cuts to the point of defying the law. However, it took a long six years from 1983 for Labour under Neil Kinnock to adopt formally a recognisably social democratic policy agenda, and a further four years before John Smith squeezed through the Labour Conference the adoption of the policy of one member, one vote. By that stage, the direction of change in Labour was all towards social democratic modernisation.

And by this time the SDP was history. After the cataclysm of 1983, David Owen as its new leader recognised that Labour was not going to collapse and would eventually recover. He tried to push the SDP and the Alliance to the centre to pick up disillusioned Conservative supporters. Recognising the strength of the criticism that the SDP had been offering a 'better yesterday', Owen felt the future lay with a party that had come to terms with Thatcherism. In his view the Conservatives could be beaten only on a policy of economic realism, accepting markets, embracing public service reforms and adopting a robust stance on defence.

Intellectually Owen was right and he dominated the airwaves with great verve. But in terms of political strategy, it became clear in the 1987 general election campaign that he was moving closer to acceptance of Thatcherism in the hope of doing a deal with the Conservatives if the Alliance were ever to hold the balance of power. This caused public division within the Alliance by upsetting David Steel and many Liberals as well as adding to the consternation many privately felt within the SDP about Owen's stance. Owen paid the price of his own refusal to accept a merger between the SDP and Liberals, or even the election of a single leader. The Alliance looked broken and ineffective as an alternative government for Britain. The 1987 election result saw Labour consolidate a little and win that decisive second place; support for Thatcher held and the Alliance's electoral support fell to 23 per cent. Owen's reward for all his efforts to maintain a separate and distinct SDP was five Members of Parliament. Those five, like the SDP itself, then spectacularly split asunder with two MPs and getting on for 60 per cent of SDP members backing merger with the Liberals. The end result was the implosion of the SDP not the Labour Party.

Labour survived. The question then became whether Labour by itself could become an effective vehicle for progressive hopes. In his wonderful book *The Progressive Dilemma*, David Marquand argued that this had been the central unanswered question on the centre left of British politics since the marginalisation of the old Liberal Party in the 1920s and that the dilemma could only be resolved by bringing together a broad based coalition of the progressive centre left. Many in the new generation of Labour leaders agreed with the analysis. The question was how to proceed.

Blair–Brown

Prior to the 1992 election, Neil Kinnock and his principal advisers, Charles Clarke and Patricia Hewitt, concluded that Labour had to show openness to electoral reform. The problem was that many in the Labour Party were firmly opposed, not unreasonably because from their perspective it was First Past the Post in single-member constituencies which more than anything else had ensured Labour's survival as a party in the 1980s. This meant that the offer of electoral reform was tentative but clearly designed to open up the possibility of a Lib–Lab coalition if the election resulted in the hung parliament which many opinion polls predicted. It was not to be. But Labour set up the Plant Commission to report on electoral reform. It was as though John Smith recognised that 'one more heave' might not be enough.

This move to electoral reform was viewed with private reservation by the rising stars of what became New Labour, Tony Blair and Gordon Brown. They were not against the notion of a progressive alliance. They did not rule out electoral reform. But they were concerned that too many people in the Labour Party would seize on electoral reform as a soft option. In particular they worried that supporters of electoral reform such as Robin Cook would argue against further modernisation on the grounds that in a pluralist polity, Labour could have it both ways: stick to socialist principles and get into government by building a progressive alliance with the Liberal Democrats.

Tony Blair in particular was not attracted to a multi-party pluralist model of Britain's political future. He was aiming to make Labour into a 'big tent' or 'broad church' party like the US Democrats. He wanted to pull Paddy Ashdown's Liberal Democrats within that big tent. His strategy towards the Liberal Democrats was first coalition, then minimal electoral reform and finally a de facto merger between the two parties, even though formally they might have retained a separate constitutional existence. To prepare the ground for this possibility, he endorsed the Cook–Maclennan negotiations to finalise an agenda of agreed constitutional reform. This was not because he personally attached particular priority to this agenda: for him it was an essential first stage in pulling the Lib Dems into the Blairite big tent.

Blair's problem was the scale of his victory in 1997. I believe Blair would have gone ahead with his plans for bringing Liberal Democrats into the Cabinet if he had only won a small overall majority of, say, thirty or forty seats. In those circumstances the backing of the Liberal Democrats would have been for him an insurance policy against the risks of left-wing rebellion within the PLP – a threat much feared prior to 1997, but in fact not significant until Labour's second term. As it was, the size of Labour's majority in 1997 made it impossible for Blair to win the internal argument for coalition. John Prescott was firmly opposed, as were many in the PLP. Gordon Brown stayed on the sidelines. As Roy Jenkins had argued privately to Blair that the long-term security of his premiership depended on his ability to command Prescott's unwavering loyalty, the Project in practice died.

Blair did agree to the setting up of the Jenkins Commission on electoral reform. But its recommendation for a proportional system, 'AV+', was a step too far for Labour traditionalists, who included Blair himself, attached to the rigid constituency link. There was a powerful contingent within the Labour Party which supported proportional representation, embracing many who at one time would have labelled themselves as soft left. But there were clear limits to New Labour pluralism, as Blair's heavy-handed interventions in the battles over the Welsh Labour leadership and London mayoralty were to show. On electoral reform Blair lined up with the traditionalists who included the remnants of the old right in the PLP and opposed any change. Labour lost the opportunity to create the conditions for progressive coalition politics at Westminster while it had the chance. Of course, it did legislate for PR systems for the European Parliament and the new Scottish Parliament as well as the Welsh, Northern Irish and London assemblies. These experiences showed that coalition politics could be made to work in Britain. However, by the time party opinion began to change towards the end of Labour's period in office, it proved too late. But should it have been?

In the period before becoming Prime Minister Gordon Brown dropped heavy hints that he wanted to promote a new constitutional settlement for the UK. The case for this had much logic. Blair's constitutional reforms had been more radical than anything since the Parliament Act of 1910, but he largely lost interest in the constitutional agenda after the failure of the project, apart from the major judicial reforms that Charlie Falconer promoted. Yet there remained large areas of unfinished business – House of Lords reform, House of Commons procedural reform, the question of a written constitution, not to mention electoral reform for the Commons. And given the huge division the Iraq war had brought about between the Labour government and the centre-left intelligentsia, there was a powerful political argument for looking at these issues again in order to rebuild a progressive consensus. Indeed the relevant minister Michael Wills, who was close to Brown, argued powerfully that a new constitutional settlement was the key to restoring trust more generally between governments and governed.

It did not happen. There was certainly activity and some symbolic changes, such as the requirement for the government to seek the approval of the Commons before taking the nation to war. But Jack Straw as Justice Secretary, while committed to reform, showed little sense of urgency. Even as the expenses scandal rocked the legitimacy of the House of Commons to its foundations in the summer of 2009, the government wavered over whether to advance a bold case for wider political reform. Gordon Brown won the Cabinet argument to include in the final Queen's Speech of the Parliament a Bill to support a referendum on AV voting reform, which, while not being proportional was still a fairer system than First Past the Post. But there was no drive to rush the Bill through Parliament before the general election. Instead the AV referendum was relegated to a manifesto pledge.

There are, of course, legitimate arguments to be made that a Labour government facing the gravest economic crisis in post-war history had more pressing and important issues to deal with than political and constitutional reform. Labour was right in my view to fight the election on the economy, where its case against the Conservatives grew stronger as the months advanced. But to Liberal Democrats who were both keen and self-interested spectators of how Labour policy on constitutional questions might develop, they can only have come away with an impression of half-heartedness and division on Labour's part. It is impossible to judge how much this might have influenced the Lib Dems' attitude in the coalition negotiations after the May election, but it cannot have enthused them to take the risk of seeming to sustain in office what the media was already representing as a defeated Prime Minister and government.

Labour in future

This essay started with a cry of anguish at the fact that Liberal Democrats could join a Conservative government. But both Labour and the Liberal Democrats have much to learn from the experience of the last thirty years. The progressive alliance has not failed because of its inherent contradictions. Even at the May 2010 election, the polls suggest a narrow majority of voters would have preferred a Lib–Lab coalition to the one they ended up with. Rather in reflecting on the 'might have beens' of the past thirty years, it has been the structural dynamics of the British First Past the Post electoral system that have made the construction of a successful centre-left alliance such a lottery of chance. It is now in Labour's interest as much as the Liberal Democrats' to consign the First Past the Post system to history.

The Labour Party is not going to disappear: it remains and will remain the major progressive force on the centre left of British politics. It will not succeed by retreating to its heartlands, geographically and ideologically. However, there are parts of Britain that will remain probably beyond Labour's reach – much of the West Country, the Scottish Borders and Highlands most obviously. And there are people who, even if Labour commands the radical centre, are firmly anti-Conservative but who find it difficult to vote for a party that they still associate with producer interest, class politics and the trade unions. And there is also the rise of the Greens. That is the case for a progressive alliance politics. But if Labour in future is to build this coalition more successfully than New Labour did, it needs honestly to confront the forces of tribalism and conservatism that remain powerful within its own ranks and have held back its radical zeal.

In 1981 Shirley Williams, Bill Rodgers and David Owen argued that they were 'not prepared to abandon Britain to divisive and often cruel Tory policies because electors do not have an opportunity to vote for an acceptable socialist alternative to a Conservative government'. Maybe the Conservatives under David Cameron will avoid a repeat of those divisive and often cruel policies of the Thatcher era. Maybe the Liberal Democrat presence in the government will make a fundamental difference to Conservative economic and social policies, and not just on civil liberties and constitutional reform. For the sake of the country one must hope so. At this moment I am somewhat jaundiced by the memory of Lady Thatcher quoting St Francis of Assisi on the doorstep of Number 10. The country will learn all too soon what it has lost with the departure of Gordon Brown. My bet is that the idea of a progressive alliance will make a comeback.

Part three

Britain and Europe

The British and Europe: how we scraped in

Stephen Wall

'We have just seen this wonderful woman on television.' This is my mother talking and the subject of her admiration, circa 1975, is Shirley Williams. She has somehow managed to get past a barrier which normally suggests to my mother that any Labour voter, let alone Labour politician, is well beyond the pale. An indeterminate, but self-evidently right-thinking, person is frequently being enjoined by my mother (safely ensconced in her Sussex garden) to 'go up to London and throw a brick through Harold Wilson's window'.

But something has now changed. Shirley Williams is helped on the road to absolution, and indeed approval, by the fact that she is Catholic and while my mother, who never swears, is not beyond describing the Pope as a 'bastard' for his pronouncements on birth control, she is a convinced and serious Catholic.

But Shirley Williams's Catholicism is only part of the secret of my mother's conversion. The main ingredients are, of course, the same qualities that have won Shirley Williams friends and admirers across the spectrum of politics, across the gap of generations and across the great British divide that is Europe.

Slightly later in time, my father (equally impressed by Shirley Williams's TV profile but with a less wide chasm of prejudice to cross) was slightly halted in his tracks by reading *Testament of Youth*. For it transpires that Shirley Williams's mother, and my father's sister, went to the same school in pre-First World War Buxton. And my paternal grandfather was one of those

Buxton bank managers who, for Vera Brittain, epitomised the stiflingly tedious atmosphere of small-town Derbyshire society. My grandfather's conformism came both with the nature of his job (in the days when bank managers told you what you could *not* spend, rather than encouraging you to spend what you could not afford) and, perhaps, because, as the son of a small-scale farmer and butcher, he felt less at ease in his bank manager's suit (one at a time only, bought each year from the fifty-shilling tailor) than he tried to pretend.

So I have a personal reason for wanting to write my chapter: to record some of the European achievements of Shirley Williams's career, which would undoubtedly have converted my mother completely to her cause, and perhaps to appease the shade of my banker grandfather for whom continental Europe held no terrors: he motored its length and breadth in the 1920s in the days when the sight of a motor car in a Pyrenean village was enough to bring all the inhabitants onto the street to stare.

If the history of post-war Britain is, in part, that of the end of empire and of our fitful attempts to moor ourselves, as General de Gaulle put it, alongside continental Europe, then that history has Shirley Williams as one of its central figures.

The first attempt

The conventional wisdom among pro-Europeans in Britain is that we missed the bus, train, or whatever, of European construction, when we declined to join the fledgling European Community in 1957, out of a blend of self-delusion and post-war hubris. The truth is a bit more prosaic, for the official documents of the 1950s show that successive British governments were conscientious and painstaking in trying to work out where British interests lay. Their calculations were both political and economic.

On the political side, there was undoubtedly an instinctive reticence about the federal model espoused by Monnet, Schuman and De Gasperi. Harold Macmillan, as a delegate to the Council of Europe in 1950, noted in his diary the concessions made to the British *functional* concept as opposed to the continental *federal* one. This was not just an innate suspicion of supranational institutions: Britain was, after all, a progenitor of the United Nations whose Charter empowered the Security Council to impose international sanctions on member countries and even to make war on them if they threatened the peace and security of the new world order. It was, rather, a suspicion bred of centuries of exposure to continental power systems from the Hapsburgs, through Napoleon, to Hitler and the threat they posed to British safety and British interests.

Macmillan, along with all his contemporaries, had lived through two world wars. He naturally shared the widespread fear that a threat to peace could again arise from Germany. Like Churchill, he saw the need to bind Germany into the family of European nations. But against that was the belief that Britain's political interest, and her love of liberty, were best preserved in a system which gave primacy to parliamentary sovereignty. So there was a respectable reason for feeling that Monnet's vision was not compatible with the British view of what was necessary to render Europe safe from further war.

Victory had been the product of Anglo-American collaboration, planning and military success. The Russian alliance had turned swiftly sour as the Iron Curtain descended across post-war Europe. Logic pointed to a continuing close relationship with America, especially in defence, and Britain already had, in intelligence and nuclear collaboration, a closer relationship with the United States than with any other nation. And no other nation had such a close relationship with the US. On top of that, particularly after the Suez crisis of 1956, there arose both a sense of fear of what could happen if Britain fell out of American favour and a seductive feeling of self-importance arising from the closeness of the relationship. That privileged partnership helped disguise our own relative political and economic decline.

On top of all that, mistakenly, was very real doubt whether the proposed European Community would prove sustainable. Here, our sense of national pride at our own wartime achievements overly influenced our judgement about both the capacity and self-interest of continental Europe to form a lasting union. And the wish was father to the thought. The idea of sharing sovereignty through supranational institutions was not one the British public relished. So, convincing ourselves that it would not happen, or would not succeed, had let us off the uncomfortable task of confronting the huge psychological and political challenges which negotiating for membership would have posed.

For much of the 1950s, that political argument was bolstered by hard economics. I think it is easier to criticise our predecessors for their political, than for their economic, assessment of what a European Community would mean. And our own generation's management of the British economy ought anyway to impose a bit of humility. The fact is that, for most of the early post-war period, including the 1950s, British trade with the old Commonwealth far exceeded in value our trade with the countries of the future European Economic Community (EEC). So, quite apart from the political difficulty of unpicking the elaborate system of Commonwealth Preference (an issue that bedevilled subsequent British efforts to join once we did decide to do so), there seemed no good economic argument for doing so.

The arithmetic of changing trade patterns began to assert itself when Britain could still, just, have negotiated to join as a founding EEC member. The Treasury, by 1956, were calculating that a successful European Community was probably something Britain could not afford economically to be absent from. But the key word was 'successful' and both ministers and officials continued to doubt if the Community would happen.

Even when it did happen, Britain had other preoccupations. Suez had been a national humiliation. The Prime Minister, Anthony Eden, was forced from office – the only time that has happened since World War II outside a general election. Harold Macmillan had to establish himself in the role as Eden's successor and win a general election, which he did, resoundingly, in 1959. Only then could he turn his attention to shifting opinion within his government, the Conservative Party and the country so that a bid for European membership was politically feasible.

By that time too the EEC had started to demonstrate its success with growth rates outstripping Britain. General de Gaulle had returned to power in France in 1958 with unparalleled power, under the constitution of the Fifth Republic, backed by the skilled use of referendums. No friend of the supranational nature of the EEC, he nonetheless used the challenge of economic competition within the Community to impose harsh economic medicine on the French people – amounting to an income reduction in real terms of up to 8 per cent. It was probably as much that achievement as any other to which Macmillan was referring when, late in life, he said that de Gaulle had 'saved France'. That hard-won success for France, sustained through robust economic policies at least until the advent of François Mitterrand in the 1980s, is an often overlooked motivation, I believe, for de Gaulle's veto of the British application to join the EEC in January 1963.

The argument about when de Gaulle decided to veto Britain's application, and why, remains unresolved. There is some evidence that the wind was blowing in that direction down the corridors of the Elysée Palace as early as April 1962. For the remainder of that year, the Brussels negotiations were bogged down in excruciating but unavoidable detail, especially over the future of Commonwealth Preference. When de Gaulle gave his famous press conference on 14 January 1963 in which he signalled his veto of Britain's candidature, he suggested that the slow pace of the negotiations in Brussels was evidence of the impossibility for Britain of adapting herself to EEC norms. Yet, only a couple of days beforehand, at lunch in Paris, Maurice Couve de Murville, the French Foreign Minister, had told Edward Heath, leader of the British EEC negotiators, that if the remaining problems in Brussels could be resolved (and it was becoming clear that they could) then nothing could stop Britain joining. There is no evidence that any of de Gaulle's ministers had prior knowledge of the bombshell he was to launch at his press conference.

Had de Gaulle, as the French propaganda machine subsequently claimed, been misled by Macmillan when the two men met at Rambouillet in December 1962? Macmillan had talked then in terms of Anglo-French collaboration across the board. He had also made distinct, but nonetheless allusive, references to continuing British dependence on US collaboration in nuclear defence. But he had been far from explicit about the deal on US supply of Polaris nuclear warheads which he was to conclude with President Kennedy in Nassau in the following week. Yet French objections to the Nassau deal as evidence that Britain was not committed to a genuinely

European future only surfaced *after* de Gaulle's press conference. The British Ambassador in Paris, Bob Dixon, saw de Gaulle on more than one occasion in the first two weeks of January and de Gaulle made no mention of Nassau.

Macmillan famously said to Alistair Horne, his official biographer, that 'if Hitler had danced in Whitehall we'd have had no trouble with de Gaulle'. Had the wounds of hurt pride festered since de Gaulle's days in London and Algeria during World War II? Some say that the wounds started early in the life of Charles de Gaulle, brought up, as he was, on memories of Fashoda when, in 1898, the British army had coolly besieged a French-held fort in the Sudan. Certainly, those perceived slights, combined with what de Gaulle himself called *une certaine idée de la France*, contributed to his vision of a Europe built economically, politically and strategically in independence from, and almost opposition to, the United States – a vision which was to hold not just Britain, but the rest of the young EEC to ransom for the best part of a decade. But de Gaulle's January press conference was also pretty hard headed, as Macmillan also recognised when he told Jack Kennedy on the phone a few days later that de Gaulle could not allow there to be 'two cocks on the same dunghill'.

The basic message of de Gaulle's press conference was that, painfully but productively, the Six had forged an economic partnership which worked, and which worked, above all, because it recognised the primacy of French agricultural interests. If Britain joined, that Common Market would be changed beyond recognition. And others would follow. We could end up with a European Community of eighteen members. If the Common Market was not to be irrevocably changed by British membership, then Britain had to change irrevocably before she could join. And that was a long way from happening.

In making that assessment was de Gaulle very far wrong? He was more farsighted than most of his contemporaries, and not a few of his successors, in seeing that enlargement to Britain would open the door much wider. I think that, far from concluding that the EEC negotiations with Britain were doomed to failure, de Gaulle realised early in January 1963 that they were, on the contrary, doomed to succeed. And he had to intervene to prevent that.

President de Gaulle had the advantage of public relations. He famously likened Macmillan's emotional appeal at Rambouillet to the 'hero' of Piaf's song 'Milord'. He told his cabinet ministers, and through his spokesman the press that, like the prostitute in the song, he had been tempted to say to Macmillan '*Ne pleurez pas, Milord*'.

That humiliation, followed by a heap of domestic troubles, contributed to the terminal decline of Macmillan's premiership. But I doubt if it is true, as Tom Mangold concludes, in his riveting study of the relationship between de Gaulle and Macmillan (*The Almost Impossible Ally*) that, in the end, Macmillan was outclassed by de Gaulle. Someone who is prepared to be totally obdurate, as de Gaulle was, will have an advantage in most negotiations. Margaret Thatcher was to demonstrate the truth of that two decades later. But de Gaulle's obduracy was directed as much towards the other five EEC members as to Britain, to the detriment of the development of the Community. In the end, de Gaulle's own vision of France at the pinnacle of a Europe which would itself be poised pivotally between the two superpowers died in August 1968 when Soviet tanks rolled into Prague. And the General's own presidency died less than a year later.

The second attempt

The Labour Party in opposition opposed, as is the British way, the emerging terms of Macmillan's EEC negotiations. Gaitskell had set the tone, rhetorically, demagogically and astutely in denouncing the approach to Europe as 'the end of a thousand years of history'. But within a very few months of coming to power in 1964, Harold Wilson had quietly abandoned the policy of building up the European Free Trade Association as an alternative to EEC membership, not least because it was quite difficult to pose as the champion of EFTA on the one hand, while, on the other, imposing a 20 per cent surcharge (illegal under EFTA rules) on EFTA imports. And this the new Labour government had done in order to improve Britain's dire balance of payments position.

Harold Wilson has had a bad press over Europe, often pilloried as the man who put party above principle; who sought to defeat Heath over terms of entry which he himself would have accepted had he still been in government, and as having subjected both Britain and her partners to a futile, empty and time-wasting 'renegotiation' of the terms of entry for the sole purpose of papering over a huge crack in the Labour Party.

The allegations are not baseless, but they are nonetheless a caricature. Wilson was, at heart, a Commonwealth man. He did not share Ted Heath's emotional sense of attachment to Europe. But, like Macmillan before him, he made a rational calculation. The EEC was too significant successfully to ignore. But, economics aside, what would be the place of Britain in the world if she were not part of a bigger European grouping? Wilson made a hard-headed calculation that, if Britain were to continue to exercise global influence, she could only do so in partnership with her fellow Europeans.

Wilson steered this change of course with patience and skill through his Cabinet and party. He got rather short shrift domestically for the tour of European capitals that he and his Foreign Secretary, George Brown, undertook in 1966. But Wilson needed to construct at home a sense that the rest of Europe wanted us, that acceptable terms were negotiable and that we were again taking control of our own future. He was received warmly but warily in European capitals. There were doubts about his commitment after the searing criticism he had made of Macmillan's European policy. Wilson and Brown assuaged those doubts.

Wilson planned his meeting with de Gaulle with care. Unlike Macmillan, he had no well of shared wartime experience to draw on, though de Gaulle had proved adept at separating sentiment from self-interest. Wilson dwelt more on the changes occurring in the British economy, on similar French and British views of the future political development of the EEC and on a vague indication that Britain would not renew the Polaris deal with the United States.

If Wilson had any advance hopes that he might get through to President de Gaulle where Macmillan had failed, he did not fool himself that he had made much real headway. De Gaulle was polite, even flattering, but his arguments against British entry remained essentially the same. When Georges Pompidou, de Gaulle's Prime Minister, came to London, he and Wilson did not get on. This was partly political antipathy on Pompidou's part; partly his uncompromising stand on British accession; partly offence taken when Wilson and Brown arrived very late for a dinner in their honour at the French embassy because they had had to vote after a major debate in the House of Commons on Vietnam.

For their part, British officials were torn between getting France onside as a route to accession or, alternatively, persuading the five other member states to gang up on France. The Foreign Office were inclined to want to isolate France. Wilson, astutely advised by his Foreign Office Private Secretary, Michael Palliser (son-in-law of Belgian Foreign Minister Paul-Henri Spaak), believed that only an accommodation with France would secure success.

That accommodation eluded the government and, when the British government, in 1967, declared its intention to renew the British application for entry, de Gaulle lost little time in once again saying no – this time before negotiations had even begun. This time, it was expected and Wilson, cleverer in this respect than Macmillan, did not withdraw the application. On the contrary, he kept it firmly on the table, asserting that Britain would not take no for an answer.

Less than a year later, in May 1968, de Gaulle came close to being ejected from office in a street-based revolution. By the end of August, his illusory dreams of France as the leader of a Europe poised as an agent of influence between the United States and the Soviet Union had expired on the streets of Prague. Early in 1969, disillusioned with Europe, de Gaulle spoke in confidence to the British Ambassador in Paris, Christopher Soames, about the idea of a different kind of Europe in which the four biggest countries, Britain included, would provide the necessary direction. Soames wisely cleared his record of the meeting with the Secretary General of the Elysée before sending it back to London. If de Gaulle's ideas amounted to more than musing, their treatment in London killed the initiative dead and destroyed any hope of an Anglo-French rapprochement while the General remained in office.

Senior Foreign Office officials, and Michael Stewart, the Foreign Secretary, suspected a trap: de Gaulle would lure the British into discussions which would then be leaked to other EEC members to demonstrate that, far from wanting to join the Community as it was, the UK was intent on undermining it. Soames's plea to be allowed back to London to talk to Stewart and Wilson was turned down, as was his proposal to explore the initiative further before rejecting it. Stewart insisted that the Five must be told. Wilson, on a visit to Bonn, understandably felt that he had to tell the German Chancellor in confidence what had happened. Reluctantly, he let Stewart and the Foreign Office have their way. In a further blunder, the Foreign Office refused to allow Soames to give the French advance warning that the other five EEC members were to be informed of the secret conversation between de Gaulle and Soames. The Foreign Office briefed the press in detail, and tendentiously, about what had happened.

De Gaulle was unsurprisingly furious and, it is said, complained of British treachery from then until his death the following year. Soames, fearing that his mission in Paris to get alongside the French as only a senior political appointee could, was in ruins, offered his resignation. Only de Gaulle's departure from office three months later prevented the Soames Affair (in which Soames was the innocent victim) from casting a lasting shadow over Anglo-French relations. Nonetheless, it was a seriously unprofessional blunder by the Foreign Office and should serve as a salutary lesson to all foreign secretaries of the need to test the advice of officials, however capable, against their own political judgement.

The third attempt, and after

In June 1970, Britain was on the verge of resuming negotiations for entry into Europe. President Pompidou, under pressure from the socialist German Chancellor, Willy Brandt, had removed France's veto, albeit at a price – the funding of the Common Agricultural Policy by a financial system that would prove crippling for Britain – which stacked the cards against the interests of the applicant.

Harold Wilson, well ahead in the opinion polls, called a general election. The Labour Party manifesto was more unequivocal in its support for EEC membership than the Conservative one, which merely spoke of opening negotiations and of joining only with 'the full-hearted consent of the British people'. Against the odds, Heath won. He now had the opportunity to fulfil the ambition, denied him seven years earlier, of taking Britain into the EEC. He set about it single-mindedly and despite considerable opposition from within his own party, as well as a distinct lack of enthusiasm on the part of the public as a whole.

There is little doubt that the terms which Ted Heath accepted were harsh ones, committing Britain to a budget contribution which soon made her a significant net contributor to the European Community, whereas all other member states except Germany were significant net beneficiaries. Tory party politics forced Heath to sacrifice British financial interest in exchange for continued New Zealand butter imports. Officials knew it was a bad deal but the truth was that Britain was more supplicant than applicant. It was believed, almost certainly correctly, that if the government were to turn down the terms on offer, the UK would be forced back to the negotiating table, and probably on worse terms, a few years later.

Heath's terms were probably no different than those which a Labour government would have obtained, but Labour were in no mood to pander to the Conservatives, whose economic policies were seen as hugely divisive. As Labour became increasingly divided over Europe, Harold Wilson was obliged to manoeuvre to save his own position as party leader. The pledge to renegotiate the terms of entry if Labour were re-elected was the price for keeping open the European option at all. And the Labour Party did have a substantive argument on their side. By no stretch of the imagination could a narrow parliamentary victory, only won with the support of Labour pro-Marketeers, including Shirley Williams, be claimed as the 'full-hearted consent of the British people'.

It is easy to dismiss the renegotiation carried out by Wilson and Callaghan after Labour returned to power in 1974 as a cynical party-political exercise. Its substantive fruits were relatively meagre. But a Labour Party unreconciled to Europe would have been a Britain unreconciled also. Wilson and Callaghan played the renegotiation for a success and the referendum for a 'yes'. To hold the party together, Wilson had to come across as more neutral than he really was. He needed champions for the European cause and in Roy Jenkins and Shirley Williams he had them. Both Roy Jenkins and Shirley Williams put their political futures on the line. Both said that if the referendum result was a 'no' they would resign from the government. It was far from clear at the time that the outcome would be a substantive 'yes'. While Wilson held the party together, Williams and Jenkins embodied the reasonable and reasoned case for Europe. The referendum of June 1975 was won as much on the electorate's judgement about, and confidence in, the individual protagonists as in the detail of their arguments.

Since then, the British people have, to the surprise of all of us who thought that the referendum would put an end to the argument, wavered mightily on the issue of European Union membership. The part of the story covered in this essay may help to explain why.

It also helps explain why the Labour and Conservative parties have succumbed to Euroscepticism in opposition, believing that to be the popular course and why, in government, prime ministers have been ambivalent about Europe. They have feared to open up divisions within their own party and to court unpopularity. Even a leader such as Tony Blair, whose instincts were pro-European, felt that the least costly policy was to try to keep Europe off the front pages, while Gordon Brown wanted to put it on the front pages only in terms of British victories won at the expense of the foreigner.

One can detect something similar at work in Britain's new coalition government: the general expectation is that the presence of the Liberal Democrats will prevent what might otherwise be the implementation of Conservative Eurosceptic policies. The coalition agreement shows as much. But, even without the Liberal Democrats, it is likely that Cameron and Hague would soon discover, as Gordon Brown did once he became Prime Minister, that there are very few British overseas interests that can be addressed without working with our EU partners and through the framework of EU policies and structures.

That fact found no acknowledgement in William Hague's first major speech as Foreign Secretary. As a nation, we still find it hard to acknowledge that, having lost an empire, we *have* found a role, and it is as one of twenty-seven EU countries, none of which, on her own, counts for a great deal in the modern world. But coalition government depends on compromise and the habit of compromise may change Britain's traditional win–or–lose approach to European negotiation. There is also a fair chance that the Labour Party, in opposition, will not revert to the old Euroscepticism. There is an opportunity for a new generation of politicians to make European policy as bipartisan as are most other aspects of our foreign and defence policy. It is to be hoped that EU membership may become not just a matter of British politics but a matter of British principle too.

Shirley Williams's life is a striking illustration of the fact that, in politics, the exercise of principle can be just as potent as the pursuit of power. That was what my mother, and millions like her, recognised and responded to all those years ago.

Governing Europe

Andrew Duff

On the evening of 28 October 1971, sixty-nine Labour MPs crossed the floor of the House of Commons to help Edward Heath, the Conservative Prime Minister, fulfil his lifelong dream. The vote was on the second reading of the Bill that gave effect to the UK's accession to the European Communities. The matter at hand split both Labour and the Tory parties. It confused and divided public opinion then, as it still does today. It was little comfort to the opponents of British entry, who lost the parliamentary vote that night and were to lose again in the nationwide referendum which confirmed membership in June 1975, that there were many within the EC who themselves remained ambivalent about the merits of being joined by the British. Even today, it is fairly apparent that many mainland European politicians continue to share, at least in private, General de Gaulle's contention that the British, being not farmers but traders, and more Atlanticist than European, are therefore basically unsuitable for membership of the European club.

The history of UK membership of the European Union has indeed been difficult. As Hugo Young chronicled so well in his 1998 book *This Blessed Plot*, Britain has remained the odd man out. The UK government has failed regularly to fulfil the expectations of those continentals who supported Britain's membership bid. No prime minister subsequent to Heath has shown the necessary combination of skill, boldness and perseverance to take the lead in Europe. The referendum settled very little. The House of Commons soon reverted to type and adopted a lackadaisical attitude to the European Union, spiced with jealousy aimed in particular at the European Parliament. Occasional signs from Britain of renewed enthusiasm for European integration proved to be fleeting and were never sustained. Rows were escalated and opportunities for reconciliation missed. The EU became an easy scapegoat for politicians who needed to excuse themselves for presiding over Britain's seemingly steady decline. Public scepticism grew to such an extent that no British political party, not excepting the Liberals, has felt able to speak the whole truth about the scale or scope of the country's interdependence with the EU, still less to argue the case for deeper integration. Instead, the language of 'red lines' and battle cries of no surrender have characterised the British discourse on Europe. British opt-outs from major areas of EU common policy, such as the monetary union, the Schengen common travel area and justice and interior policies, are trumpeted as worthy vindications of British national sovereignty. Led by the BBC, British media coverage of EU affairs is scant and ill informed. Dissembling about what is really going on in Europe is commonplace. Can there be a more shaming indictment of the recent Labour government's record on Europe than the claim by the cabinet minister involved in the constitutional negotiations that the Treaty of Lisbon was no more than a 'tidying-up exercise'?

Allergic to federalism

At the heart of the matter is Britain's strong dislike of what it takes to be Europe as a federal project. Such an aversion to federalism is mightily curious when one considers the very significant contribution the British have made over recent centuries to the growth of federal theory and practice across the globe. The British colonial gentlemen who founded the USA were, of course, federalists. As Great Britain withdrew from its empire, it installed fully fledged federal constitutions in most of its many dominions. W. E. Gladstone and successor Liberal prime ministers espoused Home Rule for Ireland. Winston Churchill, already forty years old at the outbreak of the First World War, moved decisively in the immediate aftermath of the Second World War to encourage the rapid development of the federal movement on the European mainland (albeit without Britain). As early as 1946, Churchill was calling for 'a kind of United States of Europe'. By 1948, presiding over the Congress of Europe in The Hague, Churchill was even more optimistic:

> We must proclaim the mission and design of a United Europe whose moral conception will win the respect and gratitude of mankind, and whose physical strength will be such that none will dare molest her tranquil sway . . . I hope to see a Europe where men and women of every country will think of being European as of belonging to their native land, and wherever they go in this wide domain will truly feel 'Here I am at home'.

Leading European federalists such as Altiero Spinelli drew inspiration not only from Churchill's leadership but also from the federalist writings of British political thinkers such as John Stuart Mill and Philip Kerr, Marquess of Lothian.

The Labour governments of 1945–51 were reticent about British engagement with Europe, but rightly insisted that the new constitution of post-war Germany should be of a classic federal type. At the same time, the UK pressed hard for federal solutions for its soon to be ex-colonies, embraced in the family of the Commonwealth of more or less democratic nations espousing universal fundamental rights. The federal option was a good one to choose if Britain was ever to extricate itself more successfully from its vast empire than France, Spain, Portugal or Belgium managed withdrawal from theirs. The new-found independence enjoyed by large, multi-ethnic, multi-religious states was never going to be best managed by classical European notions of centralised 'nation states'. Power had to be shared between central and provincial authorities, with neither dominating the other. Checks and balances were entrenched in constitutions that fostered pluralism and power-sharing. In many cases, as we know, the post-colonial settlements, based on federalism at home and Commonwealth abroad, proved to be over-optimistic. But in a number of cases, notably India, such post-colonial federal regimes succeeded against the odds in developing democratically and keeping dictatorship at bay.

Britain's penchant for imperial federalism has to be weighed against its evident allergy to European federalism. The phenomenon is even more curious in the light of the United Kingdom's domestic constitutional evolution. For gradually the UK itself has moved to establish devolved administrations and autonomous provincial governments and parliaments in Northern Ireland, Scotland and Wales. Today, the UK's own brand of quasi-federal monarchy has become a model closely observed in other parts of Europe from Spain to Turkey.

Going ahead despite the British

Sixty years ago, in 1950, Robert Schuman and Jean Monnet launched their famous plan for the integration of the coal and steel industries of France and Germany. This they saw as 'a first step in the federation of Europe'.

> In this way there will be realised simply and speedily that fusion of interests which is indispensable to the establishment of a common economic system; it may be the leaven from which may grow a wider and deeper community between countries long opposed to one another by bloody divisions. By pooling basic production and by instituting a new higher authority, whose decisions will bind France, Germany, and other member countries, this proposal will lead to the realisation of the first concrete foundation of a European federation indispensable to the preservation of peace.

Monnet hoped that the British would provide leadership. He and others worked in vain to get the UK government involved in the Treaty of Paris (1951) and the Treaty of Rome (1957). Rab Butler told Michael Charlton that, at that time, Britain was regarded as 'the normal chairman of Europe' (*Encounter*, 1981). But the British Labour and Conservative governments vetoed the UK's participation in these early stages of integration precisely on the grounds that British national sovereignty could not or would not be shared. Charlton's record, confirmed by Young, exposes an extraordinarily languid reaction in Whitehall to these fundamental changes taking shape on the continent. At Westminster, the tenor of the debates was complacent:

Britain had won the war; others should draw the consequences from the victory; Britain, meanwhile, had other fish to fry. Only a small minority of British figures, including William Beveridge and Lionel Robbins, begged to differ from the general view that the federal approach, while good for empire and necessary for mainland western Europe, was not on for Britain. Free trade between the UK and the six founding states of the EC would be enough; political guarantees were to be provided by NATO whose job, in the immortal words of its first secretary-general, Lord Ismay, was to keep the Russians out, the Americans in and the Germans down.

When, in the 1960s, economic and political circumstances eventually drove the UK to seek membership of the European Communities, the federal question remained a difficult obstacle around which to negotiate. Since joining the European Union in 1973, the UK has been fighting an almost constant rearguard action against the furtherance of the federal project. The common market grew into the more ambitious single market, cooperation was begun in foreign and security policy, the foundations for the monetary union were laid, police and judicial authorities entered into a tentative collaboration – and still the British sought to deny that political union of a federal type was on the cards. Successive treaty negotiations about new competences to be conferred on the Union and new powers to be granted the EU institutions struggled to cope with the British fear of federalism, leading to minimalist results clouded deliberately in obscurity. This British anti-federalist phobia has had some strange unintended consequences – none more so than when John Major's refusal at Maastricht to accept the F-word in the new treaty led inevitably to having to carry on, as we do to this day, with the perpetually centralising (and therefore non-federal) 'ever closer union of states and peoples'.

While the mainstream political parties in Britain have learned to accept EU membership as a given reality, they are still reticent about 'more Europe' – and, like Gordon Brown at the treaty signing in Lisbon, tardy. As a rule, British politicians have not wished to vest the EU with sufficient authority to enable it to govern effectively within its own areas of competence. Nor have they acted as a fluent conduit to connect the supranational politics of the EU with domestic politics at home. From time to time, Tony Blair would speak eloquently about the purpose of European integration as a response to the challenges of globalisation. But while willing the ends, he was ever reluctant to grant the means.

Eventually, despite the British, the new Treaty of Lisbon entered into force on 1 December 2009. It is a big step forward towards the federalist goal of a united Europe. Yet the problem still remains of how to establish effective and fully legitimate democratic government at the European level. The case for the UK to accept the logic of federalism in the European context is stronger than ever. Faced as we are with ever-larger global challenges, the absence of proper European government may be about to become critical.

The Treaty of Lisbon

The Lisbon treaty confers more competences upon the European Union, whose institutions now enjoy more powers and new instruments especially in the areas of justice and interior affairs and in foreign and security policy. The European Council of heads of government becomes a formal institution and has an elected permanent president, Herman Van Rompuy. His job is to oblige each prime minister to accept individual responsibility for the economic policy and foreign affairs decisions they take collectively at meetings of the European Council. The federal method, whereby the European Commission initiates policy on the basis of the common interest of all the states, is extended into the area of foreign, security and defence policy. The Council of Ministers of Foreign Affairs is chaired by the new High Representative for foreign and security policy and Vice-President of the Commission, Catherine Ashton. The European Parliament gains major new powers in terms of scrutiny, international treaties, constitutional affairs, law-making and the budget. The Council of Ministers has to meet in public, like the Parliament, when it passes law. The Charter of Fundamental Rights becomes binding. Much else happens besides as a result of the new treaty to advance the cause of European unity.

In terms of historic significance, the Lisbon treaty is certainly on a par with that signed at Maastricht in 1992, which gave birth to the euro. Yet

Lisbon proved much harder to negotiate and ratify than Maastricht, not least because the size of the Union had grown from twelve states to twenty-seven, with the commensurate loss of homogeneity that enlargement implies. Any subsequent renegotiation of the EU treaties will also be complex and protracted, especially because it is precisely those terms and conditions of economic and monetary union, first delivered at Maastricht, which will be up for revision.

The current economic crisis compels the Union to rethink the arrangements for economic and monetary union. Yet even if the economic conditions had been serene, the EU would still have to face up to the big challenge of renegotiating its financial system and budgetary settlement. From 2013 a new multi-annual financial framework is supposed to be in place. Before that date, the present financial perspectives will have to be revised – and enhanced – in order to cope with the many new demands placed on EU finances consequent on the entry into force of the Treaty of Lisbon, for example, in energy, space, immigration or foreign policy. So, inescapably, the time has come for a radical overhaul of the Union's financial system. The Lisbon treaty raises the capacity of the EU to act. The Union now needs new resources to match those rising expectations, raised for and spent through a federal budget.

A federal budget

The Union's budget – now at € 143 billion a year – must give better value for money. The budget's size, shape and administration are long overdue for reform. The current EU budget, complex and opaque, is merely an aggregate of numerous uncoordinated EU spending programmes adopted over time. There has been no overall conceptual design and little discernible budgetary policy. Now we need a coherent, strategic federal budgetary policy that will directly support the Union's top political priorities in a cost-efficient and accountable way, saving wasteful duplication at the national level.

A proper federal budget of the European Union would serve to reduce fiscal pressure by lowering costs. It would need to be much more transparent and accountable than the present hybrid system, aiming at a high degree of buoyancy to allow for changing conditions. A federal budget would also be more obviously fair than the present system to all states and citizens concerned.

Today the EU's revenue consists almost wholly of contributions wrung from, and often recouped by, national treasuries. The intergovernmental bartering process, obsessed with net balances, distorts the concept of European public goods. Instead, for the future, new and genuinely federal revenue streams are needed to finance an EU treasury that would enjoy a conventional capacity for deficit financing and borrowing. National rebates and the plethora of corrective mechanisms should be reduced and in the long run eliminated. Direct EU taxation of certain cross-border activities would help to ease distortions in the internal market and orientate the budget debate towards the overall size of EU expenditure, states' gross contributions and EU added value.

In reforming the budget, there should be no taboos. It would surely be a stimulus for post-national democracy to have some direct link established between the citizen-taxpayer and the EU. Introducing an EU carbon tax, for example, with revenue accruing straight to the EU treasury, would be acceptable as long as existing national carbon taxes were at the same time adjusted or, better, scrapped. In the context of the fight against climate change, such an EU carbon tax would fully accord with the important federalist principle of subsidiarity. Another option would be to transfer to the EU the power to raise up to 2 per cent of VAT, with commensurate reductions in the national tax take.

The McDougall Report (1977) recommended a federal EU budget (without defence) of no more than 2.5 per cent GDP. Today we might look for a doubling of the size of the present budget over a fifteen-year period – that is, over three five-year multi-annual financial framework agreements. This would imply a targeted increase in the size of the 2016 annual EU budget to 1.5 per cent GNI from the current 1 per cent.

Enlarging the size of the EU budget will only be possible by transferring expenditure on a substantial scale from the national to the EU level. A major analysis is needed in all policy sectors consistent with EU competences to identify items which, according to the principle of subsidiarity, can be more efficiently costed and economically designed by being paid for through the EU budget. The potential economies of scale in avoiding duplication and even contradiction when EU states are left to their own devices, or in correcting market failure by taking action at the EU level, are huge. The work of the European Defence Agency, for example, is beginning to show what can be achieved by pooling procurement in this one particular sector.

A thorough review of existing budgetary commitments must also play a part. While the CAP should not be dismantled, is it proper that agriculture remains the one and only EU common policy that is solely funded by the EU budget? A greater degree of co-financing of the CAP between states and the EU would undoubtedly facilitate a new budgetary agreement between France and the UK. (Indeed, it might be altogether impossible to have a new budgetary agreement without such a reform.)

By way of contrast, an integrated approach to solving the problems of Europe's higher education might win many dividends, both intellectual and financial. European R&D will hardly compete in terms of scale with that of the USA, but the salience of research for Europe's cultural and economic development should be properly reflected in the EU budget. Furthermore, the much larger national R&D programmes must be opened up to EU competition.

Europe's super-grid for electricity or high-speed railways and tram systems are unlikely to be built, or their externalities managed, without much larger direct investment from the EU budget.

The EU is the world's largest donor in terms of overseas development aid. In another reform made possible by the Lisbon treaty, the European Development Fund can and should be brought wholly within the compass of the general EU budget, leading to more coherence and accountability. At present, the EDF defies logic and is semi-detached.

Economic government

The financial crash in 2008 and subsequent economic crisis have inevitably changed the context in which the financial reform of the Union will take place. The euro is at risk and Europe's economy has virtually stopped growing; exit strategies from unsustainable public debt are largely uncoordinated, and unemployment rises sharply in the least competitive states and regions. Unbridled market forces no longer serve the interests of Europe, or indeed of the West more generally. The markets must be dealt with by a combination of regulation and common economic policies, which include fiscal measures.

Although it funked membership of the euro at its inception, the UK is heavily implicated in the experiment of the single currency area, its largest trading partner, not least because of the huge exposure of the City of London. If the euro experiment were to fail, Europe would be returned to the fierce national protectionism and beggar-my-neighbour policies that marred the inter-war period. European integration has never been condemned to succeed. Should the EU break up, aggressive devaluation, high inflation, social unrest and political extremism would follow as night follows day.

At least the EU is moving swiftly to strengthen cross-border supervision of the financial sector. It is good that initial British hostility to stronger EU regulation of the activities of the City of London appears to have been overcome. But partly because of the over-zealous safeguarding of national sovereignty, the proposed EU structure is disjointed and likely to prove too weak in another financial storm. The better policy would have been to create one fully integrated EU regulatory authority responsible for systemic risk assessment and for the supervision of transnational banking, securities and insurance. In time, this will surely come.

The financial markets will only regain confidence in the euro if the whole EU, and especially the sixteen members of the eurozone, institute firm government backed up by a credible budgetary policy. The EU's first moves in that direction have already been taken – coincidentally during the same May weekend that the Labour government fell and the coalition government arose, so that few in Britain really noticed what was happening on the mainland. Nevertheless, what happened on 10 May was the transformation of Europe's economic and monetary union. A crisis instrument of € 750 billion was set up to bail out EU states suffering severe difficulties caused by exceptional occurrences beyond their control, and which are unable to access the capital markets. The IMF stumps up € 250 billion. A new European Financial Stability Fund of € 500 billion is subscribed mainly by the sixteen eurozone states plus Poland and Sweden, who wish to show solidarity, and will become operational once the agreement is ratified by national parliaments representing 90 per cent of the shareholding. (The UK, needless to say, is nowhere in this.)

In addition, national budgetary plans will be subject to early scrutiny by the European Commission, which will be empowered to take suitable preventative action when necessary. These measures are undoubtedly serious, and they worked at least in the short term to save Greece. The size of the potential bail-out fund is vast (amounting to almost half the size of the EU budget). However, there are still questions about whether the package is sufficient to come to the aid of all the weaker states if the market declines to buy their sovereign debt. What happens if a state's severe difficulties transpire to be the norm and not the exception? And in any case, the May 2010 package is set to run out after three years – just in time for the next elections to the German Bundestag.

So more needs to be done, and soon. Essential is the transformation of the largely intergovernmental EFSF into a genuine European Monetary Fund of a federal type to verify sound national budgetary policies and to facilitate transfers to help structural adjustment aimed at raising Europe's productivity.

The Stability and Growth Pact must again be reformed, but this time radically, not to make it even easier to evade discipline but to combine measures to return to fiscal rectitude with policies aimed at enhancing economic competitiveness and at reducing structural imbalances. As Jean-Claude Trichet, President of the European Central Bank, told the *Financial Times* (15 December 2008), the original pact was merely the 'legal framework that we have as a quid pro quo for the fact that we do not have a federal budget and a federal government'. Now is the time to draw conclusions from the self-evident fact that the Maastricht arrangements for the euro have been tested and found wanting. Peer pressure aimed at fiscal discipline does not work, neither in times of boom nor bust. Mere coordination by governments of their national economic policies is not a federal solution, and does not do the business. The crisis has exposed systemic shortcomings of the voluntary intergovernmental approach that can only be addressed by the rapid emergence of a stronger EU government capable of taking necessarily tough and inevitably unpopular measures.

The eurogroup, chaired by Van Rompuy at summit level, has a prime responsibility to drive forward the reform process towards the goal of a federal economic government. It must also be reinforced so that it can speak and act through a single representative at the IMF and G20. A task force has indeed been set up by the European Council to examine the problem of economic governance. It is a pity, if inevitable, that this body has been taken over by national treasuries, whose representatives tend to act like a European ratepayers' association in local government. One should not hold one's breath for the Van Rompuy task force. Expect little by way of further reform unless and until the European Parliament learns how to force the pace and oblige the European Commission, which is fairly weak, and the European Council, which is fairly divided between the French and German camps, to raise their game.

All the elements of an economic recovery programme are already on the table, at least in the Parliament, in the Commission and in think tanks, if not in the Council. These include a concerted approach to pension reform, raising retirement ages together, which would reduce the burden on taxpayers across Europe. The introduction of a eurobond market, as first envisaged by Jacques Delors, would reduce borrowing costs for all. With the best will in the world, even with the reform of the EU budget proposed above, Europe still needs to invest more in European public goods. An issuance by the European Investment Bank of eurobonds to the tune of € 100 billion would have a meaningful macro-economic impact and boost European science and technology. The EU needs an industrial policy fit for the digital age and targeted at building the world's most competitive low-carbon economy. We must rectify the situation in which the EU found itself in 2008 when the Commission was unable to co-finance a big programme of public works (such as transport or digital infrastructure) as the core project of a genuine European recovery programme.

So the EU itself requires a capacity to lend and borrow money, to raise loans and issue bonds to invest in European public goods – notably in the field of climate change, R&D and security policies. This calls for the creation of an EU treasury, a multiplication of the instruments available to the Commission and a Europeanised guarantee fund for financial institutions.

EU fiscal policy must be aimed at supporting green, sustainable growth. We have already proposed the introduction for revenue purposes of an EU carbon tax. An important objective is the better regulation of the EU's carbon emission trading scheme, including the setting of a floor price. To ensure Europe's competitiveness, the tax must be accompanied by a duty levied on the carbon content of imported goods. Another step to boost competitiveness would be the harmonisation of the structure of corporation tax, while leaving to states discretion as to rates.

The intention of the European Commission to tackle low employment and poor productivity can be applauded. Its targets are right. But its powers are weak. The 'open method of coordination', wholly reliant on peer pressure between jealous and suspicious national governments, has never worked well. Unless a common – indeed, federal – economic policy emerges, twenty-seven different and largely uncoordinated national recovery plans will continue to compete with each other for the attention of potential investors.

The EU's new 'Europe 2020' programme should be liberated from the illusions of the old economic agenda. Repetition of (ugly) buzzwords, like 'flexicurity', has served merely to camouflage continuing structural weakness. The Commission should insist on evidence-based analysis of the national economies and on open debate about how to remove bureaucratic and political obstacles to enterprise. The use of the EU's structural and cohesion funds needs smart reappraisal in the context of Europe's new budgetary policy. The EU must launch a concerted campaign against tax evasion, corrupt public administration and international organised crime.

The Barroso II Commission intends to deliver an action plan to complete the single market by 2012 – a full twenty years after the original target set by Delors. The recent report by Mario Monti prepares the ground well. Completion of the single market, especially its extension to embrace energy and the services sectors, will increase Europe's productivity. A deeper internal market will make the EU more competitive abroad and enlarge consumer choice at home. A common immigration policy would help to manage the supply of labour across the single market.

★

Shirley Williams was one of those brave Labour MPs who followed Roy Jenkins, with the Liberals, into the government lobby on that historic night in 1971. Commitment to building a stronger and larger European Union was one of her main reasons in helping to form the SDP and, later, in staying to found the Liberal Democrats.

A similar bold commitment must be made now by the new generation of Liberal Democrats as they enter a coalition government with the Conservatives. A coalition between Britain's most pro- and anti-Europe parties is certainly startling. This is not a marriage made in heaven; but could it possibly be the long-overdue beginning of the bipartisan approach to the making of British European policy which is so sorely needed?

The fact of coalition with the Liberal Democrats has forced the Tories to accept the formerly loathed Treaty of Lisbon. The new government has dropped the Conservative's election manifesto pledge to renegotiate the terms of UK membership of the EU by scuppering the Charter of Fundamental Rights and by repatriating EU social and employment law. The Conservatives' original plug for a UK Sovereignty Act, which would try to assert the primacy of Westminster law over that of the EU, is downgraded by the coalition: such a bizarre thing will now be merely 'considered' – and, one presumes, upon consideration, dismissed.

The Liberal Democrats have also been forced to undergo a reality check on their European policy upon entering the coalition. One of their more bizarre election manifesto commitments was to hold a referendum on whether the UK should stay in or leave the European Union – a referendum which if ever mounted would have been comprehensively lost and would have triggered monumental currency and constitutional crises. Happily, we now hear no more of that.

Yet Europe's pressing federal questions remain to be addressed by the Lib–Con government, and they remain highly contentious. Some of them, including measures to reinforce the economic governance of the EU, will require treaty change. The Queen's Speech of May 2010 threatens a Bill to insist on referenda every time the UK has to ratify important amendments to the EU treaties. The long-suffering electorate is to have imposed upon it the duty to take complex decisions about the future of the European Union and Britain's place within it. One can doubt that, in such circumstances, it will be possible to hold back the forces of nationalism and xenophobia. In any case, inveterate 'Yes' campaigners will have their work cut out. According to consistent Eurobarometer polls, fewer than one third of British people approve of their country's EU membership.

One ill-considered effect of serial referenda is the sidelining of the Westminster Parliament in EU matters precisely at the time when logic (and the Lisbon treaty) demands that national parliaments upgrade the quality of their EU scrutiny. This seems a pity, notwithstanding the election of the ultra-nationalist William Cash MP as the new chairman of the Commons European scrutiny committee. Coalition has tempered the anti-European policies of the Conservatives in government, but will the Conservative back benches ever be reconciled to Europe? The early indications are discouraging.

In his first major speech as Foreign Secretary (1 July), William Hague paid scant attention to the European Union. Yet he made two shifts away from the policy of his Labour predecessor David Miliband.

> Within groupings such as the EU, it is no longer sensible or indeed possible just to focus our effort on the largest countries at the expense of smaller members . . . It is mystifying to us that the previous government failed to give due weight to the development of British influence in the EU . . . So the idea that the last government was serious about advancing Britain's influence in Europe turns out to be an unsustainable fiction. Consoling themselves with the illusion that agreeing to institutional changes desired by others gave an appearance of British centrality in the EU, they neglected

to launch any new initiative to work with smaller nations and presided over
a decline in the holding of key European positions by British personnel.

As a loyal foot soldier of the coalition, I make no comment other than to
wonder what on earth is going to happen once this government is forced
to tackle Europe's tough, perennial federal questions. Coming the way of
the coalition soon are EU negotiations on budgetary and financial reform,
the reinforcement of economic governance and the democratic renewal
of the European Parliament, itself facing electoral reform. Later on, the EU
will be making its first moves towards permanent structured cooperation in
defence. Unimpeachable relations between London and Vilnius or Ankara,
plus a few more British *fonctionnaires* in Brussels, are not going to help much
in those circumstances.

One must hope that this new government will neither be driven by spite
nor slide by accident, as all its predecessors have done, into the margins of
the European Union, and that on Europe, too, the coalition may realise
the earnest good intention of David Cameron and Nick Clegg to deliver
'great change and real progress'. British leadership in the governance of a
European federal union would help on both counts. That would surely
delight the heart of Winston Churchill, the greatest Lib–Con of them all.

Diplomacy: a lost art in an open world?

Jeremy Greenstock

Who can keep a secret? Anyone nowadays? Diplomats depend on working below the radar screen, but it is a different world out there from the hallowed diplomatic traditions of even forty years ago. Such is the power of investigative journalism and the information revolution that the quiet art of analysis and negotiation behind closed doors has become increasingly hard to practise. Are diplomats facing extinction?

There is no doubting the changed climate. Governments have lost their monopoly of control over the channels of communication; and the web, reinventing itself with new instruments every few months, connects individuals, groups, academics, businesses, the media, think tanks and even – horror of horrors – domestic ministries across borders in ways which have completely stripped foreign offices of the monopoly of position and perspective which they used to hold. Events in one place can have an instantaneous effect in another half-way round the globe, while demands for explanation of a development can come winging in before a government office even knows it has happened.

And anything can leak. You could hear the grinding of dinosaur teeth when the Foreign and Commonwealth Office decreed in 2007 that despatches from ambassadors abroad, and particularly the farewell report from a departing envoy, should be scrapped because anything beyond the jejune was likely to appear in a tabloid within days. Even e-mails, the standard reporting tool nowadays, whether encrypted or not, often hold back what an official really thinks because of the risk of a leak or, much worse, a public inquiry raking over the paths to some controversial decision. With telephones unsafe almost anywhere, what one really thinks has to be breathed quietly in a protected space to avoid coming home to roost later. Can diplomats in such a world possibly ply their trade any longer as uniquely qualified and interconnected professionals in international interpretation?

But let us stop and think. What is really going on? What is froth and noise, and what is fundamentally different? Those whose careers span the breadth of the period between the aftermath of World War Two and today's fresher version of turmoil can see that some things do not change. The age-old business of communication between peoples of radically different cultures and priorities, centred on the search for mutual interests and the avoidance of war, has to continue whatever the channels and instruments that carry the conversation. The capacity to spread volumes of information, broadcast personal views and dig out evidence is not necessarily connected to good judgement or the effective projection of power. The job of a diplomat is to represent power and manage the relationship with other sources of power. Is there not a need to assess what might matter and what might not in the flood of words which pour out every second in the global verbal agora?

In 2009 the Sixth Edition of Satow's *Diplomatic Practice* was published, ninety-two years on from its first appearance and thirty years after the previous edition. It describes how diplomacy is structured and organised, how the international and regional institutions work, how states transact their collective business and how the rule of law is supposed to operate at the global level. Much of it is taken up with the history of diplomacy; and denizens of today's world and its fast-moving journey into the unexplored will barely see the relevance of these archaic-sounding procedures to modern life. But reading through Satow is a chance to take a salutary lesson. The past is closer to us than we like to imagine. Human interaction has many unchanging characteristics. The advice on how to be a good diplomat from a century or three centuries ago can still be spot-on: listen more than you talk; stay calm in every circumstance; don't show off what you know; let your interlocutor believe he has made the proposal you favour. For the diplomat has to juggle two, often awkward, co-objectives: get your way but avoid a showdown.

Diplomacy and war are, after all, two sides of the same coin of dispute-resolution; and in the twenty-first century, war – for all the optimistic predictions of the early 1990s – remains uncomfortably close to the UK's daily experience in both its conventional and its asymmetric forms. Yet while our airwaves are full of arguments and complaints about inadequate investment in military strength and equipment, there is very little debate about our national capability in the profession which is supposed to prevent war. Is it because, little by little each day, the public perception grows that the diplomat's tool - words - is infinitely available to everyone, whereas the application of massive physical force, the resource of the armed services, is not? If so, that is to forget a cardinal point, that both words and force have to be applied with accuracy and wisdom to have the right effect, or it all becomes an awful mess. And that takes craftsmanship, perhaps even an artistry, which is not acquired overnight.

In the spring of 2010 the Ditchley Foundation held a conference on the functions and practices of modern diplomacy which confronted the career professionals with the painful question of whether they had become surplus to requirements. Postmodernists and information revolutionaries gave the diplomats some powerful reasons why they might be redundant. But the diplomats fought back. They argued, with some success, that there were a number of classic attributes which still remained relevant: the acquiring of deep knowledge about foreign countries and their leaders; the capacity for strategic analysis; calm crisis management; and negotiating skills. No other profession was required so constantly to adapt and build bridges: between national and multinational interests, between reality and values or between old and new holders of power with a global reach. So the discussion focused on how the traditional skills could be expanded to embrace the new environment. In spite of some relevant questions in justified areas, such as public diplomacy, the conversation was more about adding than replacing, because the diplomat does provide something unique. NGOs and companies tend to be single-subject; the media, for all their speed and spread of knowledge, turn out to be tactical, not strategic players; politicians are active and involved, but need support. Diplomats are still the workhorses of international interaction, with politicians setting the course and turning the wheel, but needing the engineering and the continuity which established diplomacy provides.

Globalisation

For the truth is that globalisation is not turning the world of nations into a common space, and information technology is not in itself a source of wisdom. For all the dynamism of economic exchange and communication linkage at the global level, the old tribal instincts of the human race are fostering a polarisation, not an opening up, of identities, cultures, beliefs and political choices. The engine of subjectivism is driving every conversation about solutions to global problems, whether in the security, the commercial or the environmental field. Within a world of much greater freedom of choice and action than a generation ago, a plethora of independent actors have sprung up, all of whom have to be understood and reckoned with if international peace is to be kept. The availability of a million channels for them to express themselves does not amount to a system for creating order. The analysis, the interpretation, the engagement and the negotiation have to be handled with skill. This requires professionals in more places than before, not fewer. Yet almost every diplomatic service around the world is being cut. It takes a long memory and a broad perspective to get the point that international affairs do not inevitably progress to an ever-higher level of universality just because we have invented the institutions that could organise that. Every so often, and all too often in human history, communication lapses, order breaks down and we have to start all over again.

The United Kingdom has to assess its place in this new mix with especial care. After World War Two, with the global momentum of Britain's industrial leadership exhausted, we could have sunk rapidly into second-class obscurity. For twenty years after 1945 it felt as if we were doing just that. But two things in particular gave the UK a second wind in the international arena: our competence in matters of defence and security, which gave the United States the feeling that its relationship with the UK was of especial value; and the depth, breadth and organisational strengths of our civil service, including the Diplomatic Service. The unimpressive performance of the British economy, not least its manufacturing sector, was a limiting factor, setting constraints on the modernisation of our instruments of power. But a partial recovery from the 1980s onwards, built increasingly on the dynamism of the services sector and the City of London, saw the country competing creditably for fourth place in the world's economic tables and capable of sustaining its defence forces and overseas representation at a level above most of its comparators. This, linked with the UK's well-honed and adaptable skills in the security field and in multilateral diplomacy and problem-solving, was enough to keep us close to the top table at the UN and elsewhere as the world started to reshape itself after the collapse of the Soviet Union.

Britain's role and performance at the United Nations is an interesting prism through which to illuminate the country's strengths and weaknesses in the international arena. The status of Permanent Membership of the Security Council, a product of the aftermath of World War Two, could never be achieved for the UK on the basis of its 21st-century assets. Our development assistance performance, while intelligently constructed, is not influential enough on its own. Our future is seen from outside, if not domestically, as linked to the impact of the European Union, which in the political, security and diplomatic fields makes a less weighty impression globally than some of its constituent parts. There has long been talk of a more united EU representation on the UN Security Council, with the UK and France folding their permanent seats (and non-permanent EU candidates their two other ones) into a single EU label when Security Council membership eventually achieves reform. But, even if the UN overcomes the obstacles to effective reform, it is not yet apparent that this would deliver the EU greater punch when the UN system relies on the number of votes cast, and while the UN remains a forum of nation states rather than regional blocs. Even the advent of the EU's External Action Service under the new High Representative, Catherine Ashton, will not change the capacity to deliver power and influence as a collective until and unless the EU comes much closer to forming a genuine political union of purpose and political decision-making. That is not an early prospect.

Meanwhile, the UK does not perform badly at dealing with the world as it is. Conscious of our modest qualifications for the premier league, UK representatives at the UN work hard to show that we earn our Security Council place on a continuing basis by the contribution we make to problem-solving across the whole range of UN activities. We have to be careful not to flaunt status in any way and to indicate that the work of the Security Council is in truth a subset of the UN's whole approach to development. All Permanent Members of the Security Council take generic stick, but in other respects it is surprising that the UK receives so little direct criticism for its Permanent Membership. The fact is that our competence at multilateral diplomacy and our capacity for constructing routes out of complex problems earn us enough respect to get by. Similar considerations apply in Brussels, where our EU partners grow exasperated with our lack of enthusiasm for the grand project but prefer to have us contributing our pragmatism. None of this would work to the British advantage, as it does more often than not, if our people did not have the skills to stay afloat in all sorts of weather.

Iraq dealt a blow to this image of a gently fading but still useful UK. At the UN, but also on occasions in other international forums, even including NATO, the British can gain credit, in spite of appearances, for softening, interpreting, rechannelling or sometimes even resisting the rougher or more alarming initiatives of the United States. The wider membership of the UN know that they have to live with the superpower and like to avoid direct trouble with it, but as a pack they are highly critical of the US's inclination to do its own thing with scant regard for other countries' viewpoints. The UK can often find ways of bridging these kinds of difficulties and thereby earn some forgiveness for their pro-American tendencies. Iraq exploded that trade-off. We were seen as trying but failing to gather legitimacy for the March 2003 invasion and as putting our alliance with the US above our support for the international order. For a while the issue also turned EU exasperation into something close to hostility. The saga will not be forgotten in the international sparring-grounds for a generation and has made it harder to carry off our UN-type tactics.

Against this background, the recent financial crisis has come at a bad time. With China, India, Brazil and others flexing their muscles with more confidence on the international stage, because they have grown real assets which cannot be ignored, the UK was anyway going to start sliding down the relative power scale. To have been complicit in allowing the global financial sector, where the City of London has genuinely played in the first league, to overreach itself and crash is a significant bullet in the foot. The Anglo–Saxon financial model has taken a pasting; and, worse, we have landed ourselves with a volume of debt which will make it even harder to sustain the minimum levels of armed forces, diplomatic missions and development aid projects to support a claim to be a substantive independent actor in the global arena. In these circumstances it is more important than ever that we maintain the country's capacity to live and contribute at the top table, to persuade other actors that the collective way is the best, to finesse our schizophrenic approach to the EU and to make the most of the new opportunities in the G20. Among other things, this means having the sharpest diplomats around. It also means investing in representative capacity rather than subjecting the Diplomatic Service to an ongoing series of financial cuts. The current budget of the Foreign and Commonwealth Office for running costs stands at approximately £1.5 billion, or 0.3 per cent of government expenditure. Its complement of UK-origin diplomatic staff overseas has dropped to around 1,500, compared with close to 3,000 in 1976. Once we are through the emergency measures to deal with the current debt crisis, this lack of front-line investment must be addressed.

The politicians

And our politicians? Elected leaders are the power which diplomacy serves. They determine the policies and supervise the administration of them. Their presence on the world stage is headline-catching and their relationships with each other set the mould for policy-making. But if they misunderstand the real strengths and capacities of the UK, they will take us into challenges we may not be able to live with. On the other hand, ambitious targets give the professionals something to be tested on. The experience of the Conservative Party pulling itself apart over Europe in the mid-1990s was a distressing one for those at the coal-face. Above all, it is the politicians who have to come to terms with the altered context not just of the redistribution of power and influence among 21st-century nations, but also of the information revolution and the loss of the government's primacy in the public space. Britain's recent election drama included the sight of party leaders struggling to present themselves as servants of the people, while underestimating, or failing to understand, the need to lead as well as to follow. In today's information arena communication is two-way, making leadership a circular – sometimes leading, sometimes following – rather than an apex concept.

In foreign policy it is not so different. It is a good diplomat who achieves his objective while appearing to follow. As for the voice of public opinion, it is a force to be reckoned with, but the public's understanding of all the complexities is bound to be partial. The new media, and particularly the social media, can race ahead of government processes and occupy the atmosphere, but they cannot see all the underlying trends or produce the precise solutions. To this extent, the impact of news immediacy, even if it must be managed, has to be resisted, so that the right strategic directions can be maintained. Here a partnership between political leaders and professional practitioners works better than if leaders rely closely on their own political advisers, whose tactical priorities and media orientation can be misleading.

You learn to value a politician who gets this right, who will not be diverted from a good principle or a long-term objective by an immediate crisis. While the Foreign Office has been well served from time to time in this respect, it may harbour tinges of regret that certain prominent politicians with impressive qualifications for the FCO never made it to King Charles Street. In recent times Chris Patten, George Robertson and Michael Portillo could have featured on this list; and Shirley Williams would have been a thoroughly welcome first female British Foreign Secretary for her perceptive understanding of EU and global trends and for her deep well of common sense. The UK's diplomatic strengths need careful nurturing into the uncertain future; and the country's diplomatic chief bears a huge responsibility for that. Let us hope the new team set a good course in this respect.

Not politics but arithmetic: the case for British leadership on European defence

Menzies Campbell *

The late Tim Garden, a distinguished RAF officer, security expert and Liberal Democrat peer, wrote in 2001 that European states faced a stark choice over the future of their defence policies. Either cooperate closely with each other and maintain military capabilities, or lose them altogether. This, he said, was not an ideological argument. It was nothing to do with the theologies of national sovereignty or supranationalism. It was simply to recognise the spiralling costs of running modern armed forces and the reluctance of governments to find the ever-greater sums to fund them. For Tim Garden, the decline of European military capabilities was therefore 'not a question of politics but one of arithmetic' (Chatham House Defence Conference, 29 January 2001).

This former senior Ministry of Defence planner knew better than most that without effective collaboration and partnership, European pretensions to global or even regional influence would amount to little. The inexorable rise of military procurement and personnel costs would prove unsustainable. Combined with a distinct lack of enthusiasm for defence spending from both politicians and electorate, costs would eventually erode so-called 'sovereign' national capabilities to the point of irrelevance.

The logical conclusion was that the unavoidable decline in national

* The author acknowledges the contribution of Ben Jones, former Liberal Democrat senior policy advisor, in writing this essay.

military capability must precipitate far deeper pooling, sharing and joint procurement of equipment and support. European states working through both NATO and the EU should look to sharing some of the most expensive but highly relevant assets, such as strategic airlift, reconnaissance and air-to-air refuelling. Joint training, maintenance and interoperability should become the norm as far as possible.

Tim Garden was writing almost a decade ago, but his argument was characteristically prescient. Unfortunately it also went unheeded. Today, the MoD reels from a catastrophic black hole in its budget. According to the recently published Gray Review of Acquisition, the MoD has a £35 billion gap in its forward equipment programme, much of it due to the kind of delays and cost over-runs identified by Garden. There are likely to be other mismatches between objectives and resources, for example personnel costs, which could make the situation even worse.

The parlous state of the MoD is a shocking indictment of the Labour government, particularly as Prime Minister Blair's military adventures were themselves to demand so much of the armed forces. While defence spending rose in real terms for most of Labour's term in office, it could not keep pace with demand and military capabilities have actually been scaled back as funding fell short of the ambitions of the 1998 Strategic Defence Review (SDR). As Tim Garden observed, even level defence spending in real terms 'inevitably leads to decreases in force levels year on year'.

Under the 1998 SDR, the government foresaw a Royal Navy escort fleet of thirty-two ships. Today it stands at twenty-three and may decline further. As the National Audit Office revealed last year, the order for Type 45 destroyers fell from twelve to a more likely six, and came in £1.5 billion over budget and late. The Astute tactical submarines, Future Lynx helicopters, and perhaps the aircraft carriers will suffer a similar fate. Orders will continue to be cut or delayed, thereby reducing capability and further undermining the strategic rationale for the purchase.

The scale of defence inflation is difficult to gauge, but for equipment programmes Professor Keith Hartley has estimated it runs around 10 per cent per year in real terms. And as Professor David Kirkpatrick recently told the House of Commons Defence Committee, the defence budget would need to rise around 3 per cent over the GDP deflator to maintain capabilities at planned levels (above what has been set out in the Comprehensive Spending Review).

The wars in Iraq and Afghanistan, while funded to the tune of over £10 billion, and with many billions spent on urgent equipment purchases, revealed that Britain's armed forces were simply not configured for such enduring operations of a sustained intensity not seen for decades.

The 1998 SDR was predicated on fighting one 'relatively short war-fighting deployment' and one 'enduring non-war fighting operation'. Yet since 2001, the armed forces have been operating at levels in Iraq and Afghanistan which far exceed the MoD's planning assumptions, and are not resourced adequately to meet their commitments. The result is the tired and worn-out forces we have today, though their bravery and commitment continue to win the admiration and astonishment of the British public.

Yet the Labour government was incapable of admitting that the UK was committing its armed forces to operations of a scale they were not resourced to undertake. Still less was Labour prepared to consider scaling back in some areas, for example the nuclear deterrent or aircraft carriers, to put more resources into the kinds of insurgency fighting being experienced in Iraq and Afghanistan. In fact, precisely the opposite was undertaken when in 2004, the then Defence Secretary Geoff Hoon cut back on both infantry troops and helicopters – now, of course, desperately short in Afghanistan.

Perhaps more fundamentally, when it comes to a sustainable security strategy for the future, Labour has left little by way of legacy. Nowhere is this clearer than on the question of European defence and security cooperation. Although Tony Blair paid lip-service to the issue in his early years as Prime Minister, he was soon seen off by tabloid scare stories, and the perennial tabloid scare-story of a 'European Army'. The fissure opened by the Iraq War isolated the UK from its European partners, particularly France, without whom progress in defence cooperation is impossible.

Under Gordon Brown there was some movement towards improving cooperation between France and the UK, at the initiative of President Sarkozy. But there is scant progress to show for it. Even following

France's return to the integrated military command of NATO, the Labour government did not seem to show much enthusiasm for bold new ventures. Thus the warnings of Tim Garden and others who made the same case have gone unheeded, and their proposals unexplored.

New Strategic Defence Review

It is to be hoped that the forthcoming strategic defence and security review in the United Kingdom will indeed be 'strategic'. This requires basing the balance between resources and policy on clear foreign policy objectives and threat assessments. But there is a very real danger that because costs have spiralled so far out of control, such a review might become a financial review only and not a defence review. The risk is that strategic decisions over Britain's role in the world are ignored as capabilities are pared back to the bone.

The multi-billion-pound national deficit has compounded the crisis in an already over-stretched budget. According to Malcolm Chalmers of the Royal United Services Institute, the likely scale of defence budget cuts could lead to a 'reduction of around 20 per cent in numbers of service personnel, and a commensurate reduction in numerical military capabilities (major vessels, aircraft and ground formations)'. The alternative option of putting sustained extra resources into defence was not put forward by any mainstream party at the May 2010 general election.

Military experts will be concerned that big decisions regarding the future force structure of Britain's armed forces will be ducked. Few believe that the current posture of full-spectrum capabilities can be maintained. Andrew Brookes of the International Institute for Strategic Studies has argued that the UK is 'a small island that can no longer aspire to replicate every high-tech US activity in miniature'. Yet if the UK continues to try to do so in ever more miniature forms, its capabilities will be of little relevance in the future.

The Labour government's swan-song Defence Green Paper did recognise that the UK faces tough choices over Britain's future role, and that partnerships with other states will have to play an increasingly important part in the future: but it did not spell out in any detail what this might entail.

The MoD's predicament is of course shared in various degrees by all the defence ministries of Europe. German Chancellor Angela Merkel recently announced significant military spending cuts, as no doubt will other countries grappling with their own budget deficits. The challenge of delivering defence policies on reduced budgets is therefore the most pressing factor. The European defence market and procurement practices remain greatly fractured. The time is clearly ripe for a major relaunch of European defence cooperation.

While the argument put forward by Tim Garden and others is not an ideological one, it does, of course, have a strategic dimension of the utmost importance. Without greater cooperation, the component national parts of both the NATO Alliance and the European Security and Defence Policy (ESDP) grow increasingly disparate and inefficient, thereby reducing their effectiveness. The nations of the European Union have about two million armed forces personnel in uniform, yet they can barely deploy 100,000 troops on expeditionary operations. European states are responsible for a quarter of the world's spending on defence equipment but get nothing like the value for money that the United States is able to gain through its more efficient domestic market and procurement practices.

Of course, important decisions on national security and defence procurement cannot be considered simply on the basis of what cost savings would be gained through partnerships. Some sceptics believe that the pooling of military assets and more structured European defence cooperation are simply the thin end of a supranational wedge. But they fail to face up to the seriousness of the situation. As Tim Garden noted: 'For some, the thought of real co-operation at a regional level is such an awful prospect, that they would rather have no useful military capability.'

Yet when viewed as an input into multilateral operations, the European contribution is highly inefficient by contrast with that provided by the United States. Britain's security and the vast bulk of its operations rest upon multilateral organizations, whether NATO, EU or UN. European defence cooperation based on building capabilities is not an excuse to pursue further integration for integration's sake, but to further the security of Britain, Europe, NATO and beyond. European cooperation is about boosting multilateral capability for multilateral tasks and obligations.

Therefore, the issue is about something more fundamental than affordability: it is about the very effectiveness of Britain's security alliances. Regardless of the controversy over military action in Iraq and Afghanistan, in neither case could Britain have gone it alone.

Of course, Britain can use its economic influence or assert its role in international organisations, or take part in military interventions as part of a coalition, but the ability to operate independently, diplomatically or militarily, and to achieve significant geopolitical objectives no longer exists. If Britain wishes to remain influential, it can only do so by choosing and integrating its strategies with allies or partners who share the same goals.

EU–NATO cooperation

While NATO remains the bedrock of Britain's security, the role of the EU is critical, and provides the UK with a range of adaptable means to address the security threats of the future. In Afghanistan, NATO is struggling to pull any other lever than a military one. The European Union offers policy levers across a range of broader security challenges and relationships such as those with Russia, eastern Europe and the Middle East. The EU can act on trade, aid, climate change, diplomacy and international crime. NATO does not and cannot provide these levers.

Success, of course, depends on the ability of European states to work together, and for the EU and NATO to work effectively on security policy. There is, however, great utility in the UK being able to act as part of both the EU and NATO, while ensuring that the institutional relationship remains complementary not competitive. Recent cooperation between NATO and the EU on upgrading helicopters for use in Afghanistan might provide a template for further work on developing capabilities, for example, by allowing EU access to pooled NATO C-17 aircraft to cover for delays in the delivery of the A400M.

NATO must also work closely with the EU on the updated Strategic

Concept. It will be self-defeating for both organizations, particularly the European members, if there is no thought given to how the Strategic Concept can be married with the European Security Strategy. ESDP operations have a mixed record, but Operation Atalanta, the anti-piracy operation off Somalia, and EUFOR Althea in Bosnia demonstrate that the ESDP can deliver results.

The United States has now moved firmly behind the push to improve European capabilities through more effective cooperation. The former US Ambassador to NATO, Victoria Nuland, made it clear in a 2008 speech in Paris that 'an ESDP with only soft power is not enough'. A recent RAND Europe research paper, *Revitalising the Transatlantic Agenda*, argued that 'Washington should support the development of a strategically capable ESDP that can by 2020 project power and stability well beyond Europe's borders and that can act autonomously, especially in crises where the United States does not wish to get involved, while at the same time turning civil-military security aspirations into reality'.

It is encouraging that Madeleine Albright's expert group, which advises NATO on its new strategic concept, emphasises the importance of recognising that 'the EU's Treaty of Lisbon is designed, among other purposes, to strengthen Europe's military capabilities and command structures. Allies should welcome this development and use the Strategic Concept to affirm NATO's desire for a truly comprehensive partnership with the EU, one that is cost-effective, that is based on the principle of reciprocity and that encompasses the entire range of the institutions' mutual activities'. The experts recommended further:

> In its contacts with the EU, NATO leaders should avoid the trap of categorising all threats and responsibilities as distinctly 'military' or 'non-military'. Instead, they should nurture the habit of thinking of these issues as developing along a continuum. Many situations will require a response that includes both forceful and non-coercive elements; NATO, the EU, and others should bring to bear the capabilities that add the most value in finding a solution. Accordingly, NATO should seek to agree with EU leaders on a plan for regular joint participation in meetings, fuller communications

between military staffs, and more extensive coordination with respect to crisis management, threat assessments, and sharing assets. (*NATO 2020: Assured Security; Dynamic Engagement*, May 2010)

While the US values its partnership with the UK, the partnership is valued primarily as a gateway to a strong relationship with Europe. Now more than ever, UK influence in Washington is dependent on demonstrating influence in Brussels. Moreover, an over-reliance on the UK/US relationship is neither realistic nor desirable in an increasingly multi-polar world. US attention will increasingly shift from the Atlantic to Asia. The UK needs a holistic response to the growing influence of nations such as China, India, Brazil and South Africa, and the EU remains best placed to do that.

A job for the coalition

The lead on European defence cooperation should come from the new coalition government. Although Europe was foreseen as a potential area of division, it has thus far demonstrated a surprisingly good dose of pragmatism. The coalition agreement's approach to the field of EU policy in matters of justice and home affairs, for example, grounds government decision-making in a case-by-case analysis of whether measures are in the best security interests of the country, combined with an appropriate sensitivity towards British legal traditions.

While European defence and security cooperation does not feature in the coalition agreement, it ought to be grounded in that same pragmatic approach. This should not be an ideological argument. European defence cooperation is in the clear interests of Britain's closest allies. Not only that, but as the coalition works to bring down the deficit and tackle the MoD's chaotic finances, it must consider the future sustainability of UK defence spending over twenty years, not just over the next parliament.

The coalition partners should be in no doubt about the importance of the Franco-British defence relationship. It is from this that a reinvigoration of European defence must spring. The time is ripe for a renewed push towards deeper and more strategic cooperation. But it will not happen without leadership, and that can only come from Europe's two largest military players – France and the UK.

The potential of the relationship is based on the shared values and interests as declared at the Anglo-French summit in March 2008:

> We cannot imagine a situation in which the vital interests of one of us, but not the other, are under threat. We cannot imagine a situation in which the vital interests of either of our two nations, France and the United Kingdom, could be threatened without the vital interests of the other also being threatened.

RAND Europe forecasts that by 2015, on present trends, the UK and France will between them account for 65 per cent of EU defence spending. A June 2008 report from the International Institute for Strategic Studies argued that 'the policy orientations of the United Kingdom and France, will, above all else, determine Europe's ability to have strong and coherent capabilities in the future'. It is clear that Britain and France would be wise to pioneer defence cooperation based on the assumption of increasing capabilities.

The first priority is to preserve and strengthen a European defence industrial base which is in decline. Britain, France and those states which are defence players must lead the consolidation of European defence companies – what Nick Witney of the European Council on Foreign Relations has described as a 'last supper' for industry. The debilitating practice of *juste retour* for defence contracts must eventually be phased out as incompatible with a European defence market. A good first step would be a Franco-British defence industrial strategy, as suggested recently by Paddy Ashdown.

Second, France and the UK should lead the pioneer groups of member states within the 'permanent structured cooperation' set out in the Lisbon Treaty. Membership of the pioneer group will be determined both by military capability and the willingness to deploy forces.

It will be a challenging task to formulate the pooling, sharing and procurement options that could be undertaken between NATO and EU member states without compromising sovereignty over core defence roles. Of course, there will be equipment, capabilities and certain niche industrial capacities that Britain would wish to keep solely and exclusively under a UK flag. Other nations will have similar requirements.

But obvious examples for cooperation include the operation, maintenance and training for aircraft carrier groups and building on the NATO model of the sharing of AWACS aircraft. There is a need for bold and creative solutions to the question of how shared and pooled capabilities can be reconciled with understandable concerns over sovereignty. All this must be driven from the very top of government, with high levels of representation and buy-in.

A European defence conference should be tasked with facilitating this work. This would also provide the opportunity to work out a strategic relationship between the EU and NATO to prevent needless duplication and to improve interoperability and communication. The British government should make a priority of reaching agreement on ending the 'costs lie where they fall' approach used for both NATO and ESDP operations.

Finally, much greater importance needs to be attached by the UK government to the EU's capability development plan. Governments need to set out clearly future capability targets and the alignment of orders through convergence objectives. The UK's strategic defence and security review will need to make some critical decisions on procurement very quickly. But some thinking should also go into the possibilities for future alignment of procurement timetables.

This essay is not about the phantom Euro-Armies of sceptic nightmare. It is not politics but arithmetic. European defence cooperation offers the only sustainable future for a British expeditionary capability without compromising our treaty obligations to others. We need bold, creative thinking and strong and clear political leadership on European defence and security policy. Britain should now provide that necessary leadership and commitment.

Part four

Reformation and reaction

On optimism in politics

David Howarth

It is often asserted, mainly by liberals, that liberals believe in the politics of hope, whereas conservatives (a term which now must embrace the neo-authoritarian party, New Labour) believe in the politics of fear. Nick Clegg recently confessed, 'I'm a liberal. My starting point has always been optimism about people.' Barack Obama based his whole 2008 presidential campaign on the themes of 'hope' and 'change', a theme he presaged in his 2004 Democratic National Convention speech in Boston:

> In the end, that's what this election is about. Do we participate in a politics of cynicism or a politics of hope? John Kerry calls on us to hope. John Edwards calls on us to hope. I'm not talking about blind optimism here – the almost wilful ignorance that thinks unemployment will go away if we just don't talk about it, or the health care crisis will solve itself if we just ignore it. No, I'm talking about something more substantial. It's the hope of slaves sitting around a fire singing freedom songs; the hope of immigrants setting out for distant shores; the hope of a young naval lieutenant bravely patrolling the Mekong Delta; the hope of a millworker's son who dares to defy the odds; the hope of a skinny kid with a funny name who believes that America has a place for him, too. Hope in the face of difficulty. Hope in the face of uncertainty. The audacity of hope.

But, as both Clegg and Obama have found, optimism and hope are better campaign slogans than precepts of government. They help to gather votes, but also they both set up inevitable disappointment, when the world turns out to be more resistant to change and more committed to its comfortable abuses than the candidates would have the electorate believe.

Optimism versus hope

Obama in his Boston speech distinguishes between optimism and hope, or at least between 'blind optimism' and hope. 'Blind optimism', says Obama, involves ignoring problems rather than making efforts to solve them. Hope, he implies, means believing that the effort will be worthwhile, as in the hope of slaves for freedom or immigrants for making a new life in the USA.

Václav Havel also distinguished between hope and optimism. He claimed that hope, unlike optimism, 'is not the conviction that something will turn out well, but the certainty that something makes sense, regardless of how it turns out' (*Disturbing the Peace*, 1990).

These two ways of distinguishing hope and optimism differ, not because they offer different conceptions of optimism, but because they offer different conceptions of the value of hope. Obama sees hope as worthwhile because it might be fulfilled. Havel sees hope as worthwhile because what is hoped for is right.

On further inspection, there seems little difference between Obama's version of hope and the optimism he dismisses. Singing a freedom song was not a practical plan for ending slavery. Leaving Ireland or Italy for New York was not a practical plan for improving life in Ireland or Italy. Both freedom songs and migration involve yearning for a better life, and in the case of migration, a personal route out of a worse life, but they no more engage in the relevant political problems than simply ignoring them in the belief that they would solve themselves.

Havel's distinction, however, though darker, is more substantial. His version of hope consists of a conviction that a better life is possible, but it says nothing about how likely that better life is to come about. That is why it contrasts with optimism, which is a belief, often well beyond what the evidence justifies, that a better life is not just possible but also probable, that it is within our grasp.

It is usually assumed that optimism helps people to be hopeful. But Havel's distinction throws that assumption into doubt. Optimism is far more contingent on events in the world than hope. To be hopeful because one is optimistic is, on Havel's view, to risk losing hope when one's optimism proves to be unjustified. To be hopeful without being optimistic, however, means being able to carry on in a state of hope whatever happens, to face reality even when it goes wrong. Havel's distinction hits the same note as Gramsci's declaration that he was *'pessimista con l'intelligenza, ma ottimista per la volontà'* (*Lettere dal carcere*).

Newspapers often call candidates for public office 'hopefuls'. If only that were true. Perhaps it would be more accurate to call them 'optimists'.

Optimism without hope

But there is a third possibility inherent in Havel's distinction. One can both be optimistic and have hope, and one can have hope without being optimistic, but one can also be optimistic without having hope. This is the condition of those who have no conception of a better life that makes sense, even to them, but who believe that everything will work out for the best anyway.

Optimism without hope has two distinct modes. On the one hand there is the sunny disposition inherent in 'optimism about people', that 'the wisdom of crowds' or an 'invisible hand' or the magic of 'self-organisation' will produce the best results possible. On the other is the darker thought, brought out in Voltaire's satire on Leibniz, that if it is really the case that *'tout va le mieux qu'il soit possible'*, it follows that we cannot hope for anything better (*Candide ou l'optimisme*, 1759). The world as we find it, as bad as it feels, is as good as it gets. Optimism in the second mode destroys hope, because it implies that there cannot be a state of the world better than the one we are in.

These two modes explain why market fundamentalism both attracts and repels those of a liberal disposition. We want to believe that left to themselves, people will arrive at lives that are best for them, and that no one is better qualified to decide what counts as best for them than those people themselves. But we do not want to believe that there is nothing that can be done to make everyone's life better. We do not want to believe that we already, and inevitably, live in the best of all possible worlds, and that any attempt to make it better might end up making it worse. John Maynard Keynes rejected Treasury non-interventionist orthodoxy but still ultimately advocated economic individualism, by claiming that the former was the only way to preserve the latter:

> Whilst, therefore, the enlargement of the functions of government, involved in the task of adjusting to one another the propensity to consume and the inducement to invest, would seem to a nineteenth-century publicist or to a contemporary American financier to be a terrific encroachment on individualism, I defend it, on the contrary, both as the only practicable means of avoiding the destruction of existing economic forms in their entirety and as the condition of the successful functioning of individual initiative. (*General Theory of Employment, Interest and Money*, 1936)

Likewise, liberals want to assert simultaneously that we are 'optimistic about people' and that it is rational to hope for something better. But to do that we have to reject optimism without hope, and decide what it is we can hope for.

Perhaps the rejection of optimism without hope lies at the heart of Gladstone's (often misquoted) remark, 'I think that the principle of the Conservative Party is jealousy of liberty and of the people, only qualified by fear; but I think the principle of the Liberal Party is trust in the people, only qualified by prudence' (*New York Times*, 9 February 1879). Trust in the people is a form of optimism, but prudence, although it sounds like a retreat from optimism, is a form of hope. It involves thinking through the consequences of one's actions and adjusting them if they seem to be pointing in the wrong direction. It is a plan for the future that makes sense.

Keynes also once wrote, 'A certain coolness of temper . . . seems to me at the same time peculiarly *Liberal* in flavour, and also a much bolder and more desirable and more valuable political possession and endowment than sentimental ardour' (*Liberalism and Labour*, 1931). That 'coolness' is

Gladstone's 'prudence' rather than his 'trust in the people', and it continues to be a better foundation for policy than unfocused optimism.

Nick Clegg said that optimism is his 'starting point'. Keynes and Gladstone would approve that he did not make it his end point.

Abandon all hope?

But could it be no bad thing to destroy hope? After all, as Spinoza pointed out, hope inherently involves fear, namely a fear that the hope will not be fulfilled, and so both hope and fear bring pain (*Ethics, Part IV*). Much better, he thought, to seek the calm of rational certainty rather than the turbulence of fearful uncertainty. 'Therefore, the more we endeavour to live by the guidance of reason, the more we endeavour to be independent of hope.'

Or, as John Cleese's character in Michael Frayn's film *Clockwise* put it: 'I can take the despair. It's the hope I can't stand.'

There are various forms a political strategy of abandoning hope could take. One is quietist, to leave politics altogether. Another is conservative, to support the status quo, whatever it happens to be. And a third is populist, to take optimism about people all the way to abandoning any pretence at prudence.

Political quietism is an increasingly attractive option in a society dominated by an intrusive media commercially driven to destroy lives for entertainment. Those who take part in politics risk being treated as minor celebrities to be followed, photographed, recorded and humiliated at will. The psychological toll on those who hold elective office grows as the possibility of even temporary escape disappears. A cult of openness, encouraged by the internet, threatens to reduce politics to a profession followed only by narcissistic sociopaths. Montaigne's celebrated advice 'CACHE TA VIE' increasingly looks the only way out for those who want to hold on to sanity (*Essais Livre 2*).

And yet, even for those driven into hiding, a sense of guilt remains. Politics left to actors, marketing executives and life-long professional politicians is worth fearing, and if we are to suffer the pain of that fear, why not also suffer the hope of something better? Finding people brave enough or foolish enough to take on the task is not easy, but the least those of us who are neither can do is to encourage and to protect those who are.

The conservative option is not attractive. The determined justification of everything that currently exists might bring peace of mind (which is presumably why it has often been recommended to those who suffer from a fear of death), but it amounts to a denial not just of progress but also of creativity. The conservative disposition distrusts innovation as such. It instinctively subtracts from any possible benefit from innovation (in which, in any case, the conservative is disinclined to believe) an imputed cost that arises from the mere fact that innovation involves change. In contrast, the liberal disposition values creativity and problem-solving. There are risks in political innovation – not least risks of over-optimism and utopianism – but to tell a liberal not even to look for solutions to problems, on the unbending assumption that new solutions will always be worse than the problem, is to cause a degree of pain akin to that produced by telling an athlete to sit still for a month.

That leaves populism, which for many is the most tempting of the three. There is a very strong argument for saying that morality, and by extension politics, is not about what people happen to desire. It is about what people want to desire, and what they ought to desire. But it is difficult in a democracy, especially in a democracy in which citizens do not take part in government but merely watch, cheer and boo those who do, to suggest that what is wrong is not the effectiveness of various political and economic mechanisms for delivering what people want, but what people want in the first place. In such a spectator democracy, in which those who participate in politics are seen as entirely separate from those who merely observe and vote, any political discussion of what people ought to want will sound like an attempt by the state to control individuality. As a result, politicians who are 'optimistic about people' might conclude that discussion about what they ought to want is incompatible with the principle that no one knows better what is good for a person than that person. All that could be left for politics following such a conclusion is debate and competition about how to deliver what people happen to want (contradictory though those desires might be). In other words, all that could remain is populism.

But there is a different conception of democracy, not as a summation of existing desires (in other words, a market by other means), but as an open discussion about what our collective goals should be, a discussion designed, among other things, to eliminate contradictions in our goals so that it becomes possible for them to be achieved. Such a discussion cannot work unless those who take part are prepared to revise what they want as a result of the discussion. Individuals still decide what is best for them, but after discussing what they want. In a spectator democracy, one might conclude, such a discussion can never begin, but at least that leads a supporter of the idea that democracy is more than adding up existing desires to another conclusion: that the problem lies in the existence of spectator democracy itself.

Down with optimism?

But if hope should not be abandoned, what about abandoning optimism? There is a strong case that various kinds of optimism in politics lead to various kinds of disaster.

The first form of political optimism that can have catastrophic results is optimism about the effectiveness of politics itself. For example, the previous New Labour government in Britain particularly appeared to suffer from the fantasy that legislation can cure all ills (although a more cynical view is that it cared not at all about whether its legislation made any difference in the world, only about whether voters thought that the government was doing something). In the end, that fantasy undermines the credibility of the legal system even in areas in which it could make a difference.

A variation of optimism about political effectiveness is the exaggeration of small differences, so that parties mislead voters (and possibly themselves) about how big a difference it would make to choose one party over another. A recent example in Britain is the domination of half of the 2010 election campaign, and much of its aftermath, both in the coalition negotiations and in the initial positions of the eventual coalition and its Labour opposition, by the question of whether public spending cuts should start in the 2010/11 financial year or in 2011/12. Since the amounts involved were, in terms of gross domestic product, quite small (less than 0.5 per cent of GDP) and, as a matter of administrative reality, could take effect only a few months earlier than they would have happened anyway, it is difficult to imagine that the differences between the parties made much practical difference. And yet we are asked to believe that it was the central issue of the election and that the whole of the coalition negotiations turned on whether the Liberal Democrats took one view or the other.

A second form of political optimism is acceptance of very great risk. To remain with the 2010 British election, the Liberal Democrats by entering into a full coalition under the so-called First Past the Post system have effectively put themselves in a position in which the entire future of the party depends on whether it can succeed in changing the electoral system for the House of Commons before the next general election. If the history of peacetime British coalitions under First Past the Post since the second half of the nineteenth century is any guide, failure will mean that they face either absorption into another party or oblivion. Although it might not prove to be the final chance that many assume that it will be, a very great deal depends on a single electoral campaign, the campaign for a 'Yes' vote in a referendum on the AV voting system. Liberal Democrats have bet the farm on a referendum in a country that has not experienced a national referendum campaign for thirty-five years. Moreover, they will be advocating a 'Yes' vote to an electoral system they themselves support only as a step on the way to a different, better system. Perhaps the only ground for such breathtaking optimism was that, since their senior coalition partners, the Conservatives, would be urging a vote in the opposite direction, one of the common pitfalls of referendums, that they turn into votes of confidence in the performance of the government, cannot matter, since a disgruntled voter would not know whether to vote 'No' or 'Yes'.

(Optimism is not, of course, the only source of irrationality in political negotiations. A whole course in social psychology and behavioural economics could be taught from the 2010 British post-election negotiations. It provides striking examples of, among others, all of the following: the focusing illusion, in which participants pay attention only to one part of what is valuable to them to the exclusion of all the rest (Labour's dismissal of the Liberal Democrats because the Liberal Democrats changed their minds about the 2010 versus 2011 cuts issue); the need for closure effect, in which negotiations collapse because some people's tolerance for ambiguity is much lower than others' (Gordon Brown's decision to resign the premiership prematurely, and the Civil Service's drive to resolve the situation in days, rather than the weeks taken in most countries); and the availability heuristic, in which recent events loom larger than they deserve just because they prey on participants' minds (the effect of the Spanish and Greek financial crises on the Liberal Democrats' thinking about whether they had to join a coalition as opposed to supporting a minority government).)

The third sort of political optimism that potentially leads to disaster is electoral optimism, which itself has two manifestations: optimism by parties and optimism by voters. Parties, for example, regularly exaggerate to themselves their ability to persuade voters to vote for them by putting out campaign literature. Anyone who has experienced an electoral campaign from the inside will remember it as constant activity with endless leaflets being delivered at all times of the day, and sometimes the night. Those not on the inside will remember an entirely different campaign, in which no one came round and there was very little literature, and during which life continued as normal.

But electors are often just as optimistic, voting repeatedly for parties they disagree with because they want to believe that 'really' the party maintains the values it held when those voters first voted for it. Labour voters who stuck with the same party from 1983 to 2010 – from isolationist state socialism through to neo-conservatism – must be among the most optimistic (or the least observant) voters in the world.

But the final and most apposite form of political optimism is 'optimism about people' itself. That optimism was well expressed by Will Hutton in a review of the optimistic classic, James Surowiecki's *The Wisdom of Crowds*: 'It is when we follow the crowd that it turns into an irrational mob, creating stock market bubbles or lynching the innocent. But when crowd decisions emerge of our own aggregated free will, they are astonishingly accurate and, when values are involved, decent.' (*The Observer*, 18 September 2005)

The underlying assumption is that spontaneous expressions of public opinion are to be trusted not just factually but also morally. It is only when the public is led astray by malign external forces that things go wrong. Hutton went on to describe an episode in 2005 of panic-buying of fuel: 'Petrol mainly ran out (and then only temporarily) in those towns where right-wing newspaper readership dominated, but not in those with more diverse newspaper sales and readerships.' This is Rousseau in modern dress – humans are individually moral but corrupted by interaction with the right-wing media.

The difficulty with this convenient theory is that newspapers do not force themselves on people. Their readers buy them voluntarily. The media behave as they do because they are looking for customers. Readers command content, not content readers.

If evasions such as blaming the media (or, in a previous version of the theory of false consciousness, blaming capitalist cultural hegemony) are excluded, does anyone in politics, apart from the most naïve populist, really believe in 'optimism about people' more than a few millimetres beyond their 'starting point'? Of course not.

As for the wisdom of crowds, even if there is a variation of the law of large numbers under which large numbers of human guesses about a simple measurement, as long as they are independent of one another, tend towards the right answer, there is no reason to believe that the same process tends towards a right moral or political answer. Moral and political questions are not simple measurements, and responses to them are certainly not independent of one another.

Rejection of optimism does not justify its opposite – an unwarranted disdain for the populace in general – but it does justify a hard, critical realism about people as they are. One can still, as a matter of moral and political principle, apply L. T. Hobhouse's remark that the meaning of freedom is to treat people as rational, even when they are not: '[Liberty] rests not on the claim of A to be let alone by B, but on the duty of B to treat A as a rational being.' (*Liberalism*, 1911) But that is not a matter of optimism. Rather, in Havel's terms, it is matter of hope. It makes sense, and is right, even if it is not likely to be true, or ever to become true.

Hope without optimism

The great advantage of retaining hope but abandoning optimism is that it balances the future and the present. Optimism detaches us entirely from reality. But to abandon hope would be to attach us so closely to current reality that we could do nothing apart from accept it.

Traditional conservatism would celebrate acceptance of current reality, and urge its enjoyment. It would reject both optimism and hope. Neo-conservatism, with its obsession with markets, tends towards optimism without hope, a grim Panglossian prospect. Socialists tended towards both hope and optimism, especially optimism about the state. But liberalism, the cool liberalism of Keynes and the prudent liberalism of Gladstone alike, strives to free itself from the illusions of optimism, but continues to hope.

In a period of politics in which the resilience of liberals might yet again be tested to the limit, optimism might look more foolish than ever. But that is no reason to give up hope.

Risk aversion and the culture of blame

Helena Kennedy

Shirley Williams is one of the truly great women of our times and I have the good fortune to be able to call this paragon of brilliance and virtue my close friend. One of the joys of my summer is being with her in Cape Cod, where all her brightness is on display in animated talk around dinner tables, in her head girl arrangement of expeditions, in her graceful swimming and sailing, in her dogged cycling and determined canoeing and in the casual wisdom she bestows upon us all as we bask in the sun. Shirley is not risk averse. The opposite. She embraces challenges with such enthusiasm it is hard to believe she has reached four score. Her pleasure in life is infectious. However, I know she shares my concerns about the way in which our culture is becoming more litigious and the impact this has upon so many facets of our lives.

There was a time when risk was an accepted part of life. Misfortune, providence and God's will were all invoked to explain the calamities and dreadful events that befell us. Living was a risky business and the ravaging losses which families and communities experienced were largely inexplicable and deemed to be outside the control of ordinary people. Mines collapsed and bridges fell, people lost their minds and ran amok, agricultural machinery removed limbs and industrial vats of molten metal devoured flesh. The hooves of horses crushed bones and children fell from unguarded heights. In our stumbling advance towards a just society, the right not to be exposed to unfair risk as we went about our lives slowly evolved – mostly during the nineteenth century. The right of workers to be compensated for the risks they took for their masters led to guards being placed on industrial machines, harnesses being available to people who worked at heights, face masks given to prevent the breathing into the lungs of damaging filaments and fine debris; earphones were supplied for deafening noise, head covering and gloves for similar purposes.

The right of consumers not to be harmed by poisonous foodstuffs or faulty goods arose from one of the first cases I learned as a young law student – Donaghue v. Stevenson – the case of the snail in the bottle of ginger ale, where the courts decided that a purchaser was entitled to expect the goods she bought to be uncontaminated. And while a snail may have fallen by accident into the bottle, what sort of factory environment made that possible? So Mrs Donaghue got her compensation.

Then there was the responsibility of property owners for the safe passage of legitimate visitors; and the duties of care were not confined to individuals but extended to the state, which had to protect its citizens from undue harm in a like manner. So we saw a complex, mature society reaching for legal concepts of liability to compensate for the losses and personal injuries people suffered.

This social empowerment of citizens went hand in hand with the advance of rationalism and the belief that effects usually have causes, that inexplicable 'acts of God' are rare – although the recent volcanic eruption in Iceland has reminded us that there are aspects of nature that are beyond our control. However, the rise of scientific knowledge has meant that explanations are now sought for everything that goes wrong. As the mysteries of life have been unravelled so the human spirit of inquiry reaches for understanding about whatever we experience. We want to know why something occurred and whether it was preventable. Nature may put leaves on the railway line but was the accident that followed preventable? Are there lessons to be learned? Are there people to be held responsible and possibly punished or made to pay? Then there is that vexed question: is there any financial mechanism which can place a value on the loss? While some losses are incapable of compensation, is there a sum that can at least ameliorate the suffering? Does the paying of compensation drive home the lessons of responsibility?

Reducing risk is a sane objective in a sophisticated society. A reckless disregard for risk to others can and does now also create criminal liability, and rightly so. If you drive recklessly and kill, handle a firearm recklessly and cause injury, then you will be treated as though you had offended deliberately. Failing to take reasonable steps to protect others or to behave in a way that is mindful of another's safety should have consequences.

However, the question we must all face is where lines should be drawn: what is an acceptable level of risk? And most important of all: what are the costs to us as a society of seeking to eliminate all risk?

The cost of risk

Already our aversion to risk is being debated. There are public discussions about the impact upon children of over-protectiveness. Fear of the paedophile now means that children have fewer opportunities for unsupervised play and are chauffeured even short distances to school. Family members are prevented from filming innocent events like swimming galas and nativity plays on the basis that they may be used for voyeuristic activities. Julia Somerville may not photograph her daughter playing in the bath, yet police are photographing the every move of legitimate protesters.

The exaggerated sense of threat means that huge swathes of people have to be checked for criminal convictions and the cost to volunteering is considerable. Only recently we had the authors Philip Pullman and Michael Morpurgo having to state publicly their opposition to this requirement when they went into schools to read from their books to classes of children. Private tutors are also now in revolt. Just a few weeks ago we heard that there will be a roll out of 'Sarah's Law' which will make it possible for a parent to check out whether someone who moves in next door is on record for sexual offending. Distrust, hostility and potential for lynch mob attacks is real. (A paediatrician was attacked by a crowd of vigilantes who thought the prefix 'paed-' in a word signified abuse.)

The distrust sown by the abuse of such power is never considered, although it involves the unpicking of the invisible stuff that binds societies. The newspaper columnist Deborah Orr described how a neighbour's ten-year-old child was locked out and her husband's spontaneous reaction was to invite the child in to wait out of the cold. He then thought the better of it because of the current climate of suspicion. Teachers and doctors talk about the new inhibitions about embracing a child or a patient who is distressed – as though children and adults cannot distinguish between good touchings and bad touchings. I had a discussion with Ed Balls when he was the Secretary of State for Education who described a regular feature of his job as having to remove teachers where there was no direct evidence but only suspicion of a teacher's motives – for example, if they texted a pupil frequently. It left me as a lawyer with deep misgivings about the possible injustice to a teacher who may simply be encouraging a young person who was clever but receiving little encouragement at home.

The unwillingness of schools to embark upon activities which may lead to accidents – whether it is camping trips, or fell climbing or seaside visits – has also had serious consequences for the self-confidence of young people about their own capacities. It has also caused worry about the impact upon our national sports teams because of the absence of suitably trained talent. The whole idea of outward-bound trips was that they allowed our children to test their own abilities, stretch themselves beyond what they believed was possible and gain greater self-awareness and self-esteem. For children with social problems, risk-taking with supervision can divert them from far more alarming risky behaviour such as drug abuse and crime. But less and less reasonable risk-taking is taking place.

In attempting to create safe environments we have to retain our rationality. Yet often we do the opposite. The answer to a child's drowning is not to close all swimming pools; the answer to an injury from a conker is not to ban all games involving conkers.

At another end of the spectrum – but close to my own daily round – is the response to terrorism. We do need to have strong, clear counter-terror strategies and government has the responsibility to protect its citizens. However, the response must be proportionate to the threat and we have to be aware that abandoning our civil liberties to counter terrorism is to give victory to terrorists. Most of us are more likely to be run down by a car than killed by a terrorist plot. The answer to threats of terrorism is not to junk the legal rules for the investigation and detention of suspects or the long-established methods for trial by imposing ninety days' or forty-two days' detention without charge, ID cards and centralised monolithic computer databases. The answer is not to ban all demonstrations near Parliament, or to forbid the reading of a list of the war dead outside Downing Street. It is not to stop and search every brown-skinned young man you see without reasonable suspicion, as the new laws allow. The effect of such legislation is to alienate the very communities we need to work with to gain intelligence. We have to strike a balance in establishing the appropriate steps to be taken to reduce the terrorist risk.

One well might ask: who dreams these things up?

Bureaucratic systems can so often cloud the lines of responsibility or fog the channels of communication between different parts of the whole. There can be clear signs at some corner that all is not right within a system – whether it is a work regime within a factory or the care arrangements for patients – but no one sees how it connects to the bigger picture. Surgeons tell us that repeated hand-washing has gone out of fashion. Staff reach for gloves from the box of rubber gloves and contaminate the next pair because the reaching hand is unclean. Contract cleaners sweep around a bed and run a damp cloth over surfaces, often spreading bacteria. Standard contract cleaning which is fine for city offices falls far short of the kind of cleaning needed in a ward. Some activities which may be suitable for outsourcing in any other enterprise or public service are absolutely not right in a hospital. The remedy sought to deal with risk is often a complicated risk-management system, where box-ticking takes over from professionalism.

A couple of years ago I was asked to the Royal College of Psychiatrists to chair a working party into risk. They had recently been engaged in anxious discussions about risk assessment and management because of a heightened level of public anxiety, often accelerated by the tabloid media, about a perceived increase in the number of mental patients or mentally disturbed persons presenting a threat to public safety. The government's response to public concern has included attempts to introduce wider powers of preventative detention through new legislation – strongly opposed by civil liberties groups and many professionals, especially those involved with those with learning disabilities and the mentally ill who are strange but not dangerous. But the changes also required clinicians to complete lengthy risk-assessment forms on each contact with a psychiatric patient. Sometimes as many as ninety questions were to precede the consultation proper. The questions would be formulaic and unlikely to produce helpful information, such as:

> Have you been taking your medication as prescribed, George?
> Have you been feeling any change in your mood?
> Have you had aggressive feelings, destructive feelings towards yourself or others?

George already guesses how he is expected to answer. And as any psychiatrist will tell you these are all issues a professional will undoubtedly explore in the course of a clinical meeting with a patient, usually indirectly.

Sometimes a patient will dissemble or appear to be functioning well but then some extraneous event will happen which will trigger paranoia and a dreadful outcome. But the fact is that there are no more killings by mental patients now than there were thirty years ago. It is public alarm and media coverage that has changed. A *BMJ* article by leading practitioners described the development:

> Risk has become a central feature of modern life; a veritable industry has grown up around its detection, assessment and management. The risk posed by the fraction of mentally ill people who offend has always generated concern, but as care for the mentally ill has moved out of the institutions into the gaze of an increasingly risk-obsessed public, the intensity of the reaction that it provokes has grown out of all proportion to the actual risk involved. (Turner and Salter, 2007)

Psychiatrists and patients often point to the distortion of public statistics that fails to acknowledge that there is a far greater danger to the public posed by other groups than those with mental illness, particularly because of the abuse of alcohol and drugs. On the other hand, the rarity of serious violence or homicide does not diminish the tragedy for a family when someone is killed, nor the importance of doing all possible to reduce its occurrence.

Psychiatrists have become much more alert to linking factors between violence and mental illness. It is the box ticking-methodology they take objection to. This ticking of boxes which is called a risk-management tool may in part be designed to improve clinical practice but is largely to cover the hospital trust in case of litigation. And what it also does is undermine the professionalism of the doctor.

Across the board we are seeing a gnawing de-professionalisation, where the judgement of the professional is not trusted. We see it with teachers, hamstrung by an over-prescriptive curriculum; we see it with the police and their targets. Virtually every professional in every field can give examples.

Such overweening risk-management initiatives, the over-reading of health and safety requirements, and the fear of litigation have taken the joy out of many jobs but have also greatly reduced the effectiveness of what we are all trying to do.

Social work is one of the fields most vulnerable to attack. The current concern of judges in the family division is the huge increase in children being removed from parents into care since the case of 'Baby P'. The pendulum swings from one extreme to another, with little judgement being exercised. One of the main complaints of professionals is that they spend more time on paperwork than at the front line doing the job for which they are trained.

Why are we so frightened?

The world may be frightening – but more frightening than before? Probably not, but we accepted old threats with greater equanimity. Our expectations have changed. We have lived through an era of unprecedented prosperity. Our expectations have moved on dramatically. We expect to be able to control events more and yet cannot. We think there is no such thing as an accident and are unwilling to accept that fate played a part in any event. When the volcanic ash problem was delaying flight returns from abroad, I heard a radio caller demand that the government get his family back from

New Zealand, where they were delayed because of the problem. It was all the government's fault. It was the ludicrous demand of an infantilised adult.

People claim they want small government but then demand government action the minute something does not work out for them. Increasingly we see adults behave like children. It would be easy to blame this compulsion on state-reliance but the United States, where welfare protection is meagre, is not free of this desire to blame someone, indeed anyone.

The phenomenon, in my view, is largely a product of fear and a sense of powerlessness. It is a fear that has grown with globalisation and free markets, which while they have brought some benefits have also produced many frightening adjuncts. Security at work has gone. Flexible workforces may be good for employers but not so hot for employees. There is a sense that only tomorrow there might be the removal of jobs to countries where a workforce will be cheaper. Pensions are disappearing and there is fear of old age.

Our societies have changed, bringing an enriching diversity but also fear of the 'other'. There is a loss of community, with more movement away from places of birth and growing atomisation. While people are better informed and educated, that knowledge brings a heightened awareness that national government has less power today than it did in the past, with externalities having impacts outside of its control.

There is less deference in terms of class but also towards professionals: people once respected for their expertise are now distrusted. Secularism has undermined the role of churches and other religious institutions. Materialism and consumerism means everything has a price and as a result our worth has been increasingly based on money. Einstein claimed that that which can be measured usually has little value and that which has real value can rarely be measured.

The elevation of materialism and consequent greed has been the basic cause of our two recent crises – in banking and in Parliament. What is laughable is that the banks are now to be compensated for taking risks – the very thing that everyone else is frightened of, but which bankers were supposed to be brave enough to face. It is the ordinary citizen who bore the risk – whose banking charges went through the roof, whose mortgages were withdrawn, whose public services will now be cut, whose taxes have bailed the banks out, whose jobs are now on the line.

If risk were to be properly rewarded, the reward would be to surgeons who still operate in hard cases and do not take the defensive route. It would be to fire fighters who enter burning buildings, police officers dealing with violent offenders, and psychiatric nurses confronted with patients who are out of control.

What is extraordinary is that governments have failed to regulate adequately where they should and have over-regulated where they should not. Fear and blame are two sides of the same coin. The urge to blame has a chilling effect, as witnessed by the practice of defensive medicine in the USA.

Is this new regrettable phenomenon linked to a growing sense of ourselves as citizens who have rights? Prince Charles blamed the compensation culture on the Human Rights Act. But these changes in social attitudes started long before 2000 when the Act came into force.

Clearly, lawyers do bear some responsibility. The 'no win, no fee' contingency arrangements, which let lawyers take a proportion of the winnings, have fostered a greater willingness to turn to the courts. The intention had been to cut legal aid but to provide some mechanism to enable poorer people to engage in litigation to secure civil justice. The consequences have brought damage not just to legal standards but also to the social fabric. There are now advertisements on television peddling the idea that compensation is available at every turn. Lawyers have turned into ambulance chasers.

I do not pretend to have answers to these problems other than urging a return to some sort of rationality. Life involves risk. Healthy societies accept risk. A society free of all risk cannot be created. Professionals make mistakes. Punishing all error has a chilling effect. Security will not be enhanced by becoming more punitive and accusatory. Fearful societies draw down authoritarian responses from government that in the end reduce our liberty.

British universities: the Shirley Williams démarche

Anthony King

At the University of Essex there is a vantage point from which passers-by can see, embedded in 1960s concrete, the end of one phase in the history of British higher education and the beginning of another. Looking across a large quadrangle, someone going by can easily see from the configuration of the windows opposite that, whereas the available space on the right is required to accommodate only three storeys, the same volume of space on the left is required to accommodate four. On the right, the ceilings are high and the offices and teaching rooms generously proportioned. On the left, the ceilings are low and the offices and teaching rooms and offices mean, almost poky. Everything has shrunk.

What passers-by are seeing, whether they know it or not, is a veritable archaeological site: visible remains of the moment at which the confident, adventurous, sky's-the-limit phase in the history of British higher education gave way to a phase during which universities in the UK have found themselves for all of the past four decades forced to struggle to maintain academic standards and to keep their buildings in reasonably good repair, with the very existence of several of them under threat. The glorious post-Robbins era, during which the 'new' universities (as we once called them) such as Essex, East Anglia, Warwick, Lancaster, Stirling and Sussex were founded, came abruptly to a halt. The halcyon days – and they really *were* halcyon days – were over. So was the UK government's spending spree on higher education. Universities' spending was never again to be so little constrained.

In part, the universities' descent from their own special paradise was their own fault. In September 1969, Shirley Williams, then the minister of state in charge of higher education, invited the vice-chancellors of UK universities to consider how the escalating per capita costs of higher education could be reduced, especially if – as seemed highly probable – the number of young men and women seeking university places continued to increase. Her 1969 démarche was the higher-education equivalent of Tony Crosland's later declaration to local authorities that 'the party is over'. Against the background of the looming necessity of reducing costs, Williams's tone was emollient and relaxed. It was far from dictatorial. Her circular (in the informal sense) to universities included a list of thirteen practical suggestions for reducing costs, any combination of which universities might want to act upon. Forty years later, almost every one of her suggestions still resonates:

- reduce or remove student grants and introduce a system of loans;
- the same, but at postgraduate level only;
- admit fewer overseas students;
- require that grant-aided students enter specified kinds of employment for a period after graduation;
- make greater use of part-time and correspondence courses as alternatives to full-time courses;
- make it possible for the most able students to complete a degree course in two years;
- introduce two-year courses leading to different qualifications alongside three-year degree courses;
- insert a period between school and university, giving school-leavers a period in which they could decide whether they wished to proceed to higher education;
- make more intensive use of buildings and equipment, including the possibility of reorganising the academic year;
- share facilities more often between adjacent institutions;
- encourage more students to live at home;

- develop student housing associations and other forms of loan-financed provision for student residences;
- increase student–staff ratios.

The response of the grandly named Committee of Vice-Chancellors and Principals of the Universities of the United Kingdom – that is, the universities' trade union – came a few months later. It was broadly dismissive. Most of the minister's suggestions were rejected, either explicitly or implicitly. The UK's universities were doing brilliantly, thank you very much; the government of the day should continue to fund them on the existing basis. The haughtiness of the universities' collective response is well captured by the last paragraph of the CVCP's 'statement of views':

> Much of this paper has necessarily had to deal with matters of cost and possibilities of cost economies. When we met the Minister of State last September we were asked to address ourselves to these questions and we have done so. But, significant as they undoubtedly are, we would not wish to give the impression that we regard these questions as the most important, or the most difficult, with which the universities will be faced over the next ten years. We believe that the British universities have been among the most successful in the world in pursuing the essential aims for which universities exist everywhere. We think that the great expansion which has been achieved in the past decade has not led to any slackening of their purpose. We think also that, in proportion to their real achievements, our universities are as economical in their operation as any. If, as we hope, there is to be a comparable advance in the next decade, the first aim must be to bring this about without any reduction in the quality of what the universities do, or in the contribution which their graduates can make to the society of the future. But this cannot be done if cost considerations have always to be put first.

In other words, 'Sod off (but of course continue to give us loads of taxpayers' money)'. It is scarcely too strong to say that that was the moment at which Britain's universities effectively surrendered control of their own destiny. If they themselves could not respond to rapidly changing circumstances, then successive governments and their agents would respond for them.

Some of the changes that have taken place subsequently have not been willed. They have simply happened, often driven by market forces. More degree courses are now part-time, enabling students to earn their living when not studying. More young people choose to take a gap year rather than proceed directly to university (though without apparently reducing their desire to go on to higher education). A higher proportion of students than in the past are living at home, some because they want to but far more because a combination of high travel and accommodation costs, plus the fear of going deeply into debt, effectively forces them to. For hundreds of thousands of students in the twenty-first century, attending university simply means carrying on much as they did when they were at school. For them, the school experience and the university experience are no longer qualitatively different.

But many of the changes that have taken place *have* been willed by successive governments and their agents – willed either explicitly or as the inevitable consequence of other decisions affecting higher education. Shirley Williams's démarche suggested reducing or removing student grants and replacing them wholly or in part by loans. The CVCP was instinctively opposed, commenting that any such suggestions were 'naturally unwelcome to the universities'. Unwelcome or not, they have been adopted. The proportion of students able to take advantage of outright grants has plummeted. A majority of university students now have no option but to take out loans. Shirley Williams did not suggest, but successive governments have insisted, that fees paid by students cover a substantial proportion, larger than in the past, of universities' operating costs. Forty years on, the debate over the funding of both universities and students continues.

Shirley Williams's 1969 circular mentioned the possibility of reducing the number of overseas students admitted by British universities. The relatively modest fees paid by overseas students did not begin to cover the full costs of their courses. Needless to say, the vice-chancellors were opposed to any such reduction, noting (rightly) that 'students and scholars from overseas have their own special contribution to make to the British academic community'.

In due course, a subsequent government did meet the vice-chancellors' concerns – but perhaps not in quite the way they expected. The government actively encouraged universities to attract more overseas students, not fewer, but at the same time enormously increased overseas students' fees. Many universities thus became heavily dependent on the income generated by overseas students and spent correspondingly heavily on recruitment drives overseas. Non-UK students at some British universities are so numerous that they form, in effect, tightly knit national communities, with, for example, Chinese students mixing exclusively with other Chinese students and having little or no contact with either British students or students from America, Africa and other parts of Asia.

Universities and the governments of the late 1960s and 1970s were broadly in agreement that there should be two main types of institution in the higher-education sector: universities proper and the so-called polytechnics. The polytechnics' principal purpose was to provide high-level vocational training and to conduct research relevant to commerce and industry. There was to be parity of esteem between the institutions on the two sides of the 'binary divide'; but, in the words of the CVCP, nothing 'should be allowed to obscure their essentially different purposes'. In fact, nothing much did obscure their different purposes for the better part of a generation; but then, in 1990, the then education secretary abolished the binary divide and permitted, even encouraged, polytechnics, teaching training colleges, technical colleges and even further education colleges to reinvent themselves as institutions calling themselves universities.

Abolishing the divide had two predictable effects. One was to cause the existing universities to be subjected to external checks and monitoring in much the way that the former polytechnics had always been. Successive governments had always prided themselves on having an arm's-length relationship with the universities. Post-1990, the relationship was still arm's length, but the arm was shorter. The older universities entered a strange (to them) new world of inspections, quality assessments, paper trails and audits – and of course had no choice but to hire large numbers of additional administrators to enable them to cope. The other effect was to cause most of the former polytechnics – now dubbed 'new universities' – to expand their own remits far beyond the merely vocational and practical. Now that they were called universities, they wanted to be – and to be seen to be – proper universities. They acquired departments, sometimes large departments, of sociology, economics, political science, English literature and all manner of other humanities subjects. Most of the departments in question were mediocre and conducted little research, but they consumed substantial resources.

Shirley Williams had, of course, been right in 1969 to anticipate a surge in demand for higher education. Some of the increased demand derived simply from the larger number of teenagers and young adults in the population and taking A-levels at school; but much of it also derived from the more and more widely held belief in Britain – a belief by no means unfounded – that degree-level qualifications enhanced individuals' career prospects. In addition, the rapid growth in the number of places in higher education created, as time passed, its own demand. It became harder and harder for young people *not* to go to university. For their part, successive governments, believing that the emergence of a more highly educated population would serve to promote international competitiveness and higher-than-usual rates of economic growth, encouraged the university sector to expand. There was even talk of enabling a massive 50 per cent of the age group to reap the benefits of higher education.

There was, however, a catch. There still is. It relates to Shirley Williams's thirteenth suggestion: that there should be some further increase in universities' student–staff ratios – in other words, that, as a matter of conscious choice, staff–student ratios should be allowed to continue to deteriorate.

Perhaps the fact that this particular option was Shirley Williams's thirteenth and last indicates that she was not very keen on it. In any event, the vice-chancellors responded to it with their usual hauteur. They pointed out (rightly) that 'the teaching methods characteristic of British universities have relied to a much greater extent than is the case in most foreign countries on direct personal contact and discussion between teachers and learners' and added (also rightly) that 'the whole trend of opinion among students calls for more rather than less teaching of this kind'. They concluded (more debatably) that British universities' high academic standards, short three-year degree courses and low drop-out rates depended heavily 'on the maintenance of the basic university teaching arrangements to which we are accustomed'. And the CVCP pretty much left it at that. The existing staff–student ratio, already under pressure, should on no account be allowed to deteriorate further.

Forty years on

But the world has not left it at that. On the one hand, most British universities have struggled to maintain 'the basic teaching arrangements to which we are accustomed'. On the other, the staff–student ratio has continued to deteriorate. Student numbers have increased far faster than universities' income, with the result that student numbers have increased far faster than universities' capacity to employ enough academic staff to teach them. Staff–student ratios differ widely, of course, from university to university, from department to department and even from course to course. But the trend overall has been steadily downwards. Successive governments have been reluctant to acknowledge that reduced staff–student ratios have been central to their overall higher-education strategy. But that has been the case all the same.

In an increasingly competitive environment, with every UK university forced to maintain that, while other universities' academic standards may have deteriorated, its own most certainly have not, the central fact of the decline in staff–student ratios has been largely concealed. No university wants to admit publicly that its students are less well taught than they were in the past. But, if the fact of the decline is seldom acknowledged, the consequences of the decline are – save possibly, just possibly, in Oxford and Cambridge – everywhere to be seen.

The consequences are various. One, the most conspicuous, is the enormous increase in class sizes. The size of audiences at lectures matters little; the experience of being one student among two hundred in a lecture theatre differs little from the experience of being a single student among fifty or a hundred. But in smaller classes the difference is qualitative, not just quantitative. Students in a class of half a dozen or even a dozen have a reasonably good chance of being allowed to have their say – or of being forced by their teacher to have their say. But in a class of more than fifteen – let alone of more than twenty – the sheer arithmetic probability of an individual student's contributing, or being forced to contribute to class discussion, declines sharply. The format may be the same. The pedagogical reality is different.

Less conspicuous, but if anything more serious, is the fact that a lower staff–student ratio means in practice that members of academic staff cannot give their students as much work to do as they did in the past. There are only so many hours in the day, and members of academic staff are under intense pressure, at least at the higher-quality universities, to carry out research and to publish – as well as carrying out their increasingly onerous administrative duties. The result is that most of them have considerably less time in which to teach far more students. The number of individual courses or modules that students are required to take has declined. So has the number of assignments that they are required to complete within each course or module. Whereas students might once have been required to take five courses in each term or year, they are now required to take only four or fewer. Whereas they might once have been required to complete five assignments in connection with each course, they are now required to complete only two or three. Some universities even indulge in what they archly call 'individual learning', meaning that the students are not taught at all. While teachers are thus often overworked, students are frequently underworked – and sometimes suffer from anomie as a result. Their daily lives are far less structured than they were.

Even less conspicuous, except to the students directly involved, is universities' increasing – and unavoidable – reliance on graduate students as frontline teachers. Suppose a compulsory first-year or second-year course has an enrolment of two hundred. Suppose further that 'the basic teaching arrangements to which we are accustomed' require that those two hundred students should be subdivided, for purposes of more personal instruction, into groups of fifteen or twenty. There is no way in which sufficient numbers of fully fledged members of academic staff can be deployed to teach such large numbers of these smaller groups. Graduate students are recruited to do the job instead. Many of these graduate teaching assistants, probably the majority, are keen, conscientious and intelligent, but inevitably they lack experience and wide-ranging knowledge. In addition, a large proportion of them do not have English as their native language. Given the paucity in the UK of financial support for postgraduate courses and students, the overwhelming majority of graduate students at many British universities are overseas students. A little-noticed knock-on consequence is that, already, a large proportion of British university teachers are not British. That proportion seems certain to increase in future.

The truth is that, while the research output of British universities has undoubtedly increased, and while its quality may possibly have improved, the quality of the student experience has degenerated. Forty years after Shirley Williams flagged up an imminent crisis, students do less work, spend significantly less time in the classroom and are taught too often by less qualified teachers. The fact that almost no one has noticed is the result of a conspiracy of silence, the product of an understandable desire on the part of every university to protect its own individual reputation and not to question the reputations of others. As teaching institutions, British universities increasingly resemble those elegant mansions depicted in movies set in the American post-bellum South. Their facades continue to impress the outside world, but they conceal a substantial quantum of dilapidation and decay.

In all sorts of ways, successive governments have been ambivalent in their dealings with universities. With regard to academic standards, they have, on the one hand, put great pressure on universities to maintain standards while, on the other, putting equally great pressure on them not to allow students to drop out (and also, by implication, to be exceedingly reluctant to throw them out). The result is that more and more universities are awarding standard three-year degrees to students who should have been allowed – or required – to leave at the end of their first or second years. Of course, standards have fallen. They could not have failed to. Leaning on universities to make sure that almost all of their students graduate also means that university teachers, like many school teachers, are forced to devote time and energy to their dimmer and lazier students at the expense of their bright ones.

Governments have also been ambivalent in their attitude towards student numbers. On the one hand, they have sought for decades to increase student numbers (certainly as compared with the 1960s); on the other, they are adamant that this hugely increased number of students should, by whatever means, receive the high standard of instruction that their predecessors did, this despite the fact that the increase in teacher numbers and teaching resources has not remotely kept pace with the increase in student numbers. The effect is the one mentioned above: more and more students are taught less and less – and are given less and less work to do. Small wonder that students at some universities, including quite prestigious ones, are beginning to complain about being under-taught.

Boutiques or supermarkets?

What has happened is that successive governments, along with the great majority of universities, are still attempting, despite Shirley Williams's best efforts, to run universities as though they were up-market boutiques at a time when, however, they are under tremendous pressure from all sides to function, in reality, as educational supermarkets. There is a continuing misfit between the desire to retain universities as cloistered seats of learning, reserved for the talented few, and the desire to see them function as comprehensive multiversities, open to the many, including many of the less talented. A case can be made for each of the two types of university, and a case can be made for a system of higher education in which both types of university exist side by side, but a case cannot be made for, in effect, requiring all universities to function simultaneously as both boutiques and supermarkets. But that is precisely what successive governments and most universities have attempted – and failed – to achieve.

Perhaps the coalition government that resulted from the May 2010 election and/or the universities themselves will at last get round to deciding in which direction Britain's higher-education system should go: boutiques, supermarkets or some combination of the two (but not with boutiques trying to function as supermarkets or vice versa).

Boutique universities might want to continue awarding degree classes (though even the most distinguished American universities do no such thing). Probably they would want to maintain a universities-wide system of external examiners. They would be relieved of the need to undergo periodic inspections and to equip themselves with 'equality and diversity' and 'learning and teaching' units. They would be well funded on a per capita basis, possibly being allowed to charge market-rate fees while being required at the same time to provide substantial numbers of generous bursaries for poorer students. They would be readier to divest themselves of students who persistently underperformed. Above all, they would teach intensively – in addition to requiring members of their academic staffs to think, read, write and do research.

Supermarket universities might want to issue transcripts rather than award degree classes. They would be under no compulsion to maintain the present-day clumsy and expensive – in terms of staff time – system of external examiners. As institutions providing students with technical skills and vocational qualifications, they would inevitably be subject to a variety of forms of external inspection and validation. Their teaching would be more likely than that of supermarket universities to be large-group teaching. Their focus would be more on practical and vocational training than on traditional academic learning. They, even more than the boutique universities, would be expected to offer courses likely to promote the country's economic interests. They might well absorb a larger proportion of the total higher-education budget than the boutique universities, but they would be less generously funded on a per capita basis. It is at least arguable that a large majority of those in higher education should attend such universities rather than more 'academic' establishments. A government could decide that students at supermarket universities should not pay fees at all or else should pay only very modest fees.

If all that sounds like re-establishing some form of binary divide, though not necessarily (and probably not desirably) on the pre-1990 basis, then so be it. The binary divide made sense in its day. A similar divide would make even more sense now, with student numbers far higher in the twenty-first century than they were in the 1960s and with the pressures on government budgets even more intense today than they were then. There would be no need to require the new post-1990 universities to stop calling themselves universities. They could continue to call themselves whatever they liked while offering a distinctive range of courses and being funded separately. Alternatively, they could follow the Californian example. State-funded universities in California are labelled either the University of California, Berkeley (or wherever) or California State University, Bakersfield (or wherever). Institutions of both types are called universities, but every Californian knows that the two parallel systems serve – and are meant to serve – different purposes. The important point is that universities should not be treated like the former polytechnics and that the former polytechnics should not feel the need – or be given the resources – to ape their older brethren. Boutiques and supermarkets coexist in most British towns. They should be allowed to coexist within the higher-education system.

Shirley Williams launched an important debate in 1969. The time has come for that debate to be relaunched – on financial seas that are even more stormy now than they were then.

Trends in broadcasting

John Lloyd

I last saw Shirley Williams on television a little before this was written, on one of Andrew Neil's political shows – *This Week*, on 20 April. She had been asked – with others, who included the former Conservative Defence Secretary Michael Portillo and the then Labour Minister Caroline Flint – to play a kind of game, set by Neil: it was to identify the week's most telling political moment, which she did with her usual grace.

It was a small thing, a passing of the time waiting for something larger to happen, and for the election itself. Yet it was a kind of index of the changes in the broadcasting of politics in the past sixty years, since she has been active in politics. Television politics has become, in significant part, an adjunct to the entertainment business. Politicians increasingly earn their appearances for their talent to amuse: and that has given rise to politicians who, for part of their income and fame, depend or have depended on exercising that talent – as the former (Labour) Mayor of London, Ken Livingstone; the former leader of the Liberal Democrats, Charles Kennedy; and the present (Conservative) Mayor of London, Boris Johnson.

Shirley Williams is not of that group – in part because she is a generation older than the oldest (Livingstone); in larger part because, while possessed of a good wit, she sees broadcasting, naturally, as an extension of political advocacy. Fortunately, her attractive public personality has allowed her to do that, and to continue to appear on television and radio. But it is no longer a popular position.

Trends

Five large changes have happened in the way in which the media treat our politics. One is the shift away from deference to political debate, largely within the House of Commons, to an assumption that debate does and should take place within broadcast studios: in the creation of the leaders' debates this year, the Everest has been scaled. The most important questioning in terms of public impact is done by highly experienced, often confrontational presenters: that which happens in the House of Commons is usually given prime-time airing only if particularly combustible. No newspaper now does any kind of parliamentary, Hansard-type, reporting: in Williams's youth, most Westminster reporters were engaged for that purpose, and their verbatim reports filled pages of *The Times*, and other papers.

At the same time, a channel has been dedicated to coverage of parliament and its committees: it is, however, very much minority viewing and little publicised. Hansard is now available on the Net. The BBC is right to point to this investment as one which greatly increases accessibility and ease of understanding of what happens within Westminster. But to point to these welcome innovations does not in itself compensate for the shift I am describing. The screen has become the entry into much of our political life: to a considerable degree, politics are performed on, and for most of the population only on, the media.

Shirley Williams personally benefited from this trend: she has a televisual style. That is one which is intelligent, friendly and direct, with an innate, or early learned, sense of measure in all of these. Her intelligence is not paraded; her friendliness rarely becomes mere flattery of the audience; and her directness is unforced. Television is unforgiving with pomposity and artifice. Further, being a woman – still a small minority in politics, especially high politics – meant she was on every programme producer's list for panels: she has appeared more often on *Question Time* than anyone else. She did not need the special dispensation now extended to the under-represented (non-white males) in the media, but it worked in her favour, nonetheless.

The second change is the shift from newspaper time to real time – driven first by the handful of broadcasters which existed into the 1980s, then by increased competition among TV and radio channels, then by the Net. Newspaper time is a news cycle which ends in the evening and does not start again until lunch; real media time is a space within which media storms can erupt at any time, at any strength. During the general election, the Labour campaign was described as being in 'meltdown' because of a conversation between Prime Minister Gordon Brown and his communications director, picked up on a still live Sky TV radio microphone, in which Brown called a woman with whom he had just spoken, and who had voiced concerns over immigration, 'a bigoted woman'. That is a perfect example of a real-time media age scandal.

It is a perfect exemplar because it shows what real time makes of such an event. Though a crass misreading of Gillian Duffy's comments on the part of the then Prime Minister, it was – as the Liberal Democrat leader, Nick Clegg, said at the time – the kind of comment any politician might privately have made. Nevertheless, all channels – led by the BBC's political editor, Nick Robinson – described it as a defining moment in the campaign, and as a possibly final blow to Labour's chances of holding power. By defining it as such, they were speaking implicitly to the narcissism of current affairs broadcasting: that is, its drive to incorporate the whole political world within its own ambit, and to judge political acts according to its need for drama. The Duffy moment was high drama: it raised themes of hypocrisy, racism, contempt, shock, penitence, humiliation. Television requires these, and they are especially vibrant when in a real-life setting. Such an occasion is thus 'naturally' promoted to fill the media stage.

The third trend, linked to the first two, has been a progressive shift from discussion of issues of policy substance and ideology to process and performance. For real-time media, stories must always move – and if they are to last, must have a defined future, rather like a serialised story in which the next episode is advertised as solving the entanglements created by this one. Issues of policy and ideology are too static for media of this ever-flowing kind. It is to a degree true that ideological divisions are less stark than at a time, in Williams's youth, when socialism and conservatism stood on sharply differing platforms. Policies do remain significantly different: but are seldom given wide airing. Over time, the much greater power accruing to the broadcast media meant that television's great advantage – to show an audience what its leaders are like, physically and behaviourally – has necessarily created a media–political class: leading politicians cannot become and remain so unless they can command the media, at least at times.

Commenting on the changes between his first *Anatomy of Britain* in 1962 and his last, *Who Runs This Place?* (2004) the late Anthony Sampson – like Williams, a founding member of the Social Democrats – wrote: 'Editors, journalists and cameras penetrated nearly all institutions – including parliament, the monarchy, the political parties and Whitehall – demanding answers to irreverent questions, debunking their traditions and clamouring for openness. They were not separate limbs or membranes in the anatomy so much as part of the lifeblood, or nervous system.'

Fourth, political coverage, especially (but not only) in the UK has become at once less ideological and more aggressive. In Williams's youth, newspapers were fairly reliably pro-Conservative, pro-Labour or (a few) pro-Liberal – or, in the case of the *Morning Star*, pro-Communist (when Williams began her political career as president of Oxford Labour Club in 1950, the last, of two, Communist MPs, Willie Gallagher, lost his West Fife seat). The BBC, then still a monopoly and a growing but still relatively modest presence in news and current affairs, attempted with some success to find a neutral position – though the left, in the main, believed it was pro-Conservative. (For the past three decades, it has been the right which has viewed the BBC with most suspicion.) Newspapers were edited and staffed by journalists often heavily committed to the left or right: and though good journalism was done, it was often at the service of an ideological view of the world.

That attachment is now more vestigial. Though newspapers' political preferences can still generally be predicted – less in the 2010 election than in the recent past – their endorsement means relatively little. All practise a form of political journalism which privileges revelation and scandal – some, as the expenses scandal, worth publicising, much else less so. In this they are joined by the broadcast media, whose rapid turnover of stories constantly demands refreshing by new revelations and scandals. Even in quiet times, political reporters from all media hunt for stories which will make waves – knowing these to be the ones which will advance careers.

Commenting on this shift in both written and broadcast journalism, the US writer James Fallows has written:

> The natural instinct of newspapers and TV is to present every public issue as if its 'real' meaning were political in the meanest and narrowest sense of that term – the attempt by parties and candidates to gain an advantage over their rivals. Reporters do, of course, write stories about political life in the broader sense and about the substance of issues – the pluses and minuses of diplomatic recognition for Vietnam, the difficulties of holding down the Medicare budget, whether immigrants help or hurt the nation's economic base. But when there is a chance to use these issues as props or raw material for a story about political tactics, most reporters leap at it.

Fallows says that ordinary people 'want to know how the reality of politics will affect them – through taxes, programmes, scholarship funds, wars'. Journalists, by contrast, present themselves as acting on behalf of the public, but

> in fact they ask questions that only their fellow political professionals care about. And they often do so – as at the typical White House news conference – with a discourtesy and rancour that represent the public's views much less than they reflect the modern journalist's belief that being independent boils down to acting hostile. ('Why Americans Hate the Media', *The Atlantic*, February 1996)

The shift is important. The media, especially the broadcast media, seek a style in which ideology is scorned, confrontation and conflict privileged. Another acute US commentator, Jay Rosen, a New York University professor and writer of the exemplary media blog PressThink, put it like this in a blog/essay on 14 June 2010:

Even if we had an x-ray machine that gave us perfect information about the beliefs of the journalists who report on politics, the ideological drift of the work they produce wouldn't necessarily match the personal beliefs or voting patterns of the reporters and editors on the beat because there are other factors that intervene between the authors of news accounts and the accounts they author.

Take for instance the way professional journalists try to generate authority and respect among peers, or, to state it negatively, the way they flee opprobrium. Here it is important for them to demonstrate that they are not on anyone's 'team', or cheerleading for a known position. This puts a premium on stories that embarrass, disrupt, annoy or counter the preferred narrative – the talking points, the party line – of one or both of the sides engaged in political battle. An incentive system like that tends to be an ideological scrambler, which doesn't mean that it scrambles consistently or symmetrically across political lines . . . Related to the scrambler effect is the delight most reporters take in inconveniencing with reported fact and discomfiting questions those who represent a particular point of view: whether they are office holders, spokespeople, activists, or committed ideologues. Important fact: 'True believer' is a universal term of contempt in newsrooms, 'skeptic' a universal term of praise.

The journalism which developed across the long span of Shirley Williams's career is one which proclaims its ideology to be without an ideology. That has, especially within the BBC, created reporting which tried hard and consciously to recognise its own biases and to correct them. However, it is also a gambit for power: an at least implicit claim for being above the struggle, and thus superior to it – a position which necessarily devalues politics, and increasingly sees it as a grubby trade.

Fifth, the Net has appeared, the most dynamic force in communications in general and journalism in particular for a century. This is not the place or the space to discuss its impact – Yochai Benkler's *The Wealth of Networks*, and the work of Stephen Coleman, are two of the reference points for that – but for this essay, the largest point to be made is that the Net has, so far, played a much less important part in British political life than it does in the US – and even in other European states, as France, Germany and Italy. The two best-known British political sites – Guido Fawkes and Iain Dale's Diary – are known mainly to the political classes: both are Conservative in orientation. In part this is a tribute to the power of the established, mainstream media in the coverage of political life: in part, too, it marks the fact that a relentlessly aggressive UK media leave less space for such a posture from political websites – as is the case in the more respectful US and continental European media cultures. More disappointingly, the UK web has not produced a strong political satire culture – as *The Onion* in the US.

Commentary

When Williams was beginning her political life, two US political scientists – Gabriel Almond and Sidney Verba – wrote a book, *The Political Culture*, published in 1963, which gave a picture of (among other things) British society in the 1950s. It has a nostalgic ring about it now.

> The participant role is highly developed. Exposure to politics, interest, involvement, and a sense of competence are relatively high. There are norms supporting political activity, as well as emotional involvement in elections and system affect. And attachment to the system is a balanced one: there is general system pride as well as satisfaction with specific governmental performance.

Shirley Williams has lived to a time when that cannot be said: no political scientist, and few politicians, would describe Britain as 'at ease with itself' – even if most would avoid the hyperbole, used by the Conservatives before coming to government in May 2010, of the country being 'broken'. How far a more aggressive media has been responsible for this is a matter for debate: as far as I know, there is no research on the matter. Further, it is also a matter for debate how far the more aggressive and investigative media of the post-1960s period uncovered corruption, unsavoury actions and attitudes, and downright criminality because these had increased, or because they had always existed but had been covered up by established powers and remained largely undisturbed by a more respectful journalism. Further still, the media may have been more active in fostering political identification and engagement since they were themselves more obviously politically engaged – a posture which the contemporary understanding of journalistic professionalism has hugely diluted. Journalists now, of left and right, profess to hold politicians to account: by contrast, to support one or other political movement or party with one's professional journalistic skill is seen as the domain of the hack.

The schizoid poles of journalism – that which professes a public interest role and that which, enthusiastically or cynically, serves what interests the public in the belief that such material will be (to the high minded) trivial and even demeaning – have grown further and further apart. The charges against journalism, that part of it is over-elitist and part of it is vulgar, have a common basis. That is, that both trends represent a narrowing of the public agenda: an abdication, or part abdication, from the business of making the significant generally comprehensible. It is a charge which is more powerfully made against the Net: but it considerably pre-dates the Net's arrival.

The British media are no more 'broken' than British society or politics, but they are becoming increasingly uncivil and sensationalist – in part because of the pressures of falling audiences, and the fights to the death which that situation generates. Most importantly for politicians, the news media, with the still-dominant broadcast media in the lead, now need to make an accounting of their coverage of politics, if for no other reason than that politics has become unthinkable – undo-able – without the mass media. Media were never mere transparent conductors of political debate: now, they are conductors, composers and orchestra.

In a 2005 speech at Lambeth Palace, another Williams, Rowan, the Archbishop of Canterbury, put it this way, and it is good enough to be the last word.

> We need to deflate some of the rhetoric about the media as guardians
> and nurturers of democracy simply by virtue of the constant exposure of
> 'information', and we need to be cautious about a use of 'public interest'

language that ignores the complexity and, often, artificiality of our ideas of 'the public'. We need to recognise that there is a difference between concealment that is corrupt and designed to exclude or disadvantage those who have a legitimate interest, and boundaries that are properly patrolled by professional systems of accountability and gain nothing from being opened to universal – potentially demagogic – scrutiny. It is a very difficult discrimination – it can be used easily enough as an excuse for avoiding proper questioning – but it helps simply to acknowledge that there is a discussion to be had, and that 'public interest' is not too readily to be identified with the majority prejudice of a particular readership. And finally under this head, we need a form of self-regulation that admits provisionality and provides means of assessment. We need journalistic work that equips its own critics.

Conservation

Jennifer Jenkins

In this brief article I am concerned with the conservation of archaeological and historical sites and buildings – not with the natural environment.

I first became involved in conservation in 1970, roused by plans to build a new road round the city of York, only a mile from the great cathedral at its centre. Had this scheme gone ahead a constant stream of cars and heavy goods vehicles would have circled the city, bringing noise and fumes to all the people living there or coming to visit, destroying the organic pattern created over many centuries.

I am not an architect or a professional historian, being more interested in trying to solve practical problems than in academic study. The only book I have written caused me more difficulty than grappling with the day-to-day problems of the National Trust, with its thousands of acres of countryside, its hundreds of miles of coastline or the historic buildings in its ownership. Earlier I had become Secretary of the Ancient Monuments Society, which, despite its name, concerns buildings of all periods rather than one of the more prestigious societies dealing with buildings of particular periods.

The society had little money or other resources and I installed the office in an unheated bedroom at the top of our house in Notting Hill, then an unfashionable and rather run-down area. But the society had one useful starting point: like the other amenity societies it is informed of applications to demolish buildings listed as being of historic or archaeological interest. Thus it is well informed about threats to important buildings and can make representations to government and local authorities about historic buildings at risk in England and Wales. Scotland is separately administered. I was later appointed chairman of the Historic Buildings Council for England – a statutory body responsible for advising government. My final post was to be Chairman of the National Trust.

Conservation in the UK has developed on very different lines from the system in operation in most of Western Europe. The regulatory arrangements about listing and controls over demolition are operated in much the same way, but in the UK unspoilt landscapes, and historic buildings and sites when not privately owned are looked after largely by charities, particularly the National Trust for England, Wales and Northern Ireland and the Scottish National Trust. On the continent, by contrast, the government or local authorities are responsible for regulation.

Conservation first became a subject of public interest in the late nineteenth century when William Morris, the poet and artist, established the Society for the Protection of Ancient Buildings (SPAB). Since then the movement has gradually expanded in scope. Beginning with early churches and manor houses, the legislation and controls now cover all aspects of the historic environment including parks, gardens, factories and even a colliery. The time range has been brought more up to date, most recently with the founding of the Twentieth Century Society. The number of people actively interested in conservation has grown as the public became alarmed by the destruction caused by bombing during the Second World War and more recently by widespread schemes for redevelopment of built-up areas. Visiting historic buildings has become a popular leisure pursuit.

Conservation is often thought of as backward-looking, directed to preserving old areas in aspic. Of course there are some iconic sites which do merit strict preservation – Stonehenge is one, and the continuing battle to protect the open downland in which it lies, shows that even these are not immune from being overwhelmed by roads and traffic and by the number of visitors coming to historic sites. However, in many places the conservation and reuse of older areas has proved to be the starting point for regeneration. That has, for example, been true in Liverpool, once the most thrusting city in the country but after the 1930s seeing its trade ebbing away and its older buildings left empty or demolished. Similar initiatives have revitalised the centres of Glasgow and other nineteenth-century cities where people have come back to live in streets once abandoned for life in the country or suburbs.

In London also the preservation of older buildings has been the catalyst for regeneration. In 1975 when the Covent Garden flower and vegetable market was moved to Battersea it was proposed to build a major road through the area. This plan aroused the fury of the people who lived or worked locally. Supported by the Greater London Council, which intervened to list over a hundred historic buildings in the area, the proposals were reversed. Covent Garden has since become one of the most popular venues for visitors to the capital: it is inconceivable that it could just be bulldozed.

Churches present some of the most challenging problems for conservation. The ten thousand medieval churches in England and Wales were once centres of local life. Now relatively few people attend regularly, though many more still wish to be married in church and to hold funerals there. The Church of England still plays a part in local schools, particularly in rural areas, where the vicar is often involved in appointing teachers and holding classes.

The fate of thousands of Welsh chapels now abandoned and converted into housing, shows how what was once a way of life can virtually disappear. In contrast, the conservation of the medieval churches of York shows what can be done with imagination: some have become museums or concert halls and some simply places of meditation. In the countryside caring for and opening a church can be enough to ensure that the building still has its place in family life for marriage ceremonies and funerals as is witnessed by fresh flowers on the altar or on a recently dug grave.

All urban areas have to change and adapt to new patterns of work, travel and living. Places like Glasgow and Manchester have demonstrated that change can be combined with the reuse of older buildings and the redesign of their open spaces. Balancing regeneration with good new buildings and enhancing the sense of the place of a city is a challenge to planners and owners. Successful towns and cities can be just as pleasant places in which to live as suburbs and the countryside, and perhaps more interesting.

A Catholic in politics

Richard Harries

Religion is now a major player on the political stage, both nationally and internationally, in a way which was scarcely conceivable fifty years ago. One indication of this is the contrast between the religious outlook of the political elite about 1920 and the advent of New Labour. Adrian Hastings (*A History of English Christianity, 1920–2000*, 2001) has written that in those days:

> The dominant political class was largely unbelieving. If one thinks of Asquith, Haldane, Balfour, Lloyd George, Churchill, H. A. L. Fisher, one cannot well speak in terms of degrees of Christian orthodoxy, but only of degrees of scepticism. There was hardly a straightforward Christian believer in the front rank of politics in those years.

In contrast to that more than half of Tony Blair's Cabinet described themselves as Christian Socialists, whilst Blair himself was described in the press as the first Christian Prime Minister since Gladstone. That is both untrue and unfair, but it does indicate that religious faith was much more in the public realm that had been usual in British life.

This said, there is still a reticence in British public life about the personal expression of religious belief. When Tony Blair retired and he was asked why he had not talked more openly about his faith when in office, he replied that people would have thought him 'a nutter'. There could not be a sharper contrast with the United States of America where politicians will regularly refer to God in their speeches. The idea of politicians placarding their beliefs in order to help them get elected is much disliked by the British, but one downside of this is that it is difficult for anyone to mention their faith at all in a political context without it being seen as an attempt to claim the high moral ground. Nevertheless, while avoiding an American type of culture, it may be that we are moving into an age where politicians are able to talk about their fundamental beliefs in a much more open and natural way. At the recent election all three of the main party leaders were asked about their religious beliefs. They answered in a straightforward manner, and no great fuss was made about any of the answers.

The Christian faith of Shirley Williams goes deep, but it is so much part of her being, that if called upon to mention it, she can do so in a very open and natural way. In her autobiography *Climbing the Bookshelves*, for example, it simply slips in between the lines, as it were, as when she remarks of Tony Crosland's custom of always watching *Match of the Day*. 'Tony was as regular in his Saturday habits as I was in attending mass on Sundays.' The reason for the rootedness of this faith, as we might expect, goes back to her childhood. She was brought up in a family that included not only her father and her mother, but two people who, I suppose, must be described as servants, but who were in fact very much members of the family. About Amy and George, Shirley has written: 'I adored our young cook-housekeeper Amy and her warm-hearted husband, Charles Burnett. They were my other parents, in some ways closer than my own. I felt I was their daughter too . . . Charlie brought to our rather formal household a warmth and humour that swept barriers away.'

Shirley's mother was a questioning member of the Church of England, and though her father was a Catholic, both parents rejected infant baptism, leaving her and her brother free to decide for themselves what religion they wanted to belong to when they were adults.

Amy and Charles Burnett were both Catholics, and had 'a different set of priorities . . . They took me to church with them most Sundays. I became familiar with the detached grandeur of the traditional mass, recited in Latin by a priest whose beautifully robed back was turned to the congregation, and whose movements at the altar were obscure. The insistent rise and fall of Gregorian chant and the smell of incense infused my being, and became the sensual context of the Sabbath.'

Shirley's father was a convert who had become a Catholic as a result of studying the works of Newman at Oxford during World War One. As a result of what happened in Spain under Franco his involvement with the church lapsed for a while but he had returned to an active faith by the time Shirley came back to England from America at the end of World War Two. She now went to mass not only with the Burnetts, but with her father, about whom she has said:

> His wartime experiences, among them being torpedoed on the *Western Prince*, had made him aware of life's fragility and turned his mind towards eternal truths . . . After church, often itself a plunge into deep intellectual waters given the profundity of our priest Mgr Alfonso de Zulueta, my father and I would repair to the Pier Hotel . . . where we would discuss philosophy and religion for an hour or so over a muddy brown liquid called coffee. He would regale me with comments on doctrines like infallibility, and whether there could be such a thing as a Just War.

In addition to these more specifically Catholic elements, there is the love Shirley has for the natural world, especially the New Forest, a love which has been both evoked by and expressed through another love, that of poetry. This seems to have been fostered by her formidable father who gave her a copy of T. S. Eliot's *Four Quartets* for her fourth birthday, as well as by teachers at St Paul's Girls' School.

As she describes in *God and Caesar*, Shirley was baptised while a student at Oxford.

It is not difficult to see how, with the influence of the warm and serious faith of Amy and Charles, and the intellectual but tested faith of her father, the faith of Shirley should be such an integral and natural part of her being. People know it is there, without her feeling it is necessary to bring it into the conversation.

The 1960s were a good time for Catholics to make their way in public life. The anti-Catholic sentiments that had been part of English life were, mostly, a thing of the past. William Rees-Mogg was editor of *The Times*, Charles Curran the Director-General of the BBC and George Woodcock General Secretary of the TUC – all three Catholics for whom their faith meant a great deal. In politics Shirley for Labour and Norman St John Stevas for the Conservatives (both with an education ministerial portfolio at some point) stood on the liberal side of the middle ground. As Adrian Hastings has written: 'A few decades earlier the presence of Roman Catholics in such influential positions would have been regarded by many as constituting a mysterious threat to the safety of the nation. Now it evoked little comment.'

This has been so as far as Shirley is concerned, though she has sometimes had to fight her own political parties to maintain the right of conscientious dissent over such issues as abortion. For her, a policy of a free vote on such issues is a fundamental issue, not just for herself but more widely.

Matters of conscience

In one respect she has been fortunate in being a politician in Britain, rather than the United States, where she has such strong links. In recent decades America has been beset by cultural wars, with abortion being the defining issue. Those Democratic politicians who are also Catholics have had a particularly difficult dilemma. Their party has stood firmly on the cultural divide allowing abortion. While as practising Catholics they were opposed to abortion themselves, they have wanted to take a position which allowed it for those who did not share their own convictions. This approach was regarded as unacceptable by the American Catholic hierarchy on the grounds that abortion, like murder, is regarded as wrong by natural law. In short it is regarded as wrong for all people at all times, not just for Catholics, and therefore society as a whole should always have a law forbidding it. The result of this situation is that a number of Democratic Catholic politicians have found themselves in danger of being excommunicated by their own church. Britain has not experienced culture wars to the same extent, and the tradition of free votes on such issues as abortion has enabled a person like Shirley to both be a loyal Catholic and remain within a party that is mostly liberal on such issues. But she has occasionally had to fight for those free votes.

Shirley went into politics with a passion for social justice, a profound objection to the fact that society was divided so sharply into the rich and the poor, with this divide being reflected in every area of life. It is not surprising therefore that, as she tells us in the chapter 'The Gospel to the poor' in *God and Caesar*, she has felt a strong bond of sympathy with the liberation theologians of South America, particularly for Helder Camara and Oscar Romero. Yet Shirley was critical of the even greater divides that had opened up in Soviet society, and thought that the liberation theologians were in some respects naïve. She sees the link between her political outlook and her faith quite straightforwardly in the teaching and example of Jesus. *Climbing the Bookshelves* again:

> So I was always a democratic socialist, trying to hammer out a compromise between capitalism and social justice, a compromise that might attract enough public support to make it viable. I was also a Christian socialist because Christ loved the poor, lived among them and spoke the Gospel to them. Over sixty years my convictions have not changed.

With this outlook, it is not surprising that with one part of Catholic teaching Shirley has felt totally at ease, and that is the successive Papal encyclicals on political and economic matters. For in recent decades they have been equally critical of both Marxism and unbridled market capitalism, while expressing an overriding priority for the poor. In her CAFOD lecture delivered in November 2009 for example, she cites, in support of her position, not only the teaching of Vatican II, but *Populorum Progressio* of Paul VI, and *Sollicitudo Rei Socialis* of Pope John Paul II.

Shirley has also felt at ease with the teaching of the Church on issues of war and peace, not least its attitude towards nuclear weapons. It is entirely in keeping with both her personal convictions and successive Vatican documents that in recent years she has devoted much of her expertise, energy and time working towards agreements to lessen the dangers connected with nuclear material and nuclear weapons. At the same time, she is no pacifist, and she finds the traditional Christian concept of the Just War a helpful set of criteria in judging the morality of military interventions. Like most other exponents of that tradition, such as the late Sir Michael Quinlan, she found the invasion of Iraq to be morally unjustified when judged by that test.

Among those who see themselves as part of the liberal intelligentsia – say, those who write for *The Guardian* – you could have fun drawing a Bateman-type cartoon, with everyone looking astonished and appalled as a fellow staff member reveals that they are not only a Christian but a serious Catholic. This is the world in which Shirley has moved. As she writes in *God and Caesar*: 'I have spent most of my life among colleagues, both in politics and academia, with no strong commitment to Christianity . . . In academic life, the prevailing attitude of my colleagues on both sides of the Atlantic has been one of scepticism towards religious belief tempered with tolerance and sometimes curiosity.'

In addition to this, neither of Shirley's two husbands were religious believers. It is not surprising then that, herself a liberal intellectual, and moving in that environment, she should not always find it easy to hold on to faith. As she says, her favourite text is 'Lord I believe, help thou my unbelief'. (Mark 9:24)

One inescapable implication of being at once a liberal and a Catholic is that although Shirley has felt totally at ease with the political and economic teaching of her church, the teaching on some other matters goes sharply across what she, like so many others in her intellectual milieu, might be expected to believe. For example, what about the teaching of the Church on contraception, abortion, IVF and the role of women? She disclaims any expertise as a theologian and puts forward her views with as much tact and hesitation as is possible for a strong intelligent layperson, but her positions, while not at all belligerent towards the Vatican, are clear.

On women she very much laments the secondary role that they play in the life of the Church. More strongly than that, the attitude of the Vatican makes her angry. Even leaving aside the question of ordination to the priesthood, she believes that a proper role for laypeople more generally in the decision-making processes of the Church could and should lead to senior positions for women. This is not an isolated view. As one serious Catholic has said, although opposed to the ordination of women he would nevertheless like to see Shirley running the Church, and at the very least being made a cardinal. The issue of women must be particularly galling for Shirley, given the fact that from an early age she was brought up to 'climb the bookshelves' as well as her brother. As a young woman she belonged to St Joan's Alliance, one of whose aims was the ordination of women. Now, with the very much less open attitude in the Church she writes: 'I find the prohibition, on even *discussing* the possibility of women's ordination very hard to accept'. She also believes strongly that priests should be free to marry.

On birth control she very much regrets the promulgation of *Humanae Vitae*, the encyclical of Paul VI which reiterated that all non-natural means of contraception were forbidden. As she points out, it went against the advice of the expert commission set up to advise the Pope on the issue. It is now widely ignored, and if the *sensus fidelium* means anything it is surely significant that 80 per cent of married Catholic couples do, in conscience, use such methods. The decision seems to have been made because the Pope did not wish to appear disloyal by contradicting the authoritative teaching of his predecessors. This is a reason which Shirley regards as totally inadequate. She particularly regrets the fact that the Catholic Church has come to be seen as equally opposed to both contraception and abortion, whereas in her view it is opposition to abortion that really matters, and the Church has never really faced up to the fact that abortion is widely practised in many developing countries as a form of contraception. On both moral and practical grounds, the Church cannot go on trying to oppose both contraception and abortion.

Shirley is slightly more at ease with the Church's teaching about the moral status of the early embryo, regarding fertilisation as the crucial point, after which it should be treated with the respect due to a person. In fact she has never condemned IVF, which does inevitably result in the loss of some fertilised eggs, but in debates in the House of Lords she joined with other Catholic peers to make clear her opposition to any use of the early embryo in research or to develop embryonic stem cell lines. It is important to note, however, that her main line of argument at the time was that adult stem cells (which are taken from the body and which raise no moral problem) had huge potential and that this ought to be properly explored.

She also believed that the scientific establishment at the time had developed something of a closed mind on this, so intent were they on developing stem cell lines from the early embryo. So her opposition had less to do with the status of the early embryo, as such – in fact her personal position is probably closer to the Anglican one – but with exploring the other alternative which, she believed, was not being taken seriously enough.

Shirley was shaped as a Catholic by her early Catholic influences, the warmth of the Burnetts and the intellectual rigour of her father. Baptised as a student at Oxford, she has found the internationalism of the Roman Catholic Church particularly attractive. Wherever she has been in the world she has been able to go to mass and feel at home. As discussed above, while feeling very much at home with the political and economic teaching of the Church, as well as its wider intellectual tradition, as expressed for example in the Just War criteria, she regards its attitude to women and its teaching on contraception as seriously wrong and harmful. She has been attentive to the official teaching of the Church, but this has not stopped her fearlessly stating her own conscientious position in opposition to the Church as well as, on occasions, to her own political parties. Her own views would have been much easier to hold together as a serious Anglican. Somehow, she has succeeded in being both true to herself, and at the same time being recognised as a loyal Catholic. There is obvious tension in this position, but the clue to how she has been able to live with it is perhaps revealed in a statement at which many of her secular liberal colleagues would baulk. For, as she writes in *God and Caesar*: 'I think the main reason I chose to be and remain a Catholic lay in the claims the church made for herself, and in the demands she made on her adherent . . . It was the huge claims and the huge demands that drew me to the Church of Rome.'

This reflects her temperament as someone wholehearted in all she does as a politician for wider humanity, and which enables her to be a serious Catholic, at once loyal to the faith and critical of the Church where she thinks criticism is deserved.

Modern Catholicism – has it a hope?

Clifford Longley

Shirley Williams has given us, in her short book *God and Caesar*, a remarkably accurate profile of what a modern English Catholic thinks and feels. Based on a series of lectures she gave at Notre Dame University in the United States in 2003, the book ticks virtually all the boxes for a type of intelligent and critical Catholicism so common as to be almost normative in England and Wales – in Scotland things are slightly different. It manages to be both loyal and progressive. It finds both stances difficult, sometimes painful. Success comes to it, in so far as it does at all, mainly through what John Henry Newman called a *via media*, a middle way. It is moderate, but militantly so. It does not like fanaticism, neither in the Vatican nor in the Vatican's enemies. It is reserved, likes to hide its light under a bushel; like Newman himself, it is quintessentially English. Indeed, without Newman's influence, Shirley Williams would almost certainly not be of the Catholic faith herself, for it was by reading Newman that her father, George Catlin, persuaded himself into the Catholic Church before she was born. She was powerfully influenced by her father.

If one draws a horizontal line representing the spectrum between progressive and conservative in English Catholicism, and plotted vertically the numbers who held each position, you would very likely end up with a symmetrical Bell-curve, with the largest number occupying the mid position. Across the Catholic world, however, this English single-hump camel would be unusual. Dromedary Catholicism is the exception; much more familiar across Europe, the United States and Latin America is a

Bactrian camel distribution with two humps, one to the left and one to the right. And these two groups are often at odds, sometimes almost at war.

When President Obama was invited to address students at that same Notre Dame University shortly after his election, the Catholic professors who issued the invitation were denounced by the Catholic hierarchy because of Obama's support for freedom of choice in abortion. The local bishop boycotted the event, and America's most senior Catholic cardinal, Francis George of Chicago, declared: 'It is clear that Notre Dame didn't understand what it means to be Catholic when they issued this invitation.' The invitation stood, the President spoke, and he was loudly applauded by the great majority of this exclusively Catholic academic audience. In the Presidential election he had just won, the majority of Catholics had ignored the threats and warnings of the US hierarchy and given him their vote.

When later his healthcare reform bill reached its final stage in Congress, the Bishops' Conference of the United States wrote to all the legislators who were Catholic, urging them to vote down the bill on the grounds that the safeguards built into it concerning abortion were not, in the bishops' opinion, watertight enough. The bill went through with solid support from Catholic Democrats, and with the blessing of the body representing all the Catholic hospitals in America and many of those who worked in them. The bishops had demanded obedience. They were met with almost nonchalant defiance. Verily, American Catholicism is a two-hump camel. The bishops only speak for one of the humps, and hurl anathemas at the other.

An incident from the Crosby by-election in 1981, described in *Climbing the Bookshelves*, would be almost inconceivable in the United States. The Society for the Protection of Unborn Children (SPUC), a mainly Catholic pressure group with a hard line against abortion, was not content with her known opposition to David Steel's Abortion Act. They insisted she must promise to support – and if in Parliament, campaign for – an anti-abortion amendment drafted by themselves. When she refused, thousands of leaflets attacking her were distributed to Catholic churches throughout the constituency, to be handed out after Sunday mass. As soon as she heard of this she rang her friend the Roman Catholic Archbishop of Liverpool, Derek Worlock. He promptly ordered the distribution of the SPUC leaflets to be cancelled. One rather suspects that in America, on the contrary, the local bishop would have taken part in the leafleting.

Over at least the last twenty-five years the Catholic Church worldwide has been in the throes of a counter-revolution, an attempt to halt or reverse the revolution which began after the Second Vatican Council, 1962–5. The council itself was more interested in reform than revolution, but as is often the way, it unleashed more radical forces. Catholic feminists were demanding women priests, gay rights campaigners wanted the Church to recognise homosexual relationships, priests wanted the right to marry, and in Latin America, theologians who were also militant activists promoted an amalgam of Catholicism and Marxism called liberation theology. And everywhere, Catholics disagreed with papal teaching against contraception that had been reiterated in the encyclical *Humanae Vitae* in 1968. Virtually none of these changes were advocated by Vatican II itself, but all were promoted as being part of that council's 'spirit'.

The preferred method by which these tendencies were to be brought under control was to be by means of the Vatican's exclusive right to appoint bishops, or promote junior ones to senior positions. As moderate or liberal cardinals and bishops reached retirement age all over Europe or North and South America – many of whom had been the reforming stars of the council itself – their replacements were selected from men known to be 'sound', that is to say conservative on each of the neuralgic issues that in the eyes of the Vatican were a threat to the Church's orthodoxy. They wanted men who would dance to Rome's tune. Above all, this meant being willing to stamp out any signs of a sexual revolution among the Catholic rank and file. No priest who entertained ideas about, say, the ordination of women, or even some adjustment on the Church's ban on contraception, could from then on ever hope to be made a bishop. Even to discuss such ideas was henceforth to be treated as treachery.

This doctrinal obedience came at a price. Men with first-class minds and personal charisma were too open-minded for the Vatican's taste, and they were stepped over. Those that were appointed often lacked imagination and were intolerant rather than open-minded, with inadequate leadership skills. They were tepid about social justice, fearful of controversy, and with a liking for doing things by the book. They did not see it as their role to listen to the laity, but to teach them – and what they were to be taught was the standard Vatican line, which had little room for the discoveries and insights of the modern world.

And thus as the years went by there began to emerge a 'safe' but second-rate hierarchy all over the world. It is well illustrated by the stark contrast between Cardinal Joseph Bernardin of Chicago, one of the most inspired and inspiring leaders American Catholicism has ever produced who died in 1996, and his successor Cardinal George, arch-conservative scourge of Notre Dame and Barack Obama. For some reason perhaps connected with its relative insignificance in the global Catholic scheme of things, the Catholic Church in England and Wales has been spared such treatment – which may explain why it is still a dromedary. Inevitably, there are those who lean to the left and those who lean to the right, but there is no polarisation in the Catholic community here like there is in America.

But what the Vatican did not know was that there was something else stirring in the Catholic undergrowth, far nastier than the creeping radicalism which conservative church leaders had been appointed to put a stop to. The cosy clerical culture of deference and respect for rank and office which they sought to preserve turned out to be a sinister hiding place for a hideous and unspeakable crime. Cases gradually came to light of hundreds of priests who had abused their positions of authority, trust and respect in order to sexually abuse minors, usually adolescent boys, sometimes repeatedly over long periods, sometimes despite the church authorities having been warned about them and yet taken no effective action to stop them – or to bring them to justice. What was most appalling was the treatment of victims, ignored, intimidated and sometimes bribed into silence, with their psychological and spiritual wounds, grievous by any account, left untended. The clericalists closed ranks to protect the brotherhood. It was an outrage.

It first came to notice in Ireland and the United States, and some saw it as a phenomenon linked to the Irish Diaspora. But once cases started emerging from outside the English-speaking world, it became clear that the problem was not so easily categorised. The scandal raged and still rages; it has damaged the authority of the Catholic Church beyond measure. It is no surprise that in country after country, when the Catholic bishops say do this, the Catholic laity do that. And once the mystique of power has gone, it is very hard to get it back.

Time and again, the bishops most at fault turned out to be the 'safest' ones, appointed for their caution. The very qualities for which they had been chosen – docility and obedience, conformism, fear of scandal – had become their worst enemy. And it may happen that it is on these rocks in particular that the counter-revolution inside the Catholic Church, the attempt to hold back the laity's desire to move on, will founder. When Pope Benedict XVI wrote a pastoral letter to the bishops in Ireland in 2010 he virtually accused them of having abandoned the Gospel by putting the reputation and convenience of the Church above the needs of victims. Implicit in the attack was a criticism not just of a whole generation of bishops but also of those who appointed them. It was the Vatican's own strategy that had backfired. The reckoning is still ahead, and will involve a more radical shift in the tectonic plates that lie at the foundations of Catholicism than anything that emerged from the Second Vatican Council.

Catholic social teaching

There is a far less depressing aspect of modern Catholicism, which may be where hope for the future mainly lies. It is in the power of Catholic social teaching to provide a fresh set of ideas about what it means to be Catholic. Catholic social teaching has a set of tools which have in the past been applied mainly to social and economic questions – third world development and international trade, the limitations of free markets, human rights – but which could renew and revitalise Catholicism's internal workings too.

'Catholic social teaching' is the term used to describe the body of doctrine which has developed since Pope Leo XIII's encyclical *Rerum Novarum* in 1891. Subsequent Popes have updated the teaching from time to time, and over the last half-century it has become a significant influence in international affairs. A body of academic expertise has grown up among economists and social scientists which is drawn to an alternative vision of a more humane world no longer dominated solely by profit.

Catholic social teaching lay behind the emergence of Christian Democratic movements in many parts of Europe and Latin America. It was not Marxist nor socialist, nor fascist and nationalistic; it rejected class war, national and racial superiority and the unbridled adulation of the free market. Catholic social teaching inspired the original founders of the European Economic Community, and its principles lay behind the European social model of encouraging industrial co-operation rather than conflict, with a generous welfare state for those who needed it.

Catholic social teaching had relatively little impact in Britain, however, and even Catholic politicians like Shirley Williams rarely if ever invoked it as a set of principles that were relevant to public policy. The leadership of the Catholic Church in Britain matched the indifference of the laity in their neglect of this important arm of their Church's own doctrine. It even became known as 'the Church's best-kept secret' – but those implicated in keeping it secret were precisely those responsible for shouting it from the rooftops.

Things changed a little for the better in the 1990s, when the Catholic Bishops of England and Wales published their groundbreaking study *The Common Good and the Catholic Church's Social Teaching* (invariably shortened to just *The Common Good*). It received massive attention from the media, and resonated throughout the Catholic community. Hundreds of parishes set up local discussion groups to go through the document and digest it. About 70,000 copies were sold, ten times more than the bishops had originally hoped for, and it received warm support from the Church of England and the Methodist Church. Iain Duncan Smith, a right-wing Catholic MP during Margaret Thatcher's time as Prime Minister, said later that reading it converted him to the concept of social justice and led eventually to the formation of his influential think-tank the Centre for Social Justice. Since the 2010 election this has become a central player in the formation of government policy.

Before that election the Catholic Bishops' Conference of England and Wales published a pre-election statement called *Choosing the Common Good*, which set out in summary those aspects of Catholic social teaching that were thought to be most relevant to the contemporary problems Britain faced. They helped to interpret a new 'social encyclical' published by Pope Benedict in 2010 called *Caritas in Veritate*, which includes a profound critique of the global market economy and its weaknesses, including those which have brought on the 2008 financial and economic crisis and plunged the world into recession. The previous encyclical in the series, *Centesimus Annus* of Pope John Paul II (1991), had taken a far more benign view of market forces as agencies of wealth creation, whereas *Caritas in Veritate* is cautious if not actively hostile. The laws of economics cannot be regarded as sovereign. They stand under judgement, for they could destroy the moral basis of society and exhaust the social capital, on whose existence they nevertheless depend.

What we must aim for, Pope Benedict said, is the building up of a 'civilisation of love' where everybody matters, no-one is left out, and all parts work together to advance the common good. The love he talks about is fraternal, as between brothers and sisters in the same family. But the family he is concerned with is the whole of humankind, in which each member, every person, has their immense and immeasurable human dignity fully respected. As in a family, each person accepts a serious responsibility for the good of the others, which is known in Catholic social teaching as the principle of solidarity. But a good family does not interfere in the affairs of its members beyond what is necessary, which is called the principle of subsidiarity. Those whose needs come first in the human family are those least able to help themselves, a principle sometimes called the 'preferential option for the poor' (defining 'poor' very loosely). And out of the principle of human dignity comes not only respect for basic human rights, but also the insight, applied to economics, that people are more important than money, labour more important than capital. Sometimes the complexity of society is such that great harm is done by the way things are organised, without anybody intending to do real evil. Catholic social teaching calls that 'structural sin'.

Instead of giving first place to 'liberty', for instance as stressed by libertarians or upholders of free market economics, or 'equality', the priority on the political left, Catholic teaching puts the emphasis on 'relationships'. It is not right or left, nor is it a Third Way. Instead, it is an alternative way of understanding how to run our social, economic and political affairs – the fraternal way. To Pope Benedict 'life in its true sense . . . is a relationship', and depends on relationships from birth to death. It is from our relationships we acquire the practical capacity to participate in any social setting whatever – language, culture, knowledge, know-how. It is only through our social relations that some of our deepest human needs can be realised – to be nurtured and educated, to love and be loved, to give, to receive and to share, to trust and become worthy of trust, to be recognised for oneself and to confer recognition on the value of the Other.

These benefits cannot be bought, schemed for, or coerced. But they can be undermined quite easily. Inequality may grow to the point where it undermines solidarity, and the rich and poor no longer seem to live on the same planet. With inequality of wealth and income goes inequality of power and control over one's own life. Eventually one person's freedom is at the expense of another, and those at the bottom find it is no longer possible to overcome their disadvantages. Very likely, they just go deeper into debt.

What characterised *Caritas in Veritate* was its openness to the social sciences, particularly economics and sociology. The group of experts with which the Pope had surrounded himself while writing the encyclical included several from the University of Bologna, which has become a major influence inside the Pontifical Council for Justice and Peace. What was almost as remarkable was the exclusion from these circles of right-wing Catholic neo-cons from the United States, a group who had been manoeuvring to try to influence Vatican policy on economic issues. What helped tip the balance against them was undoubtedly the crisis of confidence in the very tenets of American free market capitalism, with the success of which the neo-con case was closely identified.

Virtue ethics

Taking the papal encyclical and the English and Welsh bishops' statement together, an important common strand emerges, though it is still more implicit than explicit. It might be called the recovery of 'virtue ethics'. *Choosing the Common Good* went further than any similar Catholic document in espousing and developing this idea. It could be far-reaching.

It began by quoting the recent encyclical: 'Development is impossible without upright men and women, without financiers and politicians whose

consciences are finely attuned to the requirements of the common good.'
The English and Welsh statement went on:

> To act in this way requires more than not breaking rules. It demands the
> cultivation of moral character, the development of habits of behaviour
> which reflect a real respect for others and a desire to do good. It requires,
> in fact, the practice of virtue.
>
> The practice of virtue helps to shape us as people. By the pursuit of virtue
> we act well not because of external constraint but because it has become
> natural for us to do so. The virtues form us as moral agents, so that we do
> what is right and honourable for no other reason than that it is right and
> honourable, irrespective of reward and regardless of what we are legally
> obliged to do. Virtuous action springs from a sense of one's own dignity
> and that of others, and from self-respect as a citizen. It is about doing good
> even when no-one is looking.
>
> In place of virtue we have seen an expansion of regulation. A society that
> is held together just by compliance with rules is inherently fragile, open to
> further abuses which will be met by a further expansion of regulation. This
> cannot be enough. The virtues are not about what one is allowed to do
> but who one is formed to be. They strengthen us to become moral agents,
> the source of our own actions. The classical virtues form us as people who
> are prudent, just, temperate and courageous. The Christian virtues of faith,
> hope and charity root our human growth in the gifts of God and form us
> for our ultimate happiness: friendship with God.

It may not have been in the bishops' minds, but these words have a much
wider application than merely in the political and economic spheres. They
could apply equally to personal morality, including sexual morality. Catholic
sexual morality, at least since the Middle Ages, has been dominated by
the Ten Commandments. In the modern Catholic catechism, the entire
moral life is discussed under the heading of one or more of the Ten, and
the underlying objective is to avoid sin by avoiding offending against any
of them. But this comes close to the 'compliance with rules' approach
to morality which *Choosing the Common Good* has already criticised as

'inherently fragile'. Instead of basing Catholic moral principles on the avoidance of transgression of the Ten Commandments, this suggests there is an alternative basis – the practice of the classical virtues, which 'strengthen us to become moral agents, the source of our own actions'.

What might the application of virtue ethics have to say to such vexed Catholic questions as contraception, abortion, homosexuality and divorce? It would certainly change the terms of trade, but it would be unrealistic to predict that the outcome would be the surrender of the traditional Catholic position in favour of the demands of secular utilitarian ethics on every count. The question regarding contraception, for instance, would no longer refer to arcane discussions of natural law, but to the common good of the relationship between man and wife (which the use of effective and reliable birth control could well enhance). How would a virtuous couple – faithful and prudent – conduct themselves, faced with the need to regulate their fertility? The question almost answers itself.

On abortion, however, the outcome could be very different. Justice – one of the cardinal virtues – demands recognition of what is due, and in the case of an unborn child, what is due to it are life and the protection of its unique human dignity. So a virtue ethics approach to abortion would be more, not less, trenchant in its defence of the foetus. But it might also be less dismissive of the notion of 'freedom of choice', and recognise that the woman involved also had a unique human dignity that must be protected.

How to balance these two would become an issue of prudence. But the key question would be about the moral state of the person doing the balancing. A virtuous person would be more prudent, and would make a better decision. This suggests that the choice should lie with the woman herself; it also implies that we, being virtuous observers of the choice she has to make, could only want her to make it one way. But whether the state should take that choice from her is, in virtue ethics, another matter. It requires a different balance between prudence and justice, and the answers may vary with the circumstances. It is plain that in Britain at least, the sudden imposition of a law banning all abortion would be extremely imprudent, to the point of absurdity. The very criminal justice system itself could be jeopardised by a law, with draconian penalties, that the great majority of the population did not support. Yet that is the only outcome that traditional Catholic ethics, bound exclusively by the Ten Commandments, would allow.

It is this moral absolutism that has bedevilled the debate about abortion in the United States, where the bishops have turned a deaf ear to the argument of Catholic politicians whose main concern is for prudence. Furthermore a discussion about what is prudent or not is easily conducted with other participants in society even if their moral framework is different. Virtue ethics would allow a proper argument about abortion to take place, which is not possible as long as the Church insists there could be only one outcome.

These alternative moral frameworks – Catholic social teaching and virtue ethics – are tools that are already available, already deeply embedded in the Catholic theological tradition. Such tools could liberate the Church from the present morass in which it is stuck, could provide it with a reforming message for society, and also, which it badly needs, with a new way of doing morality. Some of the answers would be slightly different in a liberal direction, some possibly more hard line (the Church's opposition to nuclear weapons comes to mind, and in the US, to the death penalty). What would virtue ethics have to say about homosexuality? It would certainly be less concerned with its alleged 'intrinsic disorder', and would judge it by the criteria of virtue and the common good. That would mean, inevitably, on a case-by-case basis. Not unlike heterosexuality, in fact.

And its relevance to the clerical child abuse crisis? It is obvious that the bishops who failed when it came to the acid test cared not one jot for justice, and lacked the moral courage to act boldly on their own initiative. If the criteria for selecting bishops were based on virtue, rather than on strict adherence to a predetermined line, a very different leadership would have been in place, well able to do what had to be done from a deep sense of moral conviction rather than just following the rules. That is how the Catholic Church ought to be, could be, and one day, God willing, will be.

Let us exalt too in our hardships, understanding that hardship develops perseverance and perseverance character, something to give us hope; and a hope which will not let us down because the Love of God has been poured into our hearts by the Holy Spirit. (St Paul's Letter to the Romans 5:4)

Health care in America

Robert B. Reich

Had Shirley Williams been born in the United States and served this country with the same intelligence, inexhaustible energy, and political acumen she has served Britain, Americans almost certainly would enjoy many public benefits it still lacks. In particular, I expect Shirley would have focused on the single largest hole in America's tattered safety net – universal health care – and fought tirelessly and effectively for it. The Obama administration has taken an important although still inadequate step in that direction, and I can think of few better ways to celebrate Shirley's birthday than to explain what has happened on this side of the pond, why universal health care has been so difficult to achieve, and what the next steps are likely to be.

It is a humbling fact that Americans spend more on health care per person than any other nation in the world, yet we have the highest infant mortality of all the world's advanced industrialised nations, and life expectancy in the United States is shorter than in forty other nations, including Jordan and the Cayman Islands. We are the only wealthy nation that does not ensure that all citizens have coverage; as of 2010, some forty-five million people were without insurance.

That last fact is changing, fortunately. The new health care reform law – an important accomplishment of President Obama and his administration – will extend coverage to almost thirty million who now lack it, including

Americans with health problems that had previously prevented them from getting insured at all. Yet the law is just the first phase of reform, as I shall later explain. It is not nearly as momentous as Lyndon Johnson's Medicare, which provided health coverage to every senior, and dramatically reduced their rates of poverty. And most Americans will not be affected directly by the new law because they will continue to receive health insurance through their employers. Only a comparatively small minority will be required to buy insurance who do not want insurance, or to be subsidised in order to afford insurance. Only a relatively few companies will be required to provide insurance who do not now. Fundamentally, America's new health law will be built on the same system of private for-profit insurance as has failed the nation for decades.

Medicare was built on Franklin D. Roosevelt's New Deal notion of government as insurer, with citizens making payments to government and government paying out benefits. This was the central idea of Social Security, and Medicare piggybacked on Social Security. And social insurance organised this way is a core principle in the UK, and in most of Europe.

But America's new health care law derives its inspiration from a much more conservative idea, first enunciated in the Republican administration of President Dwight D. Eisenhower in the 1950s and then developed under Richard Nixon in the late 1960s. It is a market for health care based on private insurers and employers, and only subsidised by the government. Eisenhower altered the US tax code so workers did not have to pay taxes on the health insurance their employers provided them. Nixon created financial incentives for insurers to prevent diseases and worry about outcomes rather than simply provide more health care. President Obama's new plan takes Nixon's idea a step further by requiring all Americans to carry health insurance, and giving subsidies to those who need it.

The real significance of Obama's victory is more political than substantive. Mere mention of universal health insurance has always prompted a vigorous response from America's political right (which is reliably to the right of the Conservative Party in the UK), also including the ever-vigilant American Medical Association. As early as the 1930s, the editor of its journal equated national health care with 'socialism, communism, inciting to revolution'.

Years later, Ronald Reagan rejected any consideration of universal health care, telling Americans that government was the major problem in their lives. Obama's plan reasserts that government can offer a major solution. In political terms, that's a very big deal.

I have direct political experience. In 1994, Bill Clinton's health care plan was buried under an avalanche of hostility that included a now legendary advertisement featuring a fictional couple, Harry and Louise, voicing their fears that the Clinton plan would substitute government for individual choice – 'they choose, we lose'. I was serving in the Clinton administration at the time. We knew health care was imperilled but none of us knew that failure to pass health care would doom much of the rest of Clinton's agenda and wrest control of Congress out of the hands of the Democrats. In retrospect, it is clear Republicans did know.

On 5 February 1994, the National Association of Manufacturers passed a resolution declaring its opposition to the Clinton plan. Not long after that, Michigan Democrat John Dingell, who was managing the health care bill for the House, approached the senior House Republican on the bill to seek a compromise. According to Dingell, the response was: 'There's no way you're going to get a single vote on this [Republican] side of the aisle. You will not only not get a vote here, but we've been instructed that if we participate in that undertaking at all, those of us who do will lose our seniority and will not be ranking minority members within the Republican Party.'

In early March 1994, Senate Republicans invited Newt Gingrich, then House minority leader, to talk with them about health care. Gingrich warned against compromise, a view echoed by Republican Senator Phil Gramm. A few months later, at a Republican meeting in Boston, Senator Bob Dole, then Senate minority leader, promised to 'filibuster and kill' any health care bill with an employer mandate.

By then Gingrich had united House Republicans against passage of health reform and told the *New York Times* he wanted 'to use the issue as a springboard to win Republican control of the House'. Gingrich predicted that the Republicans would pick up thirty-four House seats in the November elections and that half a dozen disaffected Democrats would switch parties to give Republicans control.

By August, it was over. It did not matter that Democrats outnumbered Republicans in the Senate by 56 to 44 and in the House by 257 to 176. Health care was a lost cause. Republican Senator Bob Packwood boasted to his colleagues: 'We've killed health care reform.' In early September, William Kristol of the Project for the Republican Future spelled out the next stage of the Republican battle plan: 'I think we can continue to wrap the Clinton plan around the necks of Democratic candidates.' And that is exactly what they did. On 8 November 1992, voters roundly repudiated the Clinton plan. They brought Republicans to power at every level of government. Democrats went from a controlling majority of 257 seats in the House of Representatives to a minority of 204, and lost the Senate.

I remember how shocked we were the morning after the votes were counted. I asked one of Clinton's political advisors what had happened. 'It was health care,' he said, simply. (That advisor, by the way, is now in the Obama White House.)

The lessons of history

What are the lessons of this history in terms of understanding the American political process? This is a question Shirley's late husband, the eminent Harvard historian Dick Neustadt, would have asked. One lesson, which Obama learned, is that a new president must move quickly, before opponents have time to stoke public fears. In the first months of 1993 it looked as if Clinton's proposal would sail through Congress. But the process dragged on and by 1994 it bogged down. In the interim, battles over Clinton's budget and the North American Trade Act drained his political capital, gave his opponents ample time to rouse public concerns about government-sponsored health care and soured key allies such as organised labour and the American Association of Retired People. Lyndon Johnson could not have got Medicare enacted had he dawdled. After his 1964 landslide election victory, Lyndon Johnson warned his staff to push Medicare immediately because: 'Every day while I'm in office, I'm going to lose votes. I'm going to alienate somebody. We've got to get this legislation fast.'

Another lesson from history, learned by Obama, is that a president must set broad health reform goals and allow legislators to fill in the details, but be ready to knock heads together to forge a consensus. 'I'm not trying to go into the details,' Johnson repeatedly said of his Medicare bill, yet he flattered, cajoled, intimidated and bluffed recalcitrant members until they agreed. 'The only way to deal with Congress is continuously, incessantly and without interruption,' he quipped. Jimmy Carter, on the other hand, pored endlessly over his incipient health care plan, scribbling opinions in the margins about every detail, and dealt with Congress at arm's length. And Clinton delivered a plan so vast and complex that even a Democratic Congress chose simply to ignore it. Obama wisely set out the broad parameters of health care reform, and allowed Congressional Democrats to do the rest.

A third lesson: presidents who have been most successful in moving the United States towards universal health coverage have disregarded or overruled their economic advisors. Plans to expand coverage have consistently drawn cautions or condemnations from economic teams in every administration. An exasperated Lyndon Johnson groused to Senator Ted Kennedy that 'the fools had to go to projecting' Medicare costs 'down the road five or six years'. Such long-term projections meant political headaches. 'The first thing, Senator Dick Russell comes running in, says, "My God, you've got a one billion dollar [estimate] for next year on health. Therefore I'm against any of it now."' Johnson rejected his advisors' estimates and intentionally low-balled the cost. 'I'll spend the goddamn money.' An honest economic forecast would most likely have sunk Medicare.

It is not so much that presidential economic advisors have been wrong – in fact, Medicare is well on its way to bankrupting the United States – but that they are typically in the business of thinking small and trying to minimise risk, while the herculean task of expanding health coverage entails great vision and large risk. Economic advice is important, but it is only one source of wisdom. Yet since Johnson, presidents have found it increasingly difficult to keep their economists at bay, mainly as a result of the growth of Washington's economic policy infrastructure. Cost estimates and projections emanating from the White House's Office of Management and Budget and the Congressional Budget Office, both created during the Nixon administration, have bound presidents within webs of technical arguments, arcane rules and budget limits. Democratic presidents have felt more constrained by this apparatus than Republicans, perhaps because they have felt more of a need to prove their cost-cutting chops. President Obama was not too rattled by nay-saying economists, although the cost estimates of the Congressional Budget Office set him back.

Perhaps the most important political lesson to be drawn from the history of attempts to reform health care in the United States, and from President Obama's comparative success, is that presidents must also win the support of major health care industries by promising them they will come out ahead. The sad consequence is that Americans will have to pay more for the health care they receive than otherwise, both as individual consumers and as taxpayers. The administration rejected a proposal to allow US pharmacies and wholesalers to import prescription drugs from Europe and Canada, for example, even though American consumers pay up to 55 per cent more for their prescription drugs than Canadians, and the measure would have saved the government at least $19.4 billion over ten years (according to the Congressional Budget Office). The US pharmaceutical industry's argument that the safety of such drugs could not be assured was belied by the defeat of another proposed amendment that would have allowed drug imports only if their safety and economic benefits were certified by the Secretary of Health and Human Services.

The future of health care in America

The future of health care in America should be viewed in three phases.

Phase one, already mostly accomplished, is to extend health care coverage to the entire population. This has been Obama's signal achievement. There is more to do here; the new law excludes most new immigrants, for example.

Phase two, which is likely to begin within the next few years as the new law is implemented, will be to slow the growth of health care costs. If the experience of Massachusetts (which a few years ago embarked on its own smaller version of Obama's plan) is any guide, Americans will wake up to discover that taxpayers cannot possibly afford the costs of the plan that has been enacted. Its attempt at containing the rise in health care costs will be found completely inadequate. Extended coverage, combined with rules requiring insurance companies to offer insurance to anyone with a pre-existing medical problem, and the ageing of the giant baby-boom generation, will cause health care costs to rise far more than forecast. Hence, we can expect a future congress and president – perhaps Obama himself, should he have a second term – to seek to reduce looming medical costs much further than has already been attempted.

Phase two will necessarily involve a more direct assault on private health insurers than was politically possible during the phase one – and a more direct attempt to enact a 'single payer' system by extending Medicare to the entire population. There is no other way to achieve the necessary savings. A study by the Harvard Medical School and the Canadian Institute for Health Information shows that over 30 per cent of US health care spending – more than $1,000 per person each year – goes for administrative costs. This is nearly twice the percentage of administrative costs in Canada. By contrast, Medicare's administrative costs (in the range of 3 per cent) are well below such costs of large companies that self-insure (5 to 10 per cent of premiums), companies in the small-group market (25 to 27 per cent of premiums), and individual insurance (40 per cent).

In a more 'apples to apples' comparison, the US Congressional Budget Office has found that administrative costs under Medicare are less than 2 per cent of expenditures, compared with 11 per cent by private plans under Medicare Advantage, the private-insurance option under Medicare. Allowing Medicare to use its bargaining power with drug companies and health care providers would bring down medical costs still further. Estimates for how much would be saved by extending Medicare to cover the entire population range from $58 billion to $400 billion a year, enough to subsidise coverage for many if not all Americans who will need it, while constraining the costs of co-payments and premiums for everyone else.

The current system of reliance on private for-profit insurers will soon prove untenable even for the average member of the public who may be unaware of its toll on the federal budget but will become painfully aware of its toll on his or her earnings. To take but one example, my health insurer here in California is Anthem Blue Cross. So far, my group policy has not been affected by Anthem's planned rate increase in 2010 of as much as 39 per cent for its customers with individual policies – but the trend is unmistakable, and not just in California. In anticipation of the new health care law, private insurers have pushed up their rates all over the country. Insurers are seeking to raise premiums 24 per cent in Connecticut, 23 per cent in Maine, 20 per cent in Oregon and a wallet-popping 56 per cent in Michigan.

Big health insurers say they have no choice but to raise rates, but they are making boatloads of money. America's five largest health insurers made a total profit of $12.2 billion in 2009, 56 per cent higher than in 2008, according to a report from Health Care for America Now. Yet basically all they do is collect money from employers and individuals and give the money to providers. In most markets, consumers would not pay this much for so little. We would find a competitor that charged less and delivered more. How can insurers raise prices as much as they want without fear of losing customers?

The basic problem is private health insurers are not subject to market competition. Consequently, any efficiencies that come from large scale do not redound to the benefit of policy holders or to taxpayers. More than 90 per cent of insurance markets in more than three hundred metropolitan areas in the United States are 'highly concentrated', as defined by the Federal Trade Commission, according to the American Medical Association. A 2008 survey by the Government Accountability Office found the five largest providers of small group insurance controlled 75 per cent or more of the market in thirty-four states, and 90 per cent or more in twenty-three of those states, a significant increase in concentration since the GAO's 2002 survey. Astonishingly, the health insurance industry continues to be exempt from federal antitrust laws, which is why a handful of insurers have become so dominant in their markets that their customers simply have nowhere else to go.

President Obama has proposed giving the federal government the power to deny or roll back 'excessive' premiums.* But this power will prove

---

* http://www.nytimes.com/interactive/2010/02/22/us/politics/0222Health.html

inadequate. Half the states already have the power to approve rates and they have proven incapable of holding them back.

Anthem's parent is WellPoint, one of the largest publicly traded health insurers in America, which runs Blue Cross and Blue Shield plans in fourteen states and Unicare plans in several others. WellPoint, through Anthem, is the largest for-profit health insurer here in California, as it is in Maine, where it controls 78 per cent of the market. In Missouri, WellPoint owns 68 per cent of the market; in its home state, Indiana, 60 per cent. With thirty-five million customers, WellPoint counts one out of every nine Americans as a member of one of its plans.

US antitrust laws are supposed to prevent this kind of market power. So why are giant health insurers like WellPoint exempt? Chalk it up to an anomaly that began seven decades ago in the quaint old world of regional, non-profit Blues. They were created in part by hospitals to spread the costs of expensive new equipment and facilities over many policy holders. Collaboration was the point, not competition. The 1945 McCarran-Ferguson Act made it official, exempting insurers from antitrust scrutiny and giving states the power to regulate them, although not necessarily any power to regulate rates.

The system worked fairly well until about two decades ago when insurers began morphing into publicly held, for-profit cash machines. A new breed of medical entrepreneur saw opportunities to profit from a rapidly ageing population eager to get every new drug and technology that might extend their lives, and a government committed to doling out hundreds of billions of dollars in Medicare and Medicaid.

With size has come not only market power but political clout. Big for-profit insurers deploy enough campaign money and lobbyists to get their way with state legislators and insurance commissioners. A proposal last year to allow California's Department of Insurance to regulate rates, for example, died in committee. These companies have even been known to press states to limit how many other health insurers they license.

And when they cannot get their way, insurers go to court. In Maine – one state that aggressively regulates rates – WellPoint's Anthem subsidiary has sued the insurance superintendent for reducing its requested rate increase.

ROBERT B. REICH 229

Political clout can be especially advantageous at the federal level, as the big Wall Street banks have so brazenly demonstrated. Over the past two and a half years, WellPoint's employees and associates have contributed more than $922,000 to federal political campaigns, and the company has spent $7.8 million lobbying Washington policymakers, according to the Center for Responsive Politics. It should not be surprising that WellPoint was one of the leading opponents of the public insurance option, which would have subjected it to competition even where it had sewn up the market.

Phase three will place greater emphasis on better-quality care for every dollar spent. The American public has not yet focused on the effectiveness of health spending in this country, and is still largely wedded to the idea that more spending means better health. Once real constraints are placed on spending, the focus will shift towards achieving better health care outcomes for each dollar spent.

More data will become available – both to policymakers and to the public – comparing different hospitals and providers in terms of how well they do keeping people healthy and returning sick people to health. Few Americans today know, for example, that the main reason patients die in American hospitals is they succumb to sepsis infections caused by being in the hospital in the first place – infections that would have been avoided had hospital staff used better techniques to prevent them. To take another example: few Americans are aware that Stage 4 cancer patients in US hospitals who receive a great deal of expensive tests and treatments live no longer than Stage 4 patients who go to hospices and receive only palliative care (in fact, that data show that the latter group actually live twenty-nine days longer, on average).

Were Shirley Williams holding office on this side of the Atlantic she would quickly move American health care from phase one to phase three. But she is not, and for that unfortunate fact we will have to muddle along on our own, far more slowly.

★

Any history of the fight for universal care in America contains a subplot with a supporting actor who, although he never became president, was repeatedly heard from offstage – goading, pushing, threatening and pulling presidents of both parties toward universal coverage. Ted Kennedy first introduced his ambitious national health insurance proposal in 1969, and he never stopped promoting the cause. A deal he reached with President Nixon was the closest this country has ever come to universal care. Even before Kennedy's death last autumn, his illness had tragically sidelined him just when his powerful voice was most needed. Yet America's move towards universal coverage was due in no small measure to the tenacity and perseverance of this one remarkable man.

Comprehensive education

Robert Skidelsky

Like all contributors to this volume, I have great affection and respect for
Shirley Williams. She was – and remains – one of the most remarkable,
and lovable, politicians of the post-war era. Yet she was not a success as
Education Minister from 1964–6 and as Secretary of State from 1976–9.
I will try to explain why, calling in aid the now fashionable method of
'counter-factual' history.

'Herbert Morrison', writes Shirley Williams in her autobiography, 'was a
perfect example of the adage that there are horses for courses in government,
as elsewhere. Brilliant at the Home Office . . . he never took to the Foreign
Office . . . He knew little about foreign affairs, and was not particularly
interested in learning more.' It is an unintentionally self-revealing comment.
Shirley would have made a superb Foreign Secretary. With the formidable
Vera Brittain and George Catlin as parents, liberal internationalism is in her
blood. She loves to travel, is endlessly curious, has a wide range of sympathies,
and gets on excellently with all kinds of people. She would have brought
exactly the right radical, questioning approach to British foreign policy. But
as a woman she was 'type cast' for domestic roles, and it was her misfortune
to spend much of her time in government involved with education, to which
she brought strong feelings, but no particular feel.

Shirley is saddled with the failure of comprehensive schools. This failure
cannot be denied: ever since Jim Callaghan's speech at Ruskin College
in 1976, successive governments, Tory and Labour, have been trying to
unravel the system set up in the 1960s. Shirley was not the prime mover in

comprehensive education. As she explains in her autobiography, the decisive impulse from the top was given by Tony Crosland with his visceral hatred of grammar schools; and there was considerable groundswell from parents because of the rigid selection imposed by the Eleven-Plus examination. As Secretary of State for Education, she, like Margaret Thatcher a few years earlier, was simply engaged in unrolling a pattern already decided on.

Nevertheless, Shirley enthusiastically supported the movement. The chief benefit she saw from comprehensives was social: a common education would bridge the class divide and raise the aspirations of the majority. In other words, she put social objectives ahead of educational standards; or more exactly, did not seem to understand what the pursuit of social equality through education might do to education. In one sense, the comprehensive school project has been a great success: British society is more socially egalitarian than it used to be, and comprehensive schools must have contributed to this. But it has failed those both at the top and at the bottom of the ability range. As a result, it has entrenched a culture of mediocrity and low expectations. The structure of what Tony Blair called 'the bog-standard comprehensive' was wrong, and educational reform in the last twenty years has been largely directed at undoing it.

I wondered how far Shirley might be willing to face, or at least discuss, this issue in her autobiography *Climbing the Bookshelves*, but in fact she does not do so. Either she finds the whole subject too painful; or perhaps the capacity for reflection is not given to those whose temperament is for action and persuasion.

What her autobiography does help to explain is how she came to think about the connection between education and class the way she did, and perhaps still does. The radicalism of her upper-class parents was clearly important in creating a sympathy for the 'underdog'. But two particular episodes gave Shirley's own radicalism its particular shape. The first was going to the local elementary school between the ages of eight and ten. 'I pleaded with my parents to let me attend [it],' she writes. The other children assumed she was the cook's daughter and she maintained the deception by cultivating a cockney accent and leaving and entering her parents' grand house in Cheyne Walk by the basement. 'Many of my fellow pupils', she writes 'were pasty-faced and skinny; some had the bowed legs of rickets. Their lifeless woollen jerseys had holes in the elbow, and they wore skirts and shorts cut down after long use by older brothers and sisters. Every other morning, all of us had to go through the indignity of having our heads searched for lice.' One of her classmates could come to school only every other day, because there was only one pair of boots to go round. 'I asked my mother why I had four pairs of shoes and two pairs of sandals while they had only half of one.' What this child's question reveals is an instinctive capacity for empathy, which was to be Shirley's most attractive quality as a politician.

Few upper-class eight-year-olds, even of radical parents, ask to go to working-class schools, and one wishes Shirley had been able to recall what lay behind that 'pleading', or why her parents accepted it. (Upper-class parents, whatever their political views, usually make sure their children get an upper-class education.) Another formative influence was the impression made on her mind by the fate of her 'adored' young cook-housekeeper Amy Burnett. Amy had won a scholarship to a grammar school, but 'the doors to paradise . . . slammed shut when her parents were unable to afford the school uniform'. So Amy, like the rest of the girls in her family, 'went into service'. Again, it required an unusual strength of empathy to put herself in Amy's shoes. The fact that Shirley recalls Amy's circumstances quite precisely seventy years later suggests that she understood the unfairness of the class system from a young age. This created the guilt which was the springboard of her own radicalism.

Wider educational opportunities were opened up by the Butler Act of 1944, but this legislation contained two flaws which, in Shirley's view, made it 'at once enlightened and obsolete'. The first was the failure of technical schools, the intended middle tier of the tripartite system it set up, to get going – leaving education much too sharply bifurcated between grammar schools and secondary modern schools. The second was that the selection at eleven was too early and too rigid to allow for easy transfer between the two remaining tiers. Intellectual segregation largely confirmed social segregation. These remain powerful indictments of the system which Shirley the politician helped dismantle: the question is whether comprehensive education was the only way of getting rid of these flaws; whether, in fact, one had to throw out the baby with the bathwater.

Fast-forward to Shirley the educational reformer. In 1967 she was made Minister of State at the Department of Education and Science. Her Secretary of State was Tony Crosland, who had vowed to get rid of 'every fucking grammar school' in England. The mechanism to hand was Circular 10/65, which required education authorities to submit plans for going comprehensive, reinforced by linking building funds to their willingness to do so. Shirley shared Crosland's vision of an 'inclusive, cohesive society of which the schools would be the building blocks'. He cared 'passionately about equality, and was driven by a controlled anger against the privilege, patronage and preferment that so clutter up British society'. Now for the counter-factual: before Circular 10/65 only 8.5 per cent of children aged 11–15 attended comprehensive schools. By 1971 the figure was 35 per cent; by 1981, 85 per cent. Shirley claims that 'this extraordinary transformation was not mainly due to government policy', but to local authority and parental pressure. I am not so sure. The hostility of middle–class parents to the Eleven-Plus was a powerful factor, since if their children failed it (as most of them did) they would be consigned to the 'inferior' secondary moderns. But it was the way the political class chose to deal with the Eleven-Plus problem which determined the outcome.

The comprehensive school was seen as the only answer, whereas in fact there were quite feasible alternatives. Selection could have been postponed till thirteen or fourteen, as it was in France. It could have been made less dependent on the flawed concept of 'general intelligence'; transfer, whether at eleven or thirteen, could have been made easier. Resources poured into the comprehensive school building programme could have been diverted to building more grammar schools and constructing the middle tier of technical schools envisaged by the Butler Act of 1944. This would have created the mixed system common in Germany. It was left to Conservative Education Secretary Kenneth Baker to open up this road in the late 1980s. Shirley rightly castigates the extreme fringe of the teaching profession, but she does not see that the abolition of selection – at any point in the pupil's passage – was bound to weaken education as an academic discipline.

Such alternatives held no attraction for Shirley. As Secretary of Education herself in 1977, she tried to rally support for comprehensive schools by suggesting a 'core curriculum' to improve basic literacy and numeracy, proposing a general teaching council to isolate the 'loony left' teachers, and advocating 'diversity among schools'. These were good initiatives, which foundered in face of teacher opposition and government weakness. But Shirley never understood that the fault lay in the comprehensive structure itself.

There is an ironic coda to the tale. Had a modified tripartite system evolved, the independent sector would undoubtedly have shrunk. The abolition of the grammar schools saved the public schools. By the late 1960s, the independent sector had started to feel the strain of rising fees and still high marginal tax rates. Had acceptable state alternatives been provided, many of the lesser public schools would have gone to the wall. Instead the educational (and social) divide was reinforced, as the ladder for bright working-class children erected by the Butler Act was pulled away and ability to pay once more became the determiner of life-chances. It was a sad tale of unintended consequences.

What do I mean when I say that Shirley had 'no feel' for education? As professor of government at Harvard University she developed what she called a 'didactic' style of lecturing and I saw it in operation a number of times at the Moscow School of Political Studies, whose seminars we have both regularly attended for many years. In these presentations she saw herself as an 'educator', drawing out her students through argument and discussion. In fact she was brilliant at doing this. She was neither too highbrow nor too lowbrow, and her language was both assured and passionate. But these presentations were for adults. In her public life, too, she lived up to the ideal of politics as a form of education. But I think she accepted too readily that her own successes at this level could be generalised for all ages provided only that class- and gender-based obstacles to high aspirations could be overcome. In fact, the barriers to high achievement in any walk of life are as much genetic as social. Whereas it would be absurd to say that high-achieving genes are concentrated in the middle or upper classes, any school system which fails to recognise and provide for innate differences in ability is not going to succeed educationally, however much its succeeds socially.

The view from here

Crispin Tickell

Shirley Williams always made a difference. I suppose we first knew each other when walking along the banks of the Thames at Port Meadow in Oxford some sixty years ago. I was then looking for material to challenge the conventional wisdom in weekly tutorials, and in Shirley I found it. I am not sure that originality of approach was what my tutors really wanted then or since, but I remember that at least one of them later grabbed one of our ideas as his own.

Encouraged by talented parents, Shirley combined originality, energy, confidence, and a strong sense of fairness from the beginning of her career, and for all the inevitable vicissitudes of politics, she has hardly stopped since. Her autobiography tells some but far from all of the story. Here I want to draw attention to her ideas and feelings about the shortcomings of modern society and the ways it might go in the future, what she calls the view from here. The 'world economy' she wrote, 'is nearing the limits of the planet's capacity'.

She and I were born at a time when things were going badly wrong. Although the problems of the 1930s are very different from those of today, both are characterised by a breakdown of the conventional wisdom and a need to think differently across the whole spectrum. There are the shortcomings of the economy, and of consumer society as such; there is a widening chasm between the rich and poor of the world, with the poor wanting to follow the rich in the wrong direction; there is a marked shift in the balance of political and economic power from west to east; there is well-justified scepticism about the virtues of current political systems, including democracy as it is interpreted and applied; and there is the extraordinary proliferation of one animal species – our own – with multiple effects on the Earth's environment and resources, its land, sea and air. We are beginning to confront the phenomenon of globalisation which we have yet fully to understand.

The current situation of our society is unique. Other societies and civilisations have risen and collapsed before, but the circumstances of today are special. They go back to the beginning of the industrial revolution some 250 years ago. We have yet to recognize that that period has been a bonanza of inventiveness, exploitation and consumption which may not continue. All successful species, whether bivalves, beetles, bindweed or humans, multiply until they come up against the environmental stops, reach some accommodation with the rest of the environment, and willy-nilly restore some balance.

In September 2009 the magazine *Nature* published an article by Johan Rockstrom and others identifying nine scientific boundaries or stops which humans would cross at their peril. Three had already been crossed: climate change; loss of biodiversity; and interference with nitrogen and phosphorus levels. The other six were stratospheric ozone depletion; ocean acidification; use of fresh water; changes in land use; chemical pollution; and loading of the atmosphere with aerosols and other dust. Obviously we could all have our own lists and calculations of the dangers we face, and Shirley sets out some of them, political as well as scientific, in her autobiography.

Before setting out priorities we have to recognise the long and rickety bridge between the world of science and research on one side, and that of public understanding and policy-making on the other. The crossing between the two is never easy, and often gives rise to misunderstandings and misconceptions. The science is usually far ahead of the politics. Moreover the process itself is slow.

Scientists work on different degrees of uncertainty and work on probabilities. They have to cope with the problems of paradigm shift and phoney science (for example creationism or so-called intelligent design). Some of them like to lock themselves into specialities, and thereby miss the big picture. All face difficulties in converting the vocabulary of science into the vocabulary of politics. By contrast few politicians have scientific backgrounds or understanding of scientific problems. They usually operate short term within the electoral cycle. The mechanics of the system, at least in Britain, are usually operated by non-scientific mandarins. Politicians want black and white answers, not shades of probability. The relevance of science to policy is not always apparent: scepticism or exaggeration can lead to perverse results, including sterile and emotional debates and poor decision-making.

Not surprisingly the crossing of the long and rickety bridge has long been uncomfortable, and policy-makers of all kinds have only gradually realized the significance of what is happening. Unlike most politicians, Shirley has crossed the bridge many times in her long career, and for that reason alone her role and influence has been outstanding. She has done particularly well in promoting the role of women at all levels in society.

What are the priorities we should set for the future? It is difficult to know where to start, but it is now clearer than ever that we have to rethink a lot of economics, in particular how we measure wealth, welfare and the health not only of the human condition but of the world as a whole. At present we continue to fail to bring in externalities and true costs in our systems of measurement. As has been well said, markets are marvellous at fixing prices but incapable of recognising costs. The shortcomings of growth (as the term is normally used), and of gross domestic product/gross national product are at last being recognised, together with the artificiality of much cost benefit analysis. The idea of a 'free market' is unreal, and always has been. All markets operate within rules, whether explicit or implicit, which together constitute a framework which, if it is any good, should be in the public interest and to the public good.

Arising from all this is the clear need to establish new and more rational systems of measurement. There have been several attempts, for example in the Human Development Index, in the work of the New Economics

Foundation, and in the recent report of the Commission established by President Sarkozy and chaired by Joseph Stiglitz on possible new methodologies.

Then there have been a series of conferences and reports pointing in the same direction. Among the most significant was the Amsterdam Declaration of scientists from the four Global Research Programmes in 2001, which stated that: 'The Earth is currently operating in a no-analogue state . . . The accelerating human transformation of the Earth's environment is not sustainable.'

More recently there was the Fourth Assessment of the Intergovernmental Panel on Climate Change of 2007, which, although criticised on one or two details, well lays out the science. Then there was the Stern Review of 2006, and subsequent work on the social and economic impacts, and of course Al Gore in his book and film *An Inconvenient Truth*. There was the report of the United Nations Environment Programme of March 2009, which laid out the foundations of what was called a Global Green New Deal. Later in 2010 we shall have another report from the same source about the implications of loss of biodiversity, and the need for urgent action. We are bringing about a wave of extinctions comparable to the great extinctions of the past with consequences that cannot be foreseen.

Copenhagen

It was against this background that the conference on climate change (COP 15), a critical issue which affects all others, took place in Copenhagen in December 2009. The results were, as everyone knows, disappointing, although it was not the disaster it has sometimes been portrayed. Some positive measures have already come out of it, for example in setting targets for reducing carbon emissions and coping with deforestation. Expectations of the next COP meeting at Cancun in 2010 have not been so high, which paradoxically may lead to a better result.

An important lesson from the COP series of conferences is to appreciate the difficulty of persuading the whole international community to agree to a variety of sometimes difficult commitments and actions which affect the interests of some more than others. Within the United Nations system there are always those who are ready to block a global deal, or to extract unreasonable concessions by threatening to do so, thereby removing value from the result. Hence the second lesson we should draw is the need for what has been called plurality of agreements, in other words groups of countries which can agree among themselves on certain measures, and later try to fit them into a global framework. Such has long been the tradition of the G8 and G8+5 countries, and before that the G7 countries. Examples abound from other parts of the world of agreements between countries in very different geographical and other circumstances. The problem is how to put them effectively together.

The proposals for a Global Green New Deal, which have since been discussed among the leaders of the G20 group, are a good example of what might be done. According to an article in *Nature* of 8 April 2010 the G20 countries account for two-thirds of the world's population, 90 per cent of global economic activity, and at least three-quarters of global gas emissions. In looking to the future let us recall the sheer breadth of responsibilities which we all have in different capacities: as individuals, within communities, within regions, within governments and within the global framework such as it is.

There is a current enterprise which brings out the unique circumstances of today. In geological terms the Pleistocene epoch of intermittent ice ages was followed some 10,000 years ago by the relatively warm Holocene epoch. Now some geologists have proposed that the Holocene should be followed by an Anthropocene epoch beginning with the industrial revolution some 250 years ago to mark the extraordinary human impact on the surface of the Earth.

Sustainability should be our objective. Someone once asked what sustainability meant. The reply was 'treating the Earth as if we intended to stay'. This is Shirley Williams's message over the years, and it should certainly be ours now and in the future.